The Book of Exodus

Question by Question

Also in this series

THE BOOK OF GENESIS: Question by Question

by William T. Miller, SJ

THE GOSPEL OF MATTHEW: Question by Question

by John F. O'Grady

THE GOSPEL OF JOHN: Question by Question

by Judith Schubert, RSM

THE BOOK OF REVELATION: Question by Question

by Susan Fournier Mathews

The Book of Exodus

Question by Question

William T. Miller, SJ

Paulist Press
New York/Mahwah, NJ

Cover and book design by Lynn Else

Library of Congress Cataloging-in-Publication Data

Miller, William T., 1941–
    The book of Exodus : question by question / William T. Miller.
        p. cm.
    Includes bibliographical references (p.   ).
    ISBN 978-0-8091-4612-3 (alk. paper)
    1. Bible. O.T. Exodus—Textbooks. 2. Bible. O.T. Exodus—Commentaries.
I. Title.
    BS1245.55.M55 2009
    222'.120071—dc22

                                                              2009018058

Published by Paulist Press
997 Macarthur Boulevard
Mahwah, New Jersey 07430

www.paulistpress.com

Printed and bound in the
United States of America

Contents

Contents

In memory of three women friends:
Ms. Sheila Anderson, Sister Mary Timothy McHatten, OP,
and Mrs. Dorene Preis.
They were of different faith traditions, but all three
put their faith into action in lives of service and love

Acknowledgments

I would like to thank Father Timothy Brown, SJ, then provincial of the Maryland Province of the Society of Jesus, for providing the sabbatical time needed to complete this book. The Jesuit community at the University of Scranton provided a welcome home that made the writing almost a serene project. Many readers of the Genesis volume in this same series have assured me that the format was helpful to them, and I appreciate their enthusiasm for the scriptures as a major part of their journeys in faith.

General Introduction

This exposition of the Book of Exodus follows the format of the Genesis volume in the *Question by Question* series. For scholarly research on Exodus I rely happily and heavily on William H. C. Propp's recent volumes on *Exodus 1—18* and *Exodus 19—40* in the Anchor Bible series. His commentary is encyclopedic, yet it invites readers to further discussion of specific verses. I will also refer frequently to the well-known commentaries on Exodus by Umberto Cassuto, Brevard Childs, and Terence Fretheim, all of whom present helpful overviews of various chapters and issues found in this very complex story of the birth of Israel as a people, and of their following after God toward their future home.

I have divided Exodus into twenty-four **Sections**, some just a few verses long and others covering several chapters. Each section starts with an **Introduction**, basic information that might be useful to have at the start of each assignment. Some of these introductions are much longer than originally planned, in order to provide overviews of covenant theology, the Decalogue, basic law codes, and the like. I am inclined to mention details of Hebrew vocabulary at times, since Hebrew is so unlike English and works with far fewer synonyms. I hope those readers who know biblical Hebrew will allow for my oversimplifications in the transcription of some Hebrew letters into English. In any case, the introductions hopefully will not delay or prevent readers from moving to the **Questions**. These should be studied and answered by individuals or study groups before reference to the **Answers** at the back of the book. Some of the answers are quite long, because of the rich theological issues within Exodus. The **Conclusion** to each section is meant to tie up loose ends, but at times I use that spot to note the theological insights of one commentator or to review our progress on larger questions not yet solved at that point.

The plan is that working steadily through each section will contribute to a cohesive guided tour or classroom experience. I

1

hope that my own interest in providing so much information for general readers does not prove daunting or counterproductive. Readers may choose to scan provisionally technical segments so as not to lose their sense of progress through the book.

As I mentioned in the Genesis volume, there used to be considerable agreement among scholars that the first five books of the Old Testament (usually called the Pentateuch or the Torah) had been gathered from four sources. Analysts spoke of the Yahwist (J), a southern author from around the time of David, and of some additions from a northern school of nearly the same time, the Elohist (E). The school of Deuteronomy (D) influenced segments in Genesis to Numbers (and Deuteronomy itself, of course), as well as parts of the historical books from Joshua to Kings. The Deuteronomic writers were aware of the fall of the northern kingdom, well over a century before the Exile itself. Priestly traditions (P) were added much later (during or after the Exile). The clues to each source were key choices of vocabulary and style, and to a lesser extent the content or spiritual claim of each passage.

Even when this four-source model was popular, it was a limited working theory that did not cover all the complexities. Some traditions were much older than the estimated date of the source in which they were found. Some chapters did not seem to fit within any source, and there were often questions of who did the final editing of this or that passage. I quoted Joseph Blenkinsopp in the Genesis volume to the effect that the P and D materials clearly reflect the experience of destitution and exile and the hope for a rebirth of a viable community in continuity with the past, but that the J and E source theories seem more questionable as time goes by. The classifications of vocabulary, style, and content in J and E may be partly due to circular reasoning, and the dating of the J and E materials as far back as the time of David is now much disputed. Blenkinsopp notes, "If we continue to use the designations J and E, it will be more to maintain continuity in the scholarly tradition" than for anything else.

Propp is well aware of the limitations of the four-source theory, but he also defends its usefulness. Using the classical markers of vocabulary and style, we can see some of the editing processes.

Propp is especially interested in reviving theories about the Elohist level within Exodus. He argues that an Elohistic collection of stories made its way to Jerusalem after the fall of the northern kingdom in 721 BCE, where it was combined by redactors (RJE) with J to form what we now call JE traditions. About a century later, D materials, including Moses' final testimonies in most of the Book of Deuteronomy, supplemented JE. Later, Priestly materials were added that competed in some important ways with the JE traditions. The final editors, RF (perhaps from rival priestly factions), defused some of the competing P theology by combining as many sources as possible, adding genealogies, geographic information, and the like. So there may be five source levels within Exodus—E, J, RJE, P, and RF—in addition to some D verses. In general, the authors and editors tried to save as much as possible, adding richness and mystery while risking some inconsistencies.

Propp admits that there are only scattered strands of E in Genesis, but argues that one can identify significant E passages within the JE materials in Exodus. He questions the older scholarly practice of assigning debatable Exodus passages to J, following the Genesis model. He finds E, and P, to be more interested in Moses himself than is J. To be fair, Propp admits that some of his Exodus E material may be more D-like and that some could be J from JE rather than E. He is willing to consider renewed claims about J passages in the future.

At the start of each section, I will mention the prevailing source analyses about the verses in that section, taking Propp as the devil's advocate for E passages.

Most Americans who start studying the Pentateuch want to know "the facts," the exact dates or geographic sites or names of the persons and events about which they are reading. The problem is that we have very limited nonbiblical evidence for Jewish history prior to the reign of David (starting in 1000 BCE). Propp (2.741–44) lists the best Near Eastern archaeological data we have for the five or six centuries before David. He notes that historians cannot use the data to draw many firm conclusions about how the Israelites developed into a people prior to the time of Saul and David. This observation goes against the tide of television quasi-documentaries that hustle the latest trends and guess-work among archaeologists and pay lip service at best to scripture scholars.

We must also remember that the biblical accounts came into being two to three thousand years before the fields of modern history and archaeology were even conceived. In the oral traditions of the ancient world, the personalities of kings, priests, prophets, and gods were the keys. No one kept track of centuries-old dates and places in such a way that wise men of two separate nations could have fixed an international date for an event or agreed on a specific site for a story on a world map. Neither does the Book of Exodus, with its miracles and divine revelations, provide us with many firm historical details.

Propp refers to the Book of Exodus as one that recounts mythic events. He speaks of the difficulty of determining the historiography of mythic events—the difficulty of critical assessment of narratives whose cultural significance bears no proportional relationship to their verifiable truth content. The main story in Exodus is of good versus evil, of Egyptian high culture versus that of Egypt's surrounding, poorer neighbors. Therefore, Exodus (and the Torah) is a crafted series of mythic events, not simply oral epic or saga. Yet it is completely unlike modern historiography. Propp concludes:

> A good myth is mightier than history, immune to both evidence and analysis. I have no doubt that, the foregoing remarks notwithstanding, the Israelites' Exodus from Egypt will remain a historical fact for 99 percent of educated Americans. The story of triumph against impossible odds is narrated with the sequential...elements that we are programmed to find most affecting.... The tale of "When Israel was in Egypt's Land," imbibed by all in childhood, fundamental to two world religions, inspirational to millions seeking deliverance from their trials, cannot be lightly laid aside. If, against all the evidence, we still go through life enveloped in such myths, they are probably good for us. (*Exodus 1—18*, 746)

4

Allowing for Propp's honest skepticism, I would put it another way. When we look at Exodus chapters 1—15 or 19—24 or 32—34 we are looking at major theological claims woven so tightly into literary genres that we cannot extricate the utterly accurate historical facts, and the very effort to extricate them is wrong-headed, except as it may be part of a desire to learn God's will from history in addition to learning it from sacred writings and traditions, developed doctrines, discussion of moral principles, and so on. The stories of Exodus are not only *probably good for us,* they are God's gift of himself to us. No one wants to *lay aside* facts or go *against all the evidence* to embrace myth. We should try instead to comprehend the *story of triumph against all odds* within the myths, because that is God's triumph more than our own.

Instructions for Study Groups

1. The books in this series are arranged for individuals or study groups, rather than for students in a college classroom. Students can rely on the teacher for each week's assignments and for the time to go more deeply into difficult passages. Groups have to shepherd themselves along. The leader and members have to consider practical details—when, where, and how often to meet, which members can lead in prayer, provide refreshments, and how to keep the meeting area free of distractions. Most groups have about eight members, who can share reading aloud, praying in common, and suggesting ways to apply scripture to daily life.

2. The leader will have to read ahead far enough to estimate how many sections can best be done during each meeting, but he or she shouldn't tip everyone off about the answers. Exodus is a much more complex book than Genesis, and it will take more time to understand the theology behind the story of the escape, of the two successive covenants, and of the design and use of the Tabernacle.

3. The Answers in the book should be examined for the first time at the meeting, after everyone has shared their answers (the leader holding back). Those who tend to be shy about speaking should be given a second, personal invitation to participate at times before the group moves on. If the Answers in the book seem unsettling or untraditional at first, it may be best to review those complications at the start of the next session, after everyone has had time to think them over.

4. It will be easier for the whole group if everyone uses the same translation of the Bible. Scholars and authors usually

cite the NRSV (New Revised Standard Version) because they have found that best for the classroom. The NRSV is used in this book, unless I mention other translations or provide one of my own. Roman Catholics may be more familiar with the NAB (New American Bible) since it is used in the lectionary.

Questions

EXODUS
1:1—15:21

Section One:
Exodus 1:1-22

William Propp attributes most of verses 1–7, 13–14 to
Priestly sources or later redactors of the Pentateuch;
verses 6, 8–12, 22 to J (Yahwist); and
verses 15–21 to E (Elohist).

Introduction

This chapter falls into three sets of seven verses each, followed by an ominous final note. Verses 1–7 review the genealogy of the descendants of Jacob, 8–14 mention the hard labor now imposed on them, and 15–21 tell the story of the midwives. In the final verse, 22, the Pharaoh publicly orders death for all newborn Hebrew male infants.

Exodus uses the term *sons of Israel* (*Israelites*) many times to indicate that the Jewish people are more numerous now than the *sons of Jacob* and their immediate families who originally went to Egypt. The term *Hebrews* is often used in the Old Testament to describe their status as serfs or slaves; it is also the usual term in Exodus used by Egyptians when speaking of the Jewish people. Verse 5 speaks of the seventy original descendants of Jacob, a traditional ideal number. Another ancient tradition counted seventy-five instead, and one place that number was preserved is in Acts 7:14.

The florid description in verse 7 is a classic, using three of the same verbs for a growing population as Genesis 1:28. Another verb in verse 7, *shrz*, meaning "to be prolific" or "teeming," is also used of humanity in Genesis 9:7. In all other cases this word refers to large swarms of animal or marine life, and so here might hint at Egyptian prejudices. Another word, *rbh*, is used in verse

10 to express the Pharaoh's fear that the Hebrews will *multiply*, and in verse 12, where they do *multiply* even under very hard labor. In verse 10, the phrase "let us deal shrewdly" is based on the Hebrew verb *hkm*, the root word for *wisdom*. So one could have the Pharaoh say "Let us act with wisdom." However, his wisdom is simply a form of injustice.

The idea of a rapid increase in numbers might simply have stemmed from the high population estimate in Exodus 12:37 or it may reflect one ancient period of prosperity brought on by an absence of disease, blight, and drought. Numbers 22:3 has a similar mention of enemies being in dread of the great number of Israelites. Terence Fretheim remarks that some of the Hebrews' thriving in Egypt could well have been due to favorable or humane working conditions brought about by Egyptians. As we read chapters 1—15, it will be important for modern readers to keep an open mind about ordinary Egyptian citizens long ago.

If Propp's analysis of the sources is correct, then both P and J emphasize the rapid increase in population, but only J speaks of a Pharaoh who wants to bring death upon some of the Hebrews. E touches on the theme of growth in verse 20, although in the rest of verses 15–21 E describes the Israelites as few enough to need just two midwives. There is no need to resolve this difference in traditions by proposing that the two women were the leaders of a larger guild of midwives.

The image of oppression, especially in verses 11–14, is striking, but hard to analyze. Many ancient civilizations had variations of the corvée system, in which young adults from peasant, serf, or slave classes were drafted for periods of work without compensation, often during the slow period between sowing and harvesting times. (Later on, King Solomon did the same with his own people.) If they were kept busy for just a few months, they could return home to help with harvests and herds. When they were kept longer on bigger projects, their families back in the villages had to handle those tasks by themselves.

In Exodus, the tradition points to a period of increased corvée service, under humiliating conditions. Verses 13–14 describe this with great intensity, using forms of *ybd* (to labor) five times, *prk* (with rigor or ruthlessly) twice, and once the verb *mrr* (to make life bitter). The long servitude in Egypt was solemnly predicted in Genesis 15:13–14. Fretheim notes that there is no focus in this passage on Hebrew faith or cultural identity; such passivity and loss of identity can occur during times of oppression.

Mention is made of building *Pithom* and *Rameses*, which may be allusions to major projects in the time of Pharaohs Seti I and Rameses II. The *land* of Rameses is mentioned in Genesis 47:11 and Exodus 12:37. In various ancient biblical manuscripts, other cities are named instead of Pithom and Rameses. The hints of the time of Rameses II are only hints, and scholars have many cautions to raise against taking the Exodus setting as a solid chronicle of that specific time. Fretheim points out that, in this chapter, building storage or supply cities is taken as a way to wear down people to the point of death, whereas in Genesis 41:34–36 Joseph supervised the storing of great amounts of grain in order to preserve life for many. Nahum Sarna describes the consuming, exhausting aspects of ancient Near Eastern farming, irrigation, maintenance of canals, mud-brick making, construction, and the like. Empire was built on the backs of peasants and serfs.

Most scholars consider that the midwives were probably Hebrews, despite the ambiguity of ancient variants that referred to *midwives of the Hebrews* (who could have been Egyptians). Their names do not seem to be Egyptian in form. Whether they were Hebrews or not, they were bold in disobeying the Pharaoh. The reference in verse 19 to the quickness of the Hebrew births could also intimate Egyptian attitudes or prejudices, at least in Pharaoh's mind.

Propp notes that killing Hebrew male infants could eventually lead to more intermarriage with Egyptians and to a more subject population (as was often done with dependents of those captured and executed after battle). He also mentions that the new Pharaoh may have incited such xenophobia for his own advancement. Alternatively, he may have been afraid to mount a direct military attack and cause rebellion or loss of income.

Questions

1. As you read the opening passage about Jacob's sons and their families and how they all eventually passed away in Egypt, what is the storyteller doing for the reader? How should we work with verse 7?

2. In verse 8 we hear of the new king; he explains his concerns to his people in verses 9–10. What tone or impression do those two verses set? What is the overall effect of verses 9–14?

3. As we read of the king's instructions to the two midwives (and their later replies to him) in verses 15–19, the storyteller apparently intended us to understand that these two interactions were held in private, and that no other Hebrews or Egyptians knew about the matter. The boys were to be secretly suffocated and declared to be stillborn. How many problems or questions do you think you or other modern readers might raise about these five verses?

4. Verse 22 indicates the king's third strategy to control these slaves. Newborn Hebrew male infants are now publicly doomed. How can we judge the accuracy of the details in chapter 1? Do we have the right to dismiss implausible fictive elements? Does this chapter taken by itself stand on its own two feet?

Conclusion

We must remember that there was a vast spectrum of slavery in the ancient world; in fact, high-ranking slaves often had slaves of their own. Later on, slavery was allowed within Judaism and early Christianity. Our own disapproval of the custom now is so deep-seated that we could demonize the Pharaoh's intention to hold onto his slaves, despite the fact that it was virtually a worldwide practice, combined with systems controlling serfs and peasants.

Section Two:
Exodus 2:1–25

Most of this chapter is usually attributed to J,
except for the P comments in verses 23b–25. We should
consider 2:1–10 as a real sequel to chapter 1, rather
than simply a variant of E's story in 1:15–21.

Introduction

This chapter also divides into several short episodes. Verses
1–10 describe the birth of Moses and his adoption by the daughter of the Pharaoh. Verses 11–15a show his first contacts with
Hebrews as an adult (up to the mention of Pharaoh's anger), and
verses 15b–23a tell us of his early life in exile in Midian (up to the
mention of Pharaoh's death). The closing remarks, verses
23b–25, focus on the Israelites' suffering and God's resolve to
move forward.

The names of Moses' parents appear later, in the Priestly
genealogy in Exodus 6:16–20; and they and his sister Miriam are
identified in another genealogy in Numbers 26:29. The unnamed
sister in Exodus 2 need not have been Miriam, but biblical traditions assume that she is the same person. (Further mentions of
Miriam in Exod 15:20–21 and Num 12 are most likely from the
E level of traditions. In Num 12 she and Moses are estranged, at
least for a time.)

The mention that the boy was *good*, handsome, or *fine* clearly
echoes the creation theme that God saw his work of each day as
good. The context indicates that the infant is healthy, but not necessarily mild-mannered or quiet (the devout wish of many a parent kept up at night). The fitness of the child adds to the pathos
of the need to expose him to danger. Strictly speaking, Moses'

mother complies with the law to put her infant in the Nile, although clearly she was trying to save the child's life.

Tebah, the Hebrew word for "basket" mentioned in 2:3, is also used for the *ark* of Noah in Genesis 6—9. The word appears nowhere else in the Old Testament. (Today the same word is used for the cabinet in a synagogue that contains the sacred scrolls.) The allusion to God renewing creation in Noah's time highlights the new creation that God is about to set in motion. The word for "reeds" in 2:3 will be used in the *Sea of Reeds* in Exodus 13:18.

If the name *Mosheh* were related to the Hebrew verb for "rescue," that form, *mosheh*, would be an active participle meaning "rescuer." The princess had the right to name the child, since she was adopting him. Most scholars point out that the princess considers herself the one who rescued Moses, and that logically she should have given him a name based on a passive verbal form such as *mashuy*, indicating that he was the "rescued one." (It may also be possible that *mosheh* is a rare passive form itself.) Perhaps the point is that the princess does not know Hebrew as well as she thinks she does!

In fact, the word *Moses* is Egyptian in origin, and means "born of" or "son of." It was usually part of a longer name, but can stand alone. Those responsible for the pun in Hebrew (this baby boy, with God's help, will grow up to be the real *rescuer* of his people) were probably well aware of the Egyptian root of the name.

Name plays like this, whether in this case ribbing the princess for making a mistake or not, are quite common in the Old Testament.

Propp mentions other ancient Near Eastern legends of heroes exposed or abandoned as infants, such as the story of Sargon, a great king of Akkad, or the myths about Atrahasis or Horus. He notes that innate fear of exposure (being left outdoors to die), or respect for those who saved exposed infants and raised them, may have generated such legends, and that the ones saved in these tales might have been considered to have gained special skills or experiences during those crises. One could propose that the story of the finding of Moses fits these patterns, but that is only one possibility.

Propp also notes that we know of the custom of marriages between Egyptian nobles and foreign women, and that the children of the ruling classes of other countries were often raised and educated at the Egyptian court as part of the empire's system of influence. (The custom of training young nobles at other courts was common in the history of European monarchies.) In 1 Kings 11:14–22 we have a similar case of close relationships between an Edomite noble and the Egyptian court. One could imagine Moses as the child of parents with influence at court (or as the child of an Egyptian father); then later traditions rearranged the stories to make Moses more of an outsider or more completely Hebrew, and thus more clearly called to his role by God.

Later Jewish traditions depicted Moses as being about forty years old when he killed the Egyptian (see Acts 7:23), but the text does not specify his age; in fact, the average reader would probably assume that he was closer to the age of twenty.

The domineering Egyptian was not necessarily one of the slave drivers. (Exodus 21:20–21 allows moderate corporal punishment for slaves.) When Moses looked around and saw no one, we could speculate that he desired secrecy or that he was looking for someone to help him separate the two or to witness to his intervention as a necessary act of justice. Somewhat similar poetic phrases about seeing that there is no one to help or respond, found in Isaiah 41:28; 50:2; 59:16, lend some weight to the suggestion that Moses was looking for assistance in Exodus 2:12. On the other hand, looking around before the killing, burying the body, and later being afraid when the affair became known to others, are indicators of an original intention for secrecy.

What was the *affair* or *thing* that was known? While we ordinarily think of the killing of the Egyptian, the *thing* might instead refer to Moses' Hebrew identity. In fact, the aggressive Hebrew was able to counter Moses effectively by knowing of the incident. His challenge about Moses' right to judge makes more sense if we assume that he realized that Moses had Hebrew roots.

Commentators fall into two camps on the killing by Moses. Some consider his intervention legitimate or courageous or at least sincere. They take it to be at worst a singular overreaction in a good cause, or an incident that shows some of Moses' leadership potential and his passion for justice.

Others see Moses' anger and violence as primary, and that his intervention had no positive results. Propp judges Moses to be acting as a vigilante, and that his initial foibles point to the rocky relationships he will have with Egyptians and with Hebrews throughout the Pentateuch. Brevard Childs sees Moses as identifying with the slave being beaten, but Childs sees no evidence of Moses being driven by a commitment in faith at this point. The killing touches off a series of events that seem to flow by accident rather than anything else. In Acts 7:25 Moses comprehends his role as a rescuer sent by God, but this brief story in Exodus does not explain his motives.

The next story takes place at a well in Midian, a remote region to the east of Egypt. The Midianites are described as descendants of Abraham and his minor wife Keturah (Gen 25:1–6). Throughout the Old Testament there are various traditions in favor or against the Midianite people. Given famous stories at wells in Genesis (Abraham's servant meets Rebekah in chapter 24, and Jacob meets Rachel in chapter 29), we now see Moses in a similar situation.

In verse 17, the bullying shepherds *drove away* (*grsh*) the young women and their flocks. The same verb is used of the Pharaoh in Exodus 6:1; 10:11; 11:1; 12:39 as he *drives away* some of the Hebrews during his long struggle with them. In the same verse 17, Moses *came to their defense* (other translations are *freed, delivered,* or *saved*). Forms of this well-known verb *ysh'* are used of God in 14:13, 30; 15:2, wherein he is the *salvation* of Israel.

The girls' father, *Reuel,* is also called *Jethro* in Exodus 18, where he visits with Moses and offers him sound advice. As the young women praise Moses to their father, they say that he *helped them against* the shepherds. The same verb *nzl* is used of God *delivering* his people in 3:8; 6:6; 12:27. The daughters returned to their camp without bringing Moses along. This may have been inadvertent, or perhaps only the head of the family can issue such an invitation. As Reuel asks the whereabouts of the stranger, he may have been impatient with his daughters' lapse of manners, or just joshing them for the error.

Fretheim and other commentators admire Moses' compassion, shown in his protests against injustice. Fretheim argues that Moses learned this love of justice within his Egyptian upbringing, and not just from Hebrew culture.

Moses' first son is named *Gershom*, a common name at the time, most likely meaning "sojourner there." Moses refers to his own situation by this name, in that he was a *sojourner* or *alien* in Egypt (or perhaps in Midian, before he settled down). In another way, Moses will be a sojourner all his life, throughout the travails in Egypt to come, the long lonely wandering with people ready to complain about his leadership, and in his dying within sight of the Promised Land.

Moses' second son, Eliezer, is spoken of in Exodus 18:4, but there is little emphasis on Moses' marriage or his children in the Bible. The fact that he has sons is mentioned in passing in 4:20 and 18:1–6.

The Priestly concluding section, verses 23b–25, flows from 1:14 and leads directly to 6:2. In the final verse God *saw* the Israelites, meaning that he knew what was in their hearts. In the same way, he had gone down to *see* (the hearts of) the people of Sodom in Genesis 18:21. The final verse assures us that God *knew* his people or *took notice* of them. Propp argues for the value of a slight change in the Hebrew (reflecting the ancient Greek Septuagint translation), which would mean that God *made himself known* to his people. This form is also used in Ezekiel 20:5. Either version makes sense; God's knowing will lead to his intervention in the lives of these slaves in the next incident at the burning bush.

The king of Egypt died after *many days*; later (Exod 7:7) we are told that Moses was eighty when he confronted the next Pharaoh. If he was about forty when he killed the domineering Egyptian, then the king who forced him to flee to Midian died after forty years.

Questions

5. How reassuring to the reader are all the details given in 2:1–4?
6. Exodus 2:5–10 races to depict a very happy ending to this crisis in the life of the infant Moses. How much initiative is

shown by the princess, Pharaoh's daughter? How much by Moses' own sister and mother?

7. In these two chapters the king of Egypt is the obvious villain, but many other Egyptians seem to obey the rules or perhaps even agree that the Hebrew slaves need to be kept in their place. Given this, can you see any shortcomings in the princess? These might complicate the image of her in your answer to Question 6.

8. The compact paragraph describing the princess adopting Moses is outdone by the next four verses, 11–14, a masterpiece of brevity. One could imagine Moses as a sincere fighter for freedom for his people, and unfairly shunned by the one outspoken, aggressive Hebrew slave. However, we could also look for shortcomings within Moses himself. How well does Moses handle these two incidents? Why does the Hebrew slave rebuke Moses so forcefully? Why wasn't Moses given any sort of fair hearing by Egyptian officials?

9. In 2:15b–22 Moses drove away unscrupulous shepherds who habitually bullied the seven sisters (judging from 2:18, their father expected them to be delayed as usual). This incident at the well in Midian depicts some of Moses' good fortune. What does the passage contribute to the larger picture being developed in chapter 2 as a whole?

10. Exodus 2:23–25 mentions the ongoing harsh realities facing the Hebrews in Egypt. But now God is preparing to intervene in their lives in new ways. Are the Israelites or Moses ready for what is coming? Why did God wait so long before making his moves?

11. The name *Moses* is derived from the Egyptian language, despite the legend in 2:10. What other facts in Exodus 1—2 might be historically accurate? Start your guessing in the second chapter, and then work backward to the first chapter. (Even the experts admit that most of their conclusions at this point are educated guesses.)

Conclusion

Fretheim reminds us that we need to be alert to God's work with the Israelites prior to their Exodus. Some of that work took place during their long sojourn in Egypt. There they were able to learn of some of the positive values in Egyptian culture. To repeat one example, the princess adopting Moses can be taken as a protest against cruelty (as we see in 3:21; 9:20; 11:3, 8). In some way she and other Egyptians advance God's plans, even if unconsciously.

So too, Moses' own life images the fate of his people and anticipates their future. His disrupted childhood and adolescence reflect their travails. The rebuke of Moses by the aggressive Hebrew slave is a foretaste of many later rebukes of Moses by his own people during their forty years in the wilderness.

It is also important to appreciate the style of these chapters. For example, in chapter 2 many basic Hebrew words are repeated frequently and some verbs are used twice that might not be apparent in English. *Child* is used six times, *daughter* nine times, and *man* nine times. *Man* appears in verses 1, 11 (twice), 12, 13, 14, 19, 20, and 21; in English translations the word is only needed in verses 1, 20, and 21. The same verb *gdl* describes Moses *growing up* in verses 10 and 11, although it first refers to his reaching the age of three or so and the second time it refers to adulthood. Likewise, the references to *striking* in verse 11, and *killing* in verse 12, come from the same verb *nkh*. Finally, Moses' *settling* and *sitting* in verse 15 are two instances of the same verb *ishb*. Keeping the vocabulary simple, and repeating the same word often, are techniques or matters of style to speed things along. The simplicity and speed underplay details, leaving the emotions of the characters the more important focus.

Section Three:
Exodus 3:1–22

Propp attributes most of chapter 3 to E, except for
J elements in verses 2–4a, 5, 9, and perhaps 21–22. Other
commentators find a few more J verses in this chapter.

Introduction

The next several chapters form a complex foundation for the
story of the plagues and the march through the sea, but the traditional chapter divisions will be satisfactory for our format of
introductions and questions. Exodus 3:1—4:17 is often taken as
the opening part of this foundation, followed by Moses' starting
the actual trip to Egypt in 4:18. The Elohist clearly explains the
tradition that the name Yahweh first was revealed during the time
of Moses. He joins it to the mention of the patriarchs, and casts
Moses as a prophet called by God.

The storyteller wastes no time getting to God's appearance to
Moses, who was tending sheep for his father-in-law. Several commentators point out that shepherding is an idealized Old
Testament image for becoming a leader. Propp notes that Moses
tended sheep owned by another person; later he will become the
leader of a people owned by God.

The use of the name Jethro instead of Reuel (2:18) is consistent in the E tradition. The name Jethro may mean something
like "(a god) is great"; Umberto Cassuto considers it a name of
honor, since it is used in the long passage in Exodus 18, and
because Moses is Jethro's son-in-law.

E refers to the mountain as Horeb, instead of Sinai (used by J).
Fretheim suggests that the name Horeb, apparently meaning
"wasteland," might indicate a humble setting for this most holy

event. While we usually equate Horeb and Sinai, the varying ancient traditions disagreed on this or that location for the mountain.

The name Yahweh (replaced in most English Bibles by the title LORD) appears for the first time in Exodus in 3:2 and then in 3:4, 7. At first, this name is intended for the reader; Moses does not learn of God's name until 3:15. Fretheim suggests that future translators of the Old Testament should return to using the name Yahweh whenever it appears, since a title such as LORD is not as effective in our culture as is a proper name.

The thorn bush is called *seneh* in Hebrew, perhaps a play on the place name *Sinai*. The only other use of *seneh* in the Old Testament is in Deuteronomy 33:16. Some species of thorny desert plants can spontaneously ignite in times of severe heat and drought, but the miracle here is that the bush does not consume itself in the flames. Moses may well be drawn to the spot simply by curiosity, rather than by a firm intuition that a divine presence is within the flame. In any case he shows initiative, and his attentive approaching is noted favorably by God. Propp takes the burning bush as a small wondrous sign from nature, in line with the stick and snake sign in chapter 4; more amazing wonders will come later in the book. Fretheim notes that such a bush is a common or lowly site for such a revelation, perhaps chosen not to overwhelm Moses at the start.

The command to Moses to remove his sandals is not explained here. The custom might have been a gesture of humility or obedience or of cleanliness, if leather was considered tainted or impure. Many Orthodox Jewish worshippers today still avoid wearing leather shoes in synagogues. A similar command is found in Joshua 5:15.

The flames coming out of the bush may well hint at the pillar of smoke and fire in Exodus 13:21, or at the dramatic effects in Exodus 19:16–19. Even though he was drawn to this special encounter, Moses exemplifies the biblical tradition not to risk looking directly at God in whatever guise he appears.

When God refers to *your father* in verse 6, it could mean Moses' own father, rather than more remote ancestors, such as Abraham,

Isaac, and Jacob. Some ancient versions have the plural *fathers*, assuming that the patriarchs were the main focus of this verse.

Exodus 3:7–10 can be considered the opening section of this major revelation to Moses, an event in which he learns much about God and his plans, but also has the opportunity to ask questions. Verses 16–18 serve as the closing section, in which Moses is told what to do next after this meeting with God.

God calls the Israelites *my people* in verses 7 and 10. He is deeply concerned at their suffering. Similar compassion for the disadvantaged can be found in Exodus 22:21–27. This divine concern deepens our understanding of the more formal, hinting statements about God in Exodus 2:23–25.

Verses 7–9 do not clearly indicate that Moses will be asked to play any role in verse 10. In his question in 3:11, Moses expresses surprise, and perhaps humility. "Who am I...?" could well be equivalent to our modern retort, "Why me?" Fretheim points out that this is the first of eight questions that Moses will put forward. The complete list includes 3:13; 4:1, 10, 13; 5:22–23; 6:12, 30. This ongoing dialogue between Moses and God will reveal some of the character of each participant. God took a chance in selecting a human envoy to reach out to his people and to challenge the Pharaoh; anyone given such a responsibility could stumble or fall. Moses certainly has the right to ask questions, since he must develop leadership skills. In 3:11 we could surmise that Moses is truly humble, or perhaps not very self-confident. His question, then, seems sincere and honest.

Even so, some commentators suspect that even at 3:11 Moses is being a bit stubborn. Of course, God can choose weak patriarchs, leaders, and prophets. He can see inner strengths in these men and women, and can give them any gifts needed to help them freely fulfill their tasks. In 3:12, God reassures Moses that he will be with Moses through all this. He mentions a *sign*; most commentators assume that this will be the worship ceremonies at this location after they leave Egypt. Cassuto takes this mention of returning as a fully reassuring promise. Others say that it is also possible that this sign was instead the burning bush and this very encounter. Childs holds that the burning bush can do double duty; it confirms the present revelation from God and points to the future return to this same holy site.

The impact of God's actions in Exodus 3:1–12 should certainly remind us of the calls given to other prophets. Jeremiah (1:4–10), Isaiah (6), Hosea (chapters 1 and 3), and Amos (7:14–15) seem to have had similar overwhelming experiences.

In 3:13, Moses then asks another question. In seeking God's personal name, Moses is grasping for a deeper relationship with God. He feels the need to know in order to convince the other Israelites, and perhaps to convince himself, that this God already knows him and his people. Commentators vary in guessing at Moses' reasons for the question in verse 13. Childs allows that the people should ask such a question if, and when, Moses delivers this message to them, but Moses could certainly have had his own doubts as well, and chose to hide his own misgivings behind his focus on the Israelites.

Therefore, Childs sees verse 14 as first of all an answer to Moses himself. The words are a challenge to Moses to appreciate the consistency of God's love for his people. The larger context indicates that verse 14 is meant to be helpful or reassuring. God will be there to support Moses in any predicament. Additional notes of reassurance can be found in 4:12, 15; 6:7; 29:45. In each of these verses, as well as in 3:12, first-person Hebrew forms *I will be* or *I am* stand out. Unlike English, which always expresses personal pronouns and the verb *to be*, many ancient inflected languages, including Hebrew, did not need to express them except for emphasis.

Childs observes that introducing the name Yahweh here will show that Moses is in the mainstream of Jewish thought. The history of the prophetic movement was stormy. At times some false prophets would represent other gods, or speak for Yahweh without actually being inspired by him. There are several points in the Old Testament that allude to these false messages and messengers, and to the strife they brought about. See Deuteronomy 13:1–5; 18:15–22; 1 Kings 18:1–40; 2 Kings 10:18–28; Jeremiah 2:8 and 23:9–15 (especially verse 13) for examples.

Verses 14 and 15 of Exodus 3 each have two parts, conventionally indicated by a letter with each part of the verse:

14a God said to Moses, "I AM WHO I AM."

14b He said further, "Thus you shall say to the Israelites, 'I AM has sent me to you.'"

15a God also said to Moses, "Thus you shall say to the Israelites, 'The LORD, the God of your ancestors, the God of Abraham, the God of Isaac, and the God of Jacob, has sent me to you':

15b This is my name forever, and this my title for all generations.

Childs takes 14a as a parallel to all of 15, and 15b as a bridge back to verse 13. Most commentators note that verse 15 seems to be the most direct answer to verse 13.

Verse 14 is usually taken as a play on words; *Yahweh* is often taken as something like a third-person form of the verb *to be*, which in verse 14 is found in the first-person form *'ehyeh*. Given this connection to the verb *to be*, then *I am who I am* can also mean *I will be who I will be*, since future tenses use the present forms in Hebrew. In fact, the certain origin of the name *Yahweh* may never be found; the connection to the verb *to be* is still argued.

Cassuto assumes that Moses himself has no doubts at this point and just wants to be able to communicate well when he returns to Egypt. Cassuto claims that the inner meaning of the name in verse 14 is that God will help now and in the future. Cassuto explains God's intention in these words: "It is I who am with my creatures in their hour of trouble and need. I will always be true to my word." A similar sentiment is found in the hymn in Exodus 15:1–6. Verse 15 simply announces the name itself and solemnly establishes it as the name to use in worship. Similar solemn pronouncements can be found in Hosea 12:5; Psalm 102:12; Psalm 135:13.

Propp thinks of Moses' question as a test. Within the context of all of Genesis and Exodus, the name Yahweh would be expected by any reader of Moses' question. If we just focus on the E traditions, then Yahweh is a new name at this point, but the God of this name is not new. He has consistently loved his people. Propp appreciates the ambiguities in verse 14. He says that "I will be who I will be" does not simply mean, "I can be and can do anything," but rather, along with the rest of verse 14, serves as both an encouragement and a smooth way to terminate this conversation with Moses. Propp considers verse 14 as a cagey response, possibly petulant or sarcastic while half-serious, perhaps even humorous, for the reader. Propp may push the envelope here, but listing such varied possibilities may help our own reflections.

Fretheim finds many positive notes in this passage. Certainly, Moses can only be fully confident of God's promises as they happen. Moses should rely on God's consistent love and support in the past. Fretheim mixes the tenses in verse 14 to aid his own reflection, coming up with "I am who I will be," or "I will be who I am." Both sayings point to the meaning "I will be God for you," a God who is faithful and consistent. So verse 15 could be understood as a commitment to the future by both God and his people.

To conclude, we should consider verses 13–15 in their cohesion. We can see parallels within verse 14 and within verse 15, as well as between 14a and 15a and between 14b and 15b. There is no need for us to consider verse 14 as an inferior addition to the religious meaning of the passage.

In Exodus 3:16–18, Moses is instructed to relay this hope-filled message to the elders of Israel, and then go with them to talk to the Pharaoh. In fact, in Exodus 5:1 Aaron, not the elders, will go with Moses. In 3:18, the phrases *the God of the Hebrews* and *has met* (*qrh*) were chosen to be clear to the Pharaoh, not likely familiar with Jewish thinking. The request to make a religious pilgrimage would involve the adult Hebrew males only. Propp notes that there are ancient records of extended religious holiday periods allowed to Egyptian peasants who worked on royal building projects.

In 3:20, the phrases *I will stretch out* (*my hand*) and *he will let you go* are from the same verb *shlh*.

In 3:21–22, mention is made of gaining *favor* and *asking* for clothing and jewelry. This topic will come up again in chapters 11 and 12. In 3:22, it is called *plunder* (*nzl*). Many commentators consult Deuteronomy 15:13–15 at this point, a passage that encourages Jewish slave owners to provide generously for newly freed slaves. Some commentators doubt the link to Deuteronomy 15.

Questions

12. What can you learn about Moses and about God in 3:1–6?
13. How is Moses portrayed as he listens to God's words in 3:7–12? Is 3:10 an invitation to Moses, or a prompting about a vocation for him?
14. How are Moses and the Israelites depicted in 3:13–15? What is the impact for the reader of God's solemn responses in 3:14–15?
15. What is the tone of God's instructions in 3:16–18? What is the real point of the request made to the Pharaoh in 3:18?
16. Doesn't 3:19–20 reveal or give away the main plot of the next dozen chapters? Why would editors allow such a passage to appear so early in a story?
17. Exodus 3:21–22 also looks ahead to the time of the actual Exodus (chapters 11—12). Are these requests for jewelry and fine clothing appropriate? Will the Egyptians really *favor* or *honor* the Israelites, as God says in 3:21? In 3:22, God describes this as a way to *plunder* the Egyptians. The dictionary defines plundering as taking something by force, theft, or fraud. Is plundering allowed when there is a divine command?

Conclusion

Chapter 3 moves at a fast pace, as Moses is enlisted to be God's messenger to the Hebrew people and to the Egyptians, especially as represented by the Pharaoh. God's plans sound very convincing. He is sure the Hebrews will receive all this confidently (3:18), and that Egyptian opposition will be very temporary (3:20).

The chapter gives no indications of the range of emotions we will see when the Egyptians are offended, or when the Hebrews panic, or when they are offered a covenant, or when they abandon Moses soon after, or when they repent and involve themselves in preparing the Tabernacle. God may have known the future when he first spoke to Moses, but even he had yet to experience the fluctuations that his plans would bring upon himself.

The fast pace and oversimplification of things to come are elements of sound storytelling.

Section Four:
Exodus 4:1–31

> Propp assigns much of this chapter to E, proposing that
> J is represented in verses 19, 20a, and 24–26.
> Verse 21b could be from a redactor.

Introduction

There may be a play on words in 4:2, where the question *What is that?* (*mzh*) sounds somewhat like the word for *staff* (*mth*).

In 4:4, the instruction to grab the snake *by its tail* is odd; the much safer procedure is to immobilize it at the neck and head first. The storyteller might have ignored this point, or perhaps God was giving Moses a greater challenge in telling him to catch it this way.

Moses' hand was struck by leprosy (or some other condition that whitened his skin), perhaps for his doubts about whether the people would listen to him. In Numbers 12, Miriam was struck in much the same way for defying Moses' authority.

In 4:1, Moses says that the people will not listen to his *voice* (*qol*). In 4:8, the Hebrew refers to the *voice* of the first sign and the *voice* of the second. The context shows us that in verse 8 *voice* stands for the *deeper meaning* of the signs.

In 4:1, 5, 8, 9, 31, the author has God and Moses talking about the people *believing* (*'amn*). Here belief must indicate trust and obedience rather than simply a deep comprehension of truths about God himself. Cassuto admits that Moses may have had some self-doubts in 4:1, but denies that Moses is trying to refuse the commission itself. Cassuto asserts that the three signs in 4:3–9 met all of Moses' anxieties.

Moses' new concern in verse 10 is extensive; he knows he has not been and is not a *man of words*, even in light of this great commission. He further says that he is *heavy (kbd) of mouth* and *heavy of tongue*. (This same word, *heavy*, will be used of Pharaoh's *heart* in 7:14; 8:11, 28; 9:7, 34.) One prophet's similar concern can be found in Jeremiah 1:6–10.

There are several ways to understand Moses' remark. He could still be doubting himself, or he may have lost some Egyptian or Hebrew language skills over the years abroad. Several commentators go further and assume that Moses was speaking of a physical speech impediment.

In verse 13, Moses seems to waffle even more. The Hebrew text says, *O Lord, send I pray thee by the hand (of him whom) you will send.* The words are apparently polite, but the meaning is not entirely self-evident. The NRSV smoothes this out to "O my Lord, please send someone else." Other commentators propose "send anyone else," or "send me only as the last choice."

Clearly Moses wants out, and his reference to someone else, to anyone else, or to himself as the last choice could even be considered sarcastic or whining. Cassuto argues against this idea that Moses wants out; he takes verse 13 as a humble entreaty by someone who is troubled.

So God proposes using Aaron. The Hebrew identifies him as *Aaron, your brother, the Levite.* Propp argues that in context this means only that they are fellow Levites. Similar use of the word *brother* in this broad fashion can be found in Deuteronomy 15:12; 18:7; Numbers 16:10; Jeremiah 34:14. The various sources for the Pentateuch seem to reflect different traditions about the family relationships of Moses, Aaron, and Miriam. In Exodus 15:20, Miriam is called Aaron's sister. In Exodus 6:20, the redactor refers to Moses and Aaron as full brothers, and in the Priestly section, including Numbers 26:59, all three are full siblings.

Some commentators note that verses 27–28 should follow verse 17, to keep the details about Aaron in a better chronological order. Others consider all of verses 13–16, 27–31 as secondary material added to the main story, because these traditions about Aaron seem to contradict 4:11–12.

The image of putting words in someone's mouth is easy enough to understand. See Jeremiah 1:6–10 and 15:19 for examples. The staff Moses used in 4:3–4 is mentioned again in 4:17.

In the stories to come it will represent God's power, power delegated to Moses (and at times actually used by Aaron). In some other ancient Near Eastern religious traditions, rods or clubs used by gods seem to have more innate self-directedness, but in Exodus the staff is simply an instrument or a pointer.

At the end of verse 17, Moses is silent; one can assume that he will obey, but the silence adds to the mystery of how much Moses has taken all this into his heart.

Beginning with 4:18, we can follow Moses' return to Egypt, and then come to the first confrontation with Pharaoh, where he adds more toil to their brick making. These stories end at 6:1.

At first sight, 4:18 and 19 seem to be in reverse order. The instruction by God to return to Egypt could logically precede the conversation with Jethro. Propp suggests that an editor might have assumed that the bush at Horeb was not located within the area known as Midian. Thus the editor needed to mention speaking to Jethro and then report Yahweh's words in Midian. Verses 19 and 20a, probably from J, point back to the account of the killing of the Egyptian in Exodus 2:11–15.

There is a fine point of translation in Exodus 4:23b. The prefix on the verb *you refused* could be translated *but* or *then* (NRSV has *but*). In this case, the entire verse is a sentence of doom. On the other hand, it is possible to translate that initial prefix to mean *if.* Other translators (RSV, NAB) and commentators (Childs, Propp, Fretheim) who prefer this option see a conditional sentence, with the words warning the Pharaoh what will happen *if he refuses* to yield or repent. Fretheim speaks of the possibility that Egypt could be open to the future and to yielding, but admits that God's plans are troubling.

We jump immediately from the threat to Pharaoh's son to verses 24–26, an obscure story that involves Moses' son. Commentators note the pronoun *him* (twice in verse 24 and once in verse 26), and the adjective *his* in verse 25 (*his feet*; some translations substitute the phrase *Moses' feet* in an attempt to clarify). In all four cases the words might refer to the infant, rather than to Moses himself. There is no way to remove this ambiguity. In 4:25–26, the word *blood* is actually in the plural, *bloods* (*damim*);

oftentimes in Hebrew, plural forms represent abstract meanings of nouns.

While some commentators observe that 4:27–28 could have been placed after verse 17, the present location works well enough as a follow-up passage and conclusion to all of chapter 4. Taking verse 14 as it stands, Fretheim suggests that Aaron started the trip on his own. In this view, God's instruction in verse 27 simply confirms the care Aaron has for his brother. Aaron and Moses met at the mountain of God, presumably the same Horeb where the burning bush was revealed. Cassuto notes the use of the same form of the verb *he met* in verses 24 and 27, even though the two scenes are quite different.

In verse 30, Aaron spoke the words, but the Hebrew text does not identify the performer of the signs, using just the pronoun *he* in the verb form. Most commentators assume Aaron performed the signs (staff-snake, white hand, water to blood), but some imagine that Moses took on this task. The original audience was to have been the elders (verse 29), but apparently the people were also addressed then or soon after. Propp notes that in 3:16, 18, and here in 4:29, the elders are cooperative intermediaries who call no attention to themselves. In other parts of the Exodus story they will have more complex roles. As an essential part of the village, clan, and tribal system, elders were major players in Israel's hectic history of government. Propp suggests that in the E traditions the profile of complete cooperation described in these chapters may have been idyllic.

Questions

18. In 4:1, how do you think Moses felt when he suggested that the Israelites might not believe him? How effective do you find the snake and stick sign?

19. As the second and third signs are described in verses 6–9, what do you learn about God?

20. In this negotiation scene (verses 10–17), why does God not simply give Moses new powers of speech and persua-

sion? What does God do instead? Do verses 15–16 sound like a workable arrangement?

21. Do verses 18-20 advance the story? Do you find any unusual details in these verses?

22. Exodus 4:21–23 gives away the ending again, as did 3:19–20. How is this chapter 4 passage different from the one in chapter 3?

23. Exodus 4:24–26 is unexpected by almost all readers of the book. Why does Zipporah take the lead here? Had Moses done anything wrong?

24. What is the tone of 4:27–31? As Aaron completes the speaking and demonstrating of the signs, how do the people react in verse 31?

Conclusion

At the start of each chapter or section, I indicate mainstream estimates of which verses come from which source; I do favor Propp's tendency to attribute more verses to the Elohist. While we should not let the matter of sources disrupt our reading of the complete text, some of the results of source analysis can be helpful. Looking at all of chapters 3—4, Propp estimates only about a dozen verses to be from the Yahwist (J). These include 3:2–4a, 5, 9, 21–22 and 4:19–20, 24–26. Most of the rest is from the Elohist (E), with a few redactorial inserts. Highlighting the J verses in some way is an easy enough chore; with such a printout in hand, it is easy to follow Propp's reflections:

[B]oth J and E describe Moses conversing with Yahweh in Midian. In each source, Moses performs a special act— removing his sandals (J) or hiding his face (E)—because of the site's sanctity. In both J and E, Jahweh announces that he has perceived Israel's suffering and is going to save them from Egypt. But here there is a telling difference: in E, God first sees, then hears (3:7); in J, he first hears, then sees (3:9). In other words, for E, Yahweh is the initiator; in J, he reacts to Israel's plaint. In J, because the Deity is the actual savior, Moses needs no assistance. E, on the other hand, stresses Moses' responsibility and proportionally greater self-doubt. He must rely upon Aaron's eloquence and the elders' authority to persuade his own people and Pharaoh.... A final, formal difference between the sources is that in E Yahweh commands Moses to return to Egypt during their first conversation. In J, however, God sends him back in a subsequent communication, once the coast is clear (4:19). (*Exodus 1—18*, 194)

Section Five:
Exodus 5:1—6:1

Propp is inclined to attribute the entire chapter to E, but admits that many commentators think of the J level. There is an interesting parallel in 1 Kings 12:1–19 about Rehoboam's cruelty to his own subjects.

Introduction

This well-known tale of Pharaoh's harsh domination is more complex than it first appears. In Exodus 3:18, Moses was told to take the elders with him to this first meeting, and to ask permission for their pilgrimage to make sacrifices. Moses was not an elder himself, thus having no official status within Hebrew or Egyptian society. In fact, Moses and Aaron went without the elders, and they quoted Yahweh as saying, "Let my people go," which is a firm command form of the verb *shlh*, meaning "send away." Likewise, Moses was told in 4:21–23 to perform wonders and to mention the death of Pharaoh's firstborn. While that instruction to mention the death may not have been coupled to a specific time during the negotiations, Moses seems to bring it up for the first time much later, in chapter 11.

The introductory phrase, "Thus says the LORD," is the hallmark of the prophetic style; the occasional use of this in the Pentateuch is probably an anachronism.

The verb *hlk*, meaning "to go," is used by the people in their requests in verses 3, 8, 17, and in a dismissive, rebutting manner by the Pharaoh in verses 4, 7, 11, 18. (NRSV in verse 4 has *Get to* for *go to*.)

In the Hebrew of 5:5, the Pharaoh says *the people of the land are now many*. We presume he is referring to the Hebrew slaves

38

(connecting to the claims about numbers in chapter 1), but it might be possible that the phrase meant the *many Egyptians* whose routines were being disrupted by this slaves angling for time off.

The word for *you want them to stop working* is based on the verb *shbt*, the root of the word *sabbath*. This bold, intolerant Pharaoh does not represent the mainstream of Egyptian culture; most Egyptians were syncretistic in their religious practices, and we have Egyptian records of time off being allowed for rituals.

The Pharaoh goes well beyond shouting down Moses and Aaron. He immediately increases the workload upon all the Hebrews in a show of authority.

Note the *taskmasters* and *supervisors* mentioned in verse 6. Apparently the *taskmasters* (*ngsh*, "to enforce") are Egyptians; they are mentioned in verses 6, 10, 13, 14. The *supervisors* (*shtr*, "record keepers") are most likely Hebrew, and are mentioned in verses 6, 10, 14, 15, 19. Fretheim asks if the supervisors were drafted or took these jobs willingly.

The noun *work* in verses 9 and 11, the three instances of the word *servants* in verses 15–16, the fourth use of *servants* in verse 21 (NRSV translates it as *officials*), and the command to *work* in verse 18, are all based on the Hebrew verb *'bd*.

In 10:8, 24 and 12:31, the same verb of 5:18 to *work* will mean to *serve* or to *worship* God. In verse 22, the mention of Moses *turning aside* or *returning* to the LORD may indicate that this was a moment of private prayer, not performed in front of others. The first word in his speech, "O LORD," is the translation of the Hebrew word *Adonai*, used here rather than the proper name Yahweh. The usual custom when translating *Adonai* in English Bibles is to use three lowercase letters after the L/l, rather than small capital letters. *Adonai* was also used in 4:10, 13.

God replies in 6:1, apparently without taking any offense at Moses' forceful words. He alludes to what *he will do* (*'sh*) to Pharaoh. This same verb was used in 5:4, 8, 9, 13, and 16 to describe the *making* of bricks by the Hebrews. It is used in a more general sense in 5:15 in the phrase, "Why *do you treat* your servants like this?"

Questions

25. How does this Pharaoh handle the situation in 5:1–5? What would have been the normal extent of the festival and sacrifice proposed in verses 1 and 3?
26. In 5:6–9, why does the Pharaoh increase the workload?
27. What is the effect of 5:10–14, given that it mainly repeats the Pharaoh's program?
28. How much more do we learn in 5:15–19?
29. In 5:20–21, how do the supervisors treat Moses and Aaron?
30. In 5:22–23, does Moses have the right to complain to God in this fashion?
31. There are many mentions of *God* or LORD throughout chapter 5. What do the references achieve as devices for telling the bigger story?

Conclusion

Fretheim reminds us that the complaints of the supervisors and of Moses are partially correct; things are worse than they were before the Pharaoh became angry. He notes:

This is ultimately a recognition that deliverance from evil may entail the experience of even more evil. Overcoming oppression is a matter for struggle, *even for God*. Evil will not give up without a fight; God cannot wave a magic wand and make it all go away in an instant; protracted conflict is inevitable when evil is so deep-seated…. God does not chide Moses for his hard questions. God receives them for what they are: complaints at a difficult moment in life. God simply responds by assuring Moses that his purposes are on track. In fact, the antagonists in this struggle are now firmly set, given Pharaoh's outright refusal. Pharaoh's time is coming. Even more, the people's deliverance is coming. God's resolve is clear; Israel will be delivered. (*Exodus*, 87)

Section Six:
Exodus 6:2—7:7

> Most of this section is from P; it is likely that the
> genealogy in 6:13–30 was provided by a P redactor.
> The few previous Exodus verses from P are found
> in 1:1–7, 13, 14 and 2:23b–25.

Introduction

If we consider the P traditions in chapters 1—2 to be complete, and then continue with the P material in 6:2, the profile we
get is of Moses always living in Egypt. There was no exile in
Midian, nor a burning bush. God revealed himself as Yahweh for
the first time when he called Moses in 6:2 (see Ezek 20:5–6). The
genealogy is all we have to stand in for the stories of the childhood and early manhood of Moses.

Exodus 6:9–13 briefly describes the next steps after this revelation by Yahweh. The Israelites are too downtrodden to accept
the good news from Moses; next, God orders Moses to go to the
Pharaoh, but then Moses claims to be a *poor speaker* (the Hebrew
phrase in both 6:12 and 6:30 is *uncircumcised of lips*).

One difference in this P account is that there is no mention of
a three-day pilgrimage or journey to offer sacrifices. Readers
might have expected to see that mentioned in 6:11, 13, or in 7:2,
5. This omission is because the P traditions ignore mention of any
sacrifices before the covenant at Sinai.

In ancient tribal societies, genealogies were a way to assign status, responsibilities, and privileges among groups. In Jewish custom, the ranks of priests and Levites were hereditary; at times
conflicting genealogies became arguing points in internal disputes over matters of ceremony or authority. Scholars can follow

41

some of the shifts and counterclaims among priestly groups through the Old Testament, but that is not our purpose here. Orthodox and Roman Catholics have somewhat similar instances of narrow disputes and claims among priests and monks and other religious orders in the history of their churches, even though for them priesthood is not hereditary.

In this account in Exodus 6, Amram married his father's sister (or half sister). Many of the ancient translations modified this to say that she was a cousin. Marriage to one of such a close relationship as that of aunt is forbidden in Leviticus 18:12; 20:19. Later generations of rabbis assumed that either this marriage was from a time before such things were forbidden or that God made an exception in this case, especially to confirm full descent from Levi for Aaron (and for Moses). The marriages of other ancestors apparently needed the same ancient settings or exemptions. Abraham and Sarah were imagined to be half siblings (Gen 20:12), and Jacob married two living sisters, Leah and Rachel (Gen 29:16). These degrees of relationship are forbidden in Leviticus 18:9 and 18:18 respectively.

These genealogies make more sense as vehicles for tribal and clan values than as accurate lists of vital statistics such as we might look for in county record offices. In certain biblical genealogies, the names of some persons seem instead to be, in fact, place names.

Propp speculates that this genealogy may well have been about Aaron originally, and that Moses has now been spliced into it, as Aaron's younger brother. He raises questions about whether the Priestly author had higher regard for Aaron as compared to Moses, but this is going beyond our scope for now.

Some of the words and phrases in 7:1–5 appeared in earlier passages. God has already told Moses that the Pharaoh would not cooperate, in 3:19–20 and 4:21–23. The *hand* stretched out against Egypt recalls the *mighty hand* of 3:19–20 and 6:1. The *I am the* LORD icon was used in 6:29 in telling Moses to talk to the Pharaoh, echoing 6:2, 6, 7, and 8. God's intentions come to a dramatic level when he says in 7:5, *The Egyptians shall know that I am the* LORD.

God will use signs and wonders for his own people (4:2–9), but more especially against the Egyptians in 3:20; 4:21, 30. In 7:3, he says he will multiply (*rbh*) these signs. In 6:6 and 7:4, these powerful forces are called *mighty acts of judgment.*

Questions

32. Let us look at the Priestly material in 6:2–8 (and all of 6:2—7:7) as an alternate tradition about the call of Moses that in its own way continues the story after some foundational details from chapters 1—2. In 6:2–8 how is God depicted? What is the effect of the fourfold use of the phrase "I am the LORD" in verses 2, 6, 7, 8?

33. What does 6:9–13 tell us about the Hebrew people, about Moses, and about God? Exodus 6:28–29 repeats in brief some of the essentials of 6:9–13.

34. What seems to be the editor's purpose in inserting the genealogy found in 6:14–27? You should be able to draw some conclusions from verses 20, 23, 25–27.

35. In 6:13 and 7:1–2, 6–7, what is Aaron's status and role? Compare this with the situation in 4:14–16.

36. Even if 6:2—7:7 was originally an independent set of Priestly traditions that do not exactly match much of Exodus 1—5, it is now incorporated into the larger story and takes on new functions. It now serves as a sequel to chapters 3—5. How do 6:2–8, 10–11, 28–29, and 7:1–5 add to the momentum of the larger story up to this point? In the larger context, what is your first impression of Moses, based on 6:12 and 6:30?

37. We have seen two brief references to the Pharaoh opposing God's wishes (3:19–20 and 4:21–23). When you read 7:1–5, God describes what is to come in dramatic terms. We are at the threshold of the *great acts of judgment* (7:4) that will start in 7:8 with the wonder of Aaron's rod and will encompass ten plagues and the great escape through the Red Sea, ending in 14:31. The question of why and how the Pharaoh fights back so extensively will need much more study and reflection. However, we can ask ourselves at this point about what God wants to happen, as he pro-

claims in 7:1–5. Why does he plan to multiply his signs, to perform great acts, and to have the Egyptians know that he is the LORD? Is there anything positive in his speech in 7:1–5 for Egyptians (or for other Gentiles) of any era?

Conclusion

The problem of understanding the hardening of Pharaoh's heart will recur often in the coming chapters. There is no need to try to solve it yet; but I want to indicate Cassuto's overview (55–57) now, since it is brief and to the point. He has three observations. First, the authors of Exodus often use a "final cause" style to identify God's will in ordinary events. Therefore, for them to say that *God will harden* someone's heart is the same as saying that *that one's heart will be hard*. Second, the continuing degradation of the Hebrew slaves from the beginning of the Book of Exodus has been very unjust, and this Pharaoh and his willing fellow Egyptians merit the just punishments to come. Third, hardening someone's heart does not create sin; it simply moves a sinner toward a fitting end for injustices already committed or still being committed. Deuteronomy 2:30 shows King Sihon, his spirit hardened by God, choosing to fight rather than negotiate. He put up a good fight and lost, as God had intended.

Cassuto concludes:

> Thus, if we take cognizance of these three points, and read the passages according to their simple meaning, and according to the reasoning of their period…we shall see that in the final analysis there is no problem or difficulty here, and that everything is clear in the light of the original ideology of the Israelites. (*A Commentary on the Book of Exodus*, 57)

I find all three of Cassuto's arguments very inadequate for the topic. We need to think through a network of storytelling styles between here and the end of chapter 14, not just the point about final cause. We will need to ask many more questions about who is being cruel to whom, and about how God moves people.

I hope I can create problems about the hardening of heart if readers do not have any. In my experience, students reading Exodus inevitably become more and more puzzled as they head toward the eye of the hurricane, Passover night. Cassuto had the right to share his confident overview with us, but we have the right to have our own reactions to this coming great cascade of miracles and power struggles.

Section Seven:
Exodus 7:8—11:10

Please note: Because this section is rather long, each plague account will be titled, its sources identified, and each question or set of questions placed below; there will be one brief conclusion for the entire section. The answers will be found at the back of the book.

Introduction

These several chapters cover the initial contest with serpents between Moses and the Egyptian priests, then the first nine plagues, starting with reddening the Nile waters, and coming to the announcement of the tenth plague (11:4–8). While individual plague stories seem to have come from different sources, they now form a cohesive account. The style of the book changes dramatically at the beginning of chapter 12, and so chapters 12—13 deserve their own analysis.

Exodus 7:8–13:
The Contest with Serpents

> This preliminary episode is from the Priestly traditions.

Here the word for *snake* or *serpent* (*tannin*) may well refer to a more impressive reptile than the snake (*nahash*) of the Elohist tradition in 4:3. Cassuto uses *crocodile*, while Propp prefers the suggestion of other scholars to use *cobra*.

In 7:8, Pharaoh actually says, "Perform a wonder *for you*." The last phrase may have been sarcastic. The Egyptian *sorcerers* and *magicians* were trained priests, who took their jobs seriously; we should not think of them as entertainers or shysters. Anecdotes about magical acts and spells were common in many ancient religions. The *secret arts* mentioned in 7:11, 22 and in 8:7, 18, but not explained, are not spoken of elsewhere in the Old Testament.

The image of the one cobra eating all the others might remind us of the dream of the Pharaoh in Genesis 41, where the thin cows consumed the sleek cows. In 7:13, the verb *hzq* is active, not passive. It would be better to translate that Pharaoh's heart *became stronger* or *became harder*, rather than the NRSV's translation that the Pharaoh's heart *was hardened*.

Question

38. If we accept the sign of Aaron's rod turning into a cobra as a genuine miracle, what should we think about the report that the Egyptian priests were able to do the same? When Aaron's cobra consumed the other cobras, why did the Pharaoh not immediately cooperate with Moses and Aaron?

Exodus 7:14–25:
The First Plague: Polluting the Nile

> Propp judges that this account is mainly from E,
> with important additional details from the briefer P
> tradition included in verses 19, 20a, 21b, 22. In fact,
> these few P verses form a complete story.

In 7:14, the phrase from E is that Pharaoh's heart *became heavy* (*kbd*). The NRSV is less accurate in saying that his heart *is hardened*, since that leaves us less sure as to the one causing the hardness or heaviness. In 7:22, P says that (exactly as in 7:13) the Pharaoh's heart *became stronger* (*hzq*), an active verb form. In 7:23, E uses another phrase that the Pharaoh did not *set his heart on this*, meaning, as in the NRSV, that he did not take it to heart.

In 7:17, the staff that will strike the water could be wielded by either God or Moses, and this is done in verse 20. The speech to Pharaoh includes the challenge (verse 17) that by this sign "you shall know that I am the LORD." Given the P addition in verse 19 that Aaron is told to wave his staff over the waters, then in verse 20 Aaron becomes the striker in the expanded account.

In 7:18, the Egyptians are *unable* (passive of *lah*) to drink the water. This verb may imply that drinking the water made them sick. In verses 21 and 24, a simpler verb is used to say that they cannot use the water. When the priests do the same sign in verse 22, it is not clear where they would have found clean water for their use, but verse 24 informs us that the only remaining safe sources were found by digging near the Nile.

To visualize water literally turned into blood is upsetting, and is most likely misreading the intention of the original storytellers. Biblical authors spoke of the blood of grapes (Gen 49:11) and described a river gleaming in the sunrise as being red as blood (2 Kgs 3:22). Centuries ago, Christian theologians argued that miraculously making a river of blood was an inappropriate use of the life-giving fluids proper to animals and humans, and that the red color or temporary toxicity of such waters could be brought about in other miraculous ways, even though consistently described with the word *blood* in written traditions. On another level, early Jewish audiences would have taken the image to mean that the land of Egypt was cursed, since blood poured on the ground was an offense against God.

Question

39. At the end of this account, Pharaoh returns to his palace and ignores this miraculous damage to the Nile. Why does he act this way? Why do the Egyptian priests duplicate what Moses did?

Exodus 8:1–15:
The Second Plague: Legions of Frogs

Propp takes this passage to be mainly from E, with
important additional details from the briefer P tradition
included in verses 5–7a and 15b. Again the few P verses
form a complete story. In chapter 8, the Hebrew verse
numbers begin four verses later than do the English.
I will try to use English verse numbers throughout.

The verb in the opening instruction "*Go* to Pharaoh" is used
for *going into* or *entering* an enclosed place, here probably the
Pharaoh's palace or audience hall.

The frogs *come up* from the river, and Aaron and the priest-
magicians *made* frogs *come up*; this same verb is used in Exodus
1:10 where the Pharaoh worries that the Israelites might *come up*
(*escape*) from the land. In 8:3, the river will *produce swarms* of
frogs; the same verb appears in 1:7 where the descendants of
Jacob were *prolific*.

In the combined story, in which the P traditions of verses 5–7a
were added, the Egyptian priests bring up their frogs immediately
after Moses brings up his frogs. If we look only at the E version,
8:7b would have followed 8:4, and so Moses or Aaron may have
originally been the only ones performing the sign.

Pharaoh says *Pray to the* LORD in 8:8; other translations could
be *Entreat* or *Appease the* LORD. In the same verse, Pharaoh's offer
to allow sacrifices is not the same as letting the people leave Egypt
for good. In 8:9, Moses replies by saying, "*Kindly tell me* when I
am to pray for you." The Hebrew verb means *Take precedence over
me* or *Take honor over me.* In context, Moses may be acting with
mock humility or sarcasm. Pharaoh asks that the frogs be removed
the following day. This specification of the next day may have been
the earliest point Pharaoh expected such a thing to be possible, or
he may not have believed God to be more powerful than that, or
he may have wished to appear cool and calm during this battle of

nerves. Propp suggests that in the E traditions the plagues take place at a slower pace than those in the P stories.

In 8:15, Pharaoh *made his heart heavy.* Here we have the causative of the verb *kbd,* meaning to make heavy or dull. The NRSV has "he hardened his heart."

While we might find the image of swarms of frogs less grim than the river of blood, in fact frogs were ritually unclean (Lev 11:10–12; Deut 14:10). Leviticus 11:11 says of such scaleless, finless water creatures that "they are detestable to you, and detestable they shall remain. Of their flesh you shall not eat, and their carcasses you shall regard as detestable."

Question

40. How unexpected is Pharaoh's reaction in 8:15, given the negotiations in 8:8–11 and the priest-magicians' achievement in 8:7? Why would any Pharaoh harden his own heart at this point? How helpful to the reader is the word *respite* or *relief* in 8:15?

Exodus 8:16–19:
The Third Plague: Clouds of Gnats

> This brief passage seems to be from the
> P level of tradition.

Ancient versions of the Bible identify the biting insects as lice, mosquitoes, sand fleas, and so on. In verse 18, the Hebrew text says the priest-magicians *did likewise but could not,* apparently meaning that they copied the action of striking the ground to make a cloud of dust but did not succeed in the end. The term *finger of God* in verse 19 occurs again in Exodus 31:18, which describes the words on the two stone tablets as *written by the fin-*

ger of God. The final remark about Pharaoh's *heart being strong* is identical to 7:13 and 7:22.

Question

41. As odd as it may seem, the priest-magicians were not able to duplicate this sign, even though they had been able to bring about cobras, water red and foul, and significant numbers of frogs. What conclusions did they draw, and what advice did they offer? Why didn't the Pharaoh at least partially agree with them?

Exodus 8:20–32: The Fourth Plague: A Ruinous Swarm of Flies

This plague is from the E traditions.

Scholars note that Psalm 103:31 mentions both gnats and flies. Within the poetic style of the psalms both insects probably constituted one plague. Later on, two separate traditions developed, the P story of the gnats, and this E tradition about flies. Perhaps the authors considered the gnats and flies defiling (they are considered unclean in Lev 11:20, 23, 41–44); but certainly they are maddening as they inflict many small bites and pains on people who cannot get rid of them all.

Note that the opening verse is similar to 7:15. A new development in this warning about the flies (or other species of biting insect) is the mention that the Hebrews dwelling in Goshen will be spared altogether. In verses 20–21, the phrase *let my people go* is actually *send (slh) my people*. In verse 21, the word play continues as God says that he will *send* the flies.

The verb in verse 22, *plh*, means that God will *make distinctions* or *treat differently*. In verse 23, the Hebrew phrase *I will put a redemption* or *ransom* (*pdut*) is often emended to the Septuagint, which uses a word simply meaning *distinction*. The Hebrew seems to mean that the setting apart of Goshen is for the purpose of redeeming or saving the Hebrew people. The mention that the plague will occur the next day may enhance the authority of Moses, or it may simply be a device to build suspense. It can also remind one of the delay in 8:10.

When Pharaoh advances negotiations a bit in verse 25, he proposes that they worship *within the land* or *within the borders* of Egypt. In doing this, perhaps he takes advantage of the fact that the land of Goshen must be holy enough to serve the purpose, since it was spared the plague. Pharaoh speaks of *your god* in verse 25, instead of saying the name Yahweh, which he had used several times before; this change may have been argumentative or condescending on his part.

Moses' reply, that the people of Egypt find Hebrew sacrifices *offensive*, seems odd to historians. Ancient Egyptians were apparently tolerant of many religions. But Propp notes that there are several testimonies from Herodotus in the fifth century BCE to Porphyry in the third century CE to the effect that some Egyptians avoided the slaughter, sacrifice, or eating of cows, sheep, goats, or doves, and prohibited others from so doing. It is possible that the authors of this plague story have taken some of these more recent movements and put them back into the time of Moses. Another possibility on the literary level is to imagine Moses lying to the Pharaoh and getting away with it, just as the midwives did in Exodus 1.

Moses insists that only a trek into the wilderness will do, and that they must select animals for sacrifice when and as God says or as God commands. The issue of the herds will be brought up again in 10:9 and 10:25–26. In verse 28, Pharaoh concedes a bit more, but insists that their pilgrimage be nearby. He also asks Moses to *pray* for him (the same word is in 8:8), but the request is very brief. It probably means to pray to Yahweh to end the plague of flies. In reply, Moses warns Pharaoh not to continue to *cheat* or *deceive* (*tll*) by not sending the Hebrew people to sacrifice to the LORD. Jacob used the same verb to describe Laban in Genesis 31:7.

Even so, Pharaoh *made his own heart heavy* (*kbd*), as in 8:15. The Hebrew adds that he did this *this time also*, but does not go beyond stock phrases to explain why he reneged yet again.

Question

42. The more plague stories we read the more questions we have. Here the Pharaoh seems to try to negotiate (verses 25, 28–29) but then resists at the end for reasons we do not understand. As another approach in our analysis, ask yourself what the Pharaoh did *not* do during this episode. How could he have been a wiser king?

Exodus 9:1–7:
The Fifth Plague: Cattle and Work Animals

Propp attributes this story to the E traditions.

The opening directive to *go to Pharaoh* is like that in 8:1, meaning to enter an enclosed place. Again in verse 4, God *separates* or *treats differently* the animals belonging to the Hebrews. At the end, Pharaoh *sent* to verify that Hebrew animals were not harmed, but still he refused to *send* the Hebrew people to worship. His heart *becomes heavy* (*kbd*, in a very slight tense variation from 8:32). The massive piles of carcasses would have been defiling, as legislated in Leviticus 11:39–40.

Question

43. This description of the deaths of many tens of thousands of cattle, sheep, goats, horses, mules, and even camels (an anachronism) seems not to have hit the Pharaoh very hard. Why is he not more alert to the economic devastation of all this loss?

Exodus 9:8–12:
The Sixth Plague: Boils upon Egyptians and Animals

> This passage is the last of the P plague traditions.

As in the third plague (gnats), the introduction is minimal; Moses and Aaron come before Pharaoh but they do not engage him in a conversation. The priest-magicians are specifically mentioned, probably because boils are blemishes that will render them unfit to preside at ceremonial duties. This ceremonial restriction against blemishes is mentioned in Leviticus 21:20–21 for the Jewish priesthood, but it seems to have been a common custom in most ancient Near Eastern religions. The Old Testament also legislates that the laity abstain from public worship for the duration of skin blemishes of their own. Aaron and Moses carry the ashes, but only Moses tosses them into the air. Perhaps the Priestly authors thought it inappropriate or defiling for Aaron to handle the materials for this particular plague.

The type of boils is not clearly described. Propp reports that some researchers propose Nile Sores, which mainly settle on the lower body (see Deut 28:35; Job 2:7). Others speculate on elephantiasis or smallpox. Some of these diseases can be fatal (2 Kgs 20:7; Isa 38:21). In any case, this plague seems more dangerous than the incidents with gnats and flies. There is no mention of the

Pharaoh being personally afflicted with these boils, although he could have been included.

At the end we are told that *Yahweh strengthened* (*hzq*) Pharaoh's heart. In most of the earlier uses of this verb (7:13, 22; 8:19), Pharaoh was the one strengthening. God said that he himself would do this in 4:21.

Question

44. We have seen six of the ten plagues at this point, as well as the opening confrontation in 7:8–12. Now the priests who fought back until the episode with the gnats are banned from public life by virtue of their boils or blemishes. Are you enjoying these stories as much as the ancient authors who first wrote them? If not, why not?

Exodus 9:13–35:
The Seventh Plague:
Hail, Thunder, Lightning, and Rain

> Propp attributes the entire passage to E, with the exception of the last verse (35), which may come from a redactor using Priestly vocabulary.

Verse 13 describes Moses standing before Pharaoh, and reminds us of the standard phrases in 7:15 and 8:20 where the two met outdoors by the Nile. The broad reference to *plagues* in verse 14 can also be translated *torments* or *afflictions*. In verse 15, another Hebrew word for *plague* or *pestilence* (*daber*) is used, which usually refers to very contagious, deadly outbreaks, perhaps comparable to bubonic plague. In verse 17, Moses tells the Pharaoh that he *exalts himself* over the Hebrews. The same verb is used in Proverbs 4:8 where the listeners are urged to *prize* or *cherish* Wisdom.

The message of Yahweh in 9:14–16 is revealing. God wants the Egyptians to know that there is no one like him anywhere, that he could have already ended their lives several times over, and that he wants them to see his power and he wants to make his name resound everywhere. He knows Pharaoh is still trying to fight back, and this is the reason for the coming hailstorm. The Hebrew word for *thunder* is *voices* (*qolot*). One might consider these words domineering, but they are counterbalanced by the unusual twenty-four-hour grace period to shelter those servants and animals that live in the open.

In verse 27, the Pharaoh's admissions about himself *sinning* (*ht'*), and about him and his people being *in the wrong* (*rsh'*), can be taken in a public, legal sense, and need not imply that he is thinking in religious dimensions. He is more likely admitting to mistakes, rather than to moral defiance or blasphemy. Again in verse 28, Pharaoh asks Moses to *pray* to or *entreat* Yahweh for an end to the hail; he had earlier asked for such prayers by Moses in 8:8, 28. In 9:28, Pharaoh seems to yield completely to Moses' basic demand to let everyone go wherever they wish to make the sacrifices. Moses makes a broad remark in verse 30 that the Egyptians do not yet *fear the LORD*. On one (less religious) level, some of them already fear him—those who sheltered their laborers and livestock in 9:20.

In 9:34 (E), the Pharaoh *sinned* (*ht'*) again and made heavy his own heart, and at the start of the next plague in 10:1 (E) God says, "I have made heavy his heart." These uses of *kbd* (make heavy) are familiar from earlier verses (Pharaoh acting in 8:15, 32; 9:7). To use the same verb with the two different subjects implies that one complex process is taking place; otherwise the two verses (9:34 and 10:1) seem to contradict completely each other.

In the intervening verse 9:35 (P or redactor), the other verb *hzq* is used; Pharaoh's heart *becomes strong* (as seen in 7:13, 22; 8:19).

The effect of God's revealing speech and grace period, coupled with the yielding of Pharaoh, is to raise the hopes of the readers. It is a bizarre, sorry pattern repeating itself when Pharaoh acts in bad faith at the end of this great storm, even if this stubbornness is supposed to fit into God's larger purposes.

Questions

45. In chapter 9, the Hebrew word *eretz*, meaning "ground, land, or earth," is used in verses 14, 15, 16, 23, 29, 33. In which three of these verses should we take the word in its widest meaning—the entire world inhabited by all its people?

46. In 9:27, why does Pharaoh say that he is wrong *this time*? What do you make of his mentioning *I and my people* in that same verse?

47. How can you make sense of the matter of Pharaoh's heart, focusing mainly on 9:34—10:1? Why do the authors use three different verbal phrases for one process?

Exodus 10:1–20:
The Eighth Plague:
Ravenous Locusts

> Propp argues that this entire passage is from the E level, with verse 20 by a redactor using the Priestly style.

In 10:1, the Hebrew text has *in his midst* instead of *in their midst*, as found in ancient versions. The NRSV translates the phrase as "among them" going with the versions. Propp suggests the translation *in his inner being* or *in his core* to show that the Hebrew form might be correct. The phrase in 10:2 that God *made fools* (*ll*) of the Egyptians or *toyed* with them seems harsh or cruel, but that is the main thrust of the verb. The meeting with Pharaoh is apparently indoors, as in 8:1 and 9:1. The question in verse 4, "How long will you refuse to *humble yourself* before me?" involves the verb *'nh*, which means to *bow down* (but not in worship). The phrase *how long* will be repeated by the officials in verse 7. The *snare* they speak of is a hunter's trap. The Hebrew has "How long will *this* be a snare to us?" Translators supply phrases

57

like *this man* or *this fellow*, but the Septuagint translators used *this matter*. They apparently thought it meant this matter of restraining the Israelites. Propp notes that in verse 7 ordinary Egyptians by now know that Yahweh is the name of the god of the Hebrews.

In verse 10, as he reacts against Moses' demand to have everyone and all the herds participate in the pilgrimage, Pharaoh takes Yahweh's name in his own oath not to allow this. This seems to be a sarcastic or cynical imprecation. He wants the *little ones (tap)* to stay behind as hostages; this term could mean dependents of any age rather than just young children. Pharaoh's assumption that only the men need to participate in the pilgrimage and sacrifices fits with widespread ancient custom. Even in Exodus (23:17 and 34:23) and Deuteronomy (16:16), the men have more religious obligations than do their families. In other passages, women and children are mentioned (Deut 16:11–14; 31:12; 1 Sam 1, the story of Hannah). Propp suggests that the matter of the extent of women's religious duties may not have been settled at the time this episode became fixed in writing.

In verse 11, Pharaoh *drives out (ngsh)* Moses and Aaron. This verb will be used again in 11:1 and 12:39, when tensions are even higher than now. In 10:16, Pharaoh rushes Moses and Aaron into his presence and again admits (as in 9:27) that he has been *wrong* or *sinful*; but in verse 17 he exhibits special pleading by using terms like *only this once* and that *at the least he remove this deadly thing from me*. In this last remark, he does not bother to plead for his own people.

The P phrase in 10:20 that Yahweh *strengthened (hzq)* Pharaoh's heart occurred earlier in 9:12.

Question

48. Examine the style of the various speeches in chapter 10:1–20, and the direct narration by the authors in verses 13–15 and 18–19. Which of these five parties (God, Moses, Pharaoh, his advisors, and the storytellers) are getting emotional or melodramatic? Give your reasons.

Exodus 10:21–29:
The Ninth Plague: Deep Darkness

Propp assigns this passage to E, with the exception of verse 27, another redactional verse in the Priestly style. Propp notes that this E material may have replaced a P version of the same story, bringing some inconsistencies with it.

There is no introductory dialogue with Pharaoh here, as there was none before the plagues of gnats or boils (8:16; 9:8). The image of extended darkness may have come from common experiences of eclipses, thunderstorms, or sandstorms, or it may have been a motif about God reversing the forces of creation. This last is found often in the Old Testament (for example, Jer 4:23–28).

The phrase about a darkness *that can be felt* assumes a rare form of the verb *mshsh*, and many alternative translations have been proposed in place of it, with little consensus.

In 10:27, Yahweh again *strengthens* Pharaoh's heart, as in 9:12 and 10:20. The angry exchange between Pharaoh and Moses in the last two verses is surprising; we know that they will meet again. Perhaps one or the other is lashing out in anger. The Pharaoh's death threat seems irrational, given that he has not been able to prevent any of the plagues so far. Propp offers the explanation that Pharaoh's warning and Moses' oath to never *see* Pharaoh's *face* again might refer to coming to an official audience with him. This idiom is used often for audiences (Gen 43:3, 5; 2 Sam 3:13; 14:24, 28, 32). Later, when Pharaoh speaks to Moses and Aaron in 12:31–32, Propp suggests that Pharaoh came to them at their camp (since the Israelites were indoors celebrating the Passover) and so Pharaoh sought an impromptu audience with Moses, unlike their earlier official audiences where Pharaoh presided.

Questions

49. Is Pharaoh's request to leave the herds behind while on pilgrimage completely selfish? Could Moses have made any concessions at this point?

50. We have noted the introductions indicating outdoor confrontations with Pharaoh in the first, fourth, and seventh episodes involving the Nile waters, the flies, and the hail. Likewise, in the second, fifth, and eighth plagues telling of frogs, cattle pestilence, and locusts, Moses and Aaron met the Pharaoh indoors, presumably in his palace. The third and sixth plagues about gnats and boils have minimal introductions, as does this ninth one. Why do these three introduction patterns occur in this repeating series?

51. Another way to look at the ten plagues is to consider them in turn in pairs. If we were to consider the red Nile waters and the frogs as a pair, and then the gnats and flies, and then the afflictions to the cattle and the boils, and then the hail and locusts, and finally the darkness and the death of the firstborn, what does this order of pairs of stories suggest?

Exodus 11:1–10:
The Announcement of the Tenth Plague: Death for the Firstborn

> Propp credits E for verses 1, 4–8. He notes that verses 2–3 are most likely from the J level, although verse 3 might be redactional. Verses 9–10 seem to be from P redactors.

Chapter 11 is a bit of a patchwork. God proclaims what he will do next, and reminds Moses about getting silver and gold from the Egyptian people. Verse 3 is an aside to the reader, followed by Moses' speech to Pharaoh in verses 4–8a. Given the angry exchange and the death threat at the end of chapter 10, we might not expect that Moses and Pharaoh would meet face-to-face again, but they are. The mention in 8b that Moses left *in hot anger* may indicate the stress under which Moses was working, but in 11:1 God had mentioned that their freedom is close at hand; indeed, soon the Pharaoh will *drive them away (grsh)*. Perhaps verse 8b picks up on Moses' anger in 10:29.

This warning about death for the firstborn is brought to a notable pause at 11:10, since the actual slaying will not be described until 12:29–32. The many paragraphs in 12:1–28 and 12:33—13:16 are devoted to complex matters of worship related to Passover.

The references to Israelites asking Egyptians for objects of silver and gold build on the first mention of this back in 3:21–22. The *favor* attributed to the Israelites by Egyptian neighbors and the *greatness* of Moses among Egyptians need not be hollow tributes, but 11:2–3 does not explain the inner motives of the Egyptians at any length. The officials of the Pharaoh are specifically mentioned in 11:3, 8; they seem less sure of themselves and their fate, in comparison with the Pharaoh.

The mention of the Lord coming at midnight (verse 4) makes sense in ancient cultures where the dark of night was the stage for the most dangerous religious forces. Propp holds that context limits the firstborn ones spoken of; they are probably males, no older than juveniles, or who have parents still living. Their dead bodies, unburied, will once again defile the land. The mention of the *female slave behind the handmill* is a stereotypical image of Egyptian peasantry. When the deaths occur, the Egyptians will let out great *cries* (verse 6), just as the Israelites did in 3:7–9.

This solemn warning to Pharaoh should have been credible, given the astounding extent of the damage and suffering of all the plagues so far. Proclaiming the deaths of the firstborn now satisfies the command originally given to Moses in 4:22–23.

P redactors guide us to this pause with summary remarks at 11:9–10, using the phrase once again that Yahweh *strengthened (hzq)* Pharaoh's heart. Pharaoh did not release the Israelites, even after the fearsome wonder of the deep darkness.

Question

52. Look at the P plague traditions: they include
    The sign of the cobras (7:8–13)
    A few verses about the Nile (7:19, 20a, 21b, 22)
    A few verses about frogs (8:5–7)
    The plague of gnats (8:16–19)
    The plague of boils (9:8–12)

    What do these traditions have in common? How does
    Moses end each one? What seems to be the Priestly profile
    of God influencing Pharaoh, given these traditions and the
    isolated P redactorial verses in the E plagues (8:15b; 9:35;
    10:20, 27; 11:9–10)?

Conclusion to the Entire Section

As I read the account of the plagues just to the end of chapter
11, I see two dynamics. There is the ratcheting pattern of greater
and greater punishments, inevitably leading toward the death of
the firstborn. However, there is also an oddly sterile, static pattern. The various plagues, woven from P and E sources, lead to
continual, incomprehensible defiance by the Pharaoh (and who-
ever or whatever supports him), even as he apparently becomes
more isolated from his own people. The effect is surreal; God
wants to win, the Pharaoh does not want to lose, the Egyptians
are taking shock after shock, and Moses and his people are
unaware of the new duties and trials their own faith will require
of them in the near future.

Section Eight:
Exodus 12:1—13:16

A fair amount of stitching together takes place in this block covering nearly two chapters. Propp credits the Priestly sources for 12:1–20, most of 12:40–51, and 13:1–2. Redactors, perhaps in line with Priestly traditions, added 12:24, 28, 42, and 13:10. Propp finds E behind the other materials in 12:21–34, 37–39, and 13:3–9, 11–16. The ideas in 12:25–27 and 13:3–9, 11–16 are also in the mainstream of Deuteronomic traditions.

The Jahwist may have contributed just the reference to gold and silver in 12:35–36. Many of the ceremonial details and regulations can be found in Numbers, Leviticus, Deuteronomy, and elsewhere; at points in those books small details conflict with each other and with Exodus.

Introduction

It may help us to look for the differing patterns in the E and P materials. Propp points out that E themes in 11:4–8 can be directly joined to 12:29–34, and then to 12:39. In 12:21–27, E describes Moses instructing everyone to mark their doors with the blood of the Passover lambs; only in verse 27 is the lamb described as part of a *sacrifice* (*zbh*). Some of the phrases in 12:21–22 might hint at temporary altars or burnt sacrifices. We read in 12:34 of the people moving bread dough before it had had the time to rise properly. In 13:3–8, E focuses on a weeklong feast centered on removing leaven and using unleavened bread instead; E explains this as the way to commemorate getting out of Egypt. Further instructions from E follow in 13:11–16 regarding consecrating and redeeming firstborn males, human and animal. E continues the narrative of the Hebrews' journey in 13:17.

Propp notes that the Priestly traditions (12:1–20, 40–51, and 13:1–2) follow the same basic outline, but P adds many fine details and some modifications. We cannot tell if such details were already in E; we can only work with our final version of the combined traditions.

Here are a few examples of differences between the E and P traditions. Explanations for some of the differences will be offered as the verses are studied.

- In 12:22, E has families stay inside that night; in 12:46, P speaks of the lamb staying inside.
- In 12:23, E speaks of a *destroyer*; in 12:13, P has *no plague shall destroy you*.
- In 12:34, 39, E speaks of dough carried away before it had risen; in 12:11, P legislates that the meal is to be eaten hurriedly, while wearing sandals and holding a staff.
- P does not refer to the *elders* that E mentioned in 12:21.
- P omits mention of the *hyssop* (or *marjoram*) branches that the elders used to sprinkle the blood in 12:22 (E).
- P has no parallel to E/D references to parents teaching future generations (12:26–27; 13:8, 14–15).
- P has laws about unleavened bread (12:15–17), while E tells a story instead, in 12:39.
- P's command about firstborn (13:1–2) is much shorter than the E/D version in 13:11–16.
- P does not identify the Passover meal as a *sacrifice*, as E/D does in 12:27.
- There is no P account of the actual death of the firstborn; E's version is in 12:29–33.

Propp is convinced that the redactors of these two sets of traditions put things together in a fairly logical way, repeating laws but holding to one story line. They started with the P account, since the basic Passover rules are described as direct revelations from God to Moses and Aaron (12:1–20). The E traditions in

12:21–27 follow, since they are cast as a direct quotation from Moses to the elders. P or a redactor wraps up the combined account easily with 12:28, saying that everyone obeyed the directives that they were given.

The redactors kept the narration of events brief by using only the E version of the final plague and the flight (12:29–39). They then added more Priestly comment and regulations up to 13:2, with the likely exception of editorial remarks in 12:42. Much of this P material (12:43–49 and 13:1–2) is again in the form of direct revelation by God to Moses and Aaron. The rest of that section (the E material in 13:3–16) is presented as direct comment and instruction by Moses to the people.

When layers of traditions are combined in this manner, new connections can be made by those reading the final version and sometimes small contradictions are left unresolved. For example, in this longer combined account, most readers would take the references to *destruction* in 12:13 (P) and to a *destroyer* in 12:23 (E) to be the same, and not question who the destroyer might be. On the other hand, the rules about those eligible to share in the ceremonies (12:43–49) could raise questions about 12:38, where it is not completely clear whom the *mixed crowd* included.

Although we call it *Passover*, the name of this meal, *Pesach*, is not easily translated. The Exodus tradition is that *Pesach* is related to *pasach*, the verb translated as *pass over* in 12:13, 23, 27; but scholars are fairly sure that this is not a correct use of this verb but more of a play on words.

Propp suggests that the same verb should be translated in these three instances in Exodus 12 as *protect*. This would match the use of the verb at the end of Isaiah 31:5: "[H]e will *spare* and rescue it." Propp also suggests reexamining a related remark used twice in 12:42, "for the Lord a night of *vigil* (or *celebration*)." The root meaning of that verb, *shmr*, is "to watch or keep," but it can also mean "to guard." If we spoke of the LORD's *guarding* in 12:42, that would support the theme of protection in the rest of chapter 12. So the word *Pesach* might originally have meant *protection*.

Questions

53. As you look at the basic rules and instructions for the Passover meal in 12:1–11, how much sense do they make as directives for an enduring, annual ritual? (Assume appropriate and customary removal of skin, hooves, and inedible segments from the animals.) Could any of the rules come from a time before the life of Moses?

54. Exodus 12:12–13 describes the final plague, which is to happen during this meal. Earlier mentions of this are found in 4:23 and 11:4–8. How closely knit is 12:12–13 with 12:1–11?

55. The next passage, 12:14–20, describes ceremonies involving unleavened bread and rules for removing leaven from every house. When we compare these verses with 12:1–11, do the two ceremonies seem to be of equal importance?

56. Exodus 12:21–28 returns to the topic of instructions for the Passover and the final plague, last mentioned in 12:12–13. How does 12:21–28 differ from 12:1–13?

57. Exodus 12:29–34 recounts the actual death of the Egyptian firstborn. Why is the prisoner mentioned in 12:29 rather than the slave woman, as in 11:5? The Hebrew of 12:31 says that Pharaoh *called to* Moses (NRSV translates that Pharaoh *summoned* him). How is Pharaoh portrayed in this passage? How can a ruler *summon* the man whose God has just ended the lives of so many Egyptian firstborn? In verse 33, do the Egyptian people say the same thing as the Pharaoh had said just before? In verse 33, they *urged* the people to depart. The Hebrew verb is that they *became stronger* (in asking them to depart); this verb *hzq* is the same one used many times earlier in the story to describe Pharaoh's heart *becoming stronger* or Pharaoh *strengthening* his own heart or God *strengthening* Pharaoh's heart. What irony is there in using this same verb in 12:33?

58. The acquiring of gold, silver, and fancy robes is mentioned in 12:35–36. Did the Hebrews ask for these amid all the dying, or is this just the point where an editor reported the

66

acquisition in writing? What is the overall effect of 12:33–39? Who makes up the *mixed crowd* of verse 38? Why had no one *prepared any provisions for themselves* (verse 39)?

59. Characterize the style of 12:40–41. Characterize the style of 12:43–51. Do these rules enhance the ones we read in 12:1–13?

60. Exodus 13:1–2 and 13:11–16 may be two complementary versions regarding another custom—consecrating firstborn males. Judging just from these verses, how and why are they so consecrated?

61. Exodus 13:3–10 refers to leaven and unleavened bread, as did 12:15–20. Why would an editor repeat similar regulations in two passages relatively close to each other?

62. What effect is there for the reader in the way 12:1–28 and 12:33—13:16 wrap around the actual death of the firstborn in 12:29–32?

Conclusion

Before moving on to chapter 14, I think we should reflect more deeply on the theological insights behind Jewish liturgical ceremonies. We can begin with some overviews by Propp (427–61) about Exodus 12—13. Although these rules and details surround the few verses that describe the final plague, they have a logic of their own. They create suspense but, even more, they help us to share the experience and the emotions of the ordinary Hebrews of that Passover night. All future Passovers reenact that first one. Egypt too lives on, representing the injustice of empires and the clash of economic forces of any era.

The Exodus account functions as a foundational story, with its precise divine and Mosaic instructions and clever explanation of unleavened bread in the baking bowls. Foundation stories, which may contain unprovable traditions and claims, explain essentials of belief; they thrive even if details may be questioned by historians.

Scholars generally agree that *Pesach* had its origins in ancient domestic rites of prayer for divine protection, while *Mazzot*, the longer pilgrimage week of avoiding leaven in any form was centered at regional shrines. Eventually *Pesach* came to be a Temple sacrifice in Jerusalem, and *Mazzot* became a domestic observance.

At this time in the spring, *Mazzot* would be made from the final grain supplies of the past year; it was also the time when the first new grains were being presented as offerings of praise. The key to the week is banning old leaven. Leaven, the agent of fermentation in the production of wine and the baking of risen loaves of bread, was considered dangerous or impure in itself, an element of decay. Leaven in any form was not used in Jewish sacrifices, whereas salt, a preservative agent, was acceptable. Banning the old leaven throughout the country made the entire land a zone of purity, an altar for worshipping God.

It may also be the case that unleavened bread represented simpler, holier times—an instance of the earlier nomadic fireside cooking. Nomads never had the time or resources to make wine. (Abstaining from alcohol was part of the ascetic antiquarian regimen for Nazirites during the time of their vows.) Having the week of *Mazzot* in the spring made sense. This period of using unleavened bread, made with the older grain supplies, was a way to commemorate the departure from Egypt and the wandering in the wilderness, another period of sacrifice and asceticism.

Regarding leaven, Propp draws another parallel with Jewish laws for what is clean and unclean. Plant and animal products, which are very different in some way from the mainstream, were often proscribed. One example would be shellfish, which do not have scales and which do not move about as do other fish. Leaven was unlike other food or spices in that it could multiply itself. A small bit of leavened starter dough affects many pounds of new bread loaves. Breaking the cycle of multiplication once a year may have been considered a way to keep leaven under control, to keep it from becoming more unnatural.

Pesach may well be one example of protecting rites, of which we have many instances in ancient cultures. At times of danger, animals were sacrificed (in place of or in some way representing people), and some of the blood was placed on the people or objects of concern. In simpler ceremonies, red dye could substitute for blood. The meat of the sacrificed animals was usually cooked and shared at a subsequent meal. Times of danger could include droughts, famine, or epidemics, but major life transitions for individuals were also considered times of danger, times when evil spirits could take the offensive. The spring season was a time for some of these rites for a whole society, to seek protection for all in the coming year.

The logic of marking with blood or red dye in these ceremonies seems to be to fool evil spirits into thinking that someone has already died at this location, so that they would go elsewhere looking for victims. The communal meal in these rites is also important; participants celebrate their relationships with the gods, and with each other, in unity against the forces of evil. Sharing the meat of the sacrifice was a way of joining with the good qualities of the very animal that took the place of the participants.

In several Jewish rituals, the sprinkling or application of blood was an essential. See Exodus 24:8 (part of the covenant ceremony); Exodus 29:12, 20–21 (ordination of Aaron and his sons); Leviticus 14:1–7 (cleansing rites for lepers); and Leviticus 16:11–19 (the yearly cleansing of the Temple). Clearly blood had many symbolic meanings.

In our story of the first *Pesach,* the destroyer is alerted by the blood on the doorposts and lintels. The image is not simply that of an angel following God's commands; we can also imagine mysterious, indiscriminate forces of death, now unleashed, who are warned away (or deceived) by the blood. Another way of thinking about this night of danger is to see the blood as purifying or sanctifying the doorways and the dwellings; God can protect such holy places, and the people inside. Therefore, in a sense the purified doorway functions like an altar, a site for holiness. The P and E traditions modify the power of the evil spirit within their story, turning him into an angel sent by God; on another level, their extensive description of a supremely stubborn Pharaoh provides us with enough evil, enough terror for the Israelites to bear.

Another possibility is that the Exodus traditions considered the Egyptian firstborn (animal and human) to be the sacrificial substitutes, rather than the lambs used in the *Pesach* meal. Propp takes this as a specification or rationalization of the basic logic of the protecting ritual.

In the past, scholars suggested that this *Pesach* ritual meal made sense for a sheepherding community. In the spring, the newborn lambs are vulnerable, and the flocks with newborn lambs have to be moved to summer grazing grounds; this is another complex and dangerous task (even in modern times). Propp finds little parallel evidence for similar rites among shepherds elsewhere, but he does note that in the study of ancient rituals there seem to be many held near the spring and fall equinoxes. He notes the *Pesach-Mazzot* complex in the spring and the *Succoth–Yom Kippur* complex in the fall as fitting into this general pattern.

If protection rituals had ancient roots, why did this *Pesach* story become a vehicle to describe the meal first shared the night all the firstborn died in Egypt? Propp replies that belief in Yahweh who broke the Pharaoh's grip and brought the Israelites out of Egypt is belief in a God who protects his people. He saved them not only from death or from special danger, but, more important, he saved them from injustice, bondage, and servitude. Reworking elements of such ancient rituals into the Exodus story makes complete theological sense.

In later centuries, the Passover celebrations were centralized in Jerusalem; everyone who could came to the Temple on that day, with the purchased sheep or goat, and brought it forward for slaughter and flaying. The blood was sprinkled on the altar and poured on its base, but none was kept by the laity since no doors would be marked. (In the decades prior to the destruction of the Temple by the Romans, tens of thousands of animals were sacrificed at Passover, with the assistance of virtually the entire corps of priests and Levites.) The offerers then shared the meal with family and friends that same evening, in crowded circumstances. It was customary to thank hosts for providing space and shelter by giving them the flayed sheepskins, which could be sold to weavers and tanners.

The observances of *Mazzot* were gradually overshadowed by the importance of Passover, and by the logistics of the trip to Jerusalem. It seems that this change of the Passover ceremony from homes throughout Israel to one massive ceremony in Jerusalem was encouraged by kings and priests over a long period, probably to enhance the religious and national unity that this sacrifice so richly renews.

In Exodus 12—13, the Priestly editors preserved traditions about Moses and the Hebrew slaves having this simple meal at home in Egypt that night, even though the editors were steeped in the Jerusalem traditions of one ceremony at the Temple. In a sense, the elders or family heads performed roles that were restricted to priests later on, such as slaughtering the lambs and sprinkling the blood.

Perhaps the authors built up the events involving Moses using notions from other protection rituals, but they then went beyond the Exodus account with other ceremonial rules in the Pentateuch and elsewhere. For example, in Numbers 9:1–14 those who had unavoidable contact with the recently deceased, or who had been on a journey, could celebrate Passover in the second month of the year. In Leviticus 17:3–9 during the wandering in the desert, Moses prohibited individual families from slaughtering any animal for any purpose without bringing it to the priests for blessing or supervision. Both passages are far from the family meal of Exodus 12–13, far from basic prayers for protection.

The importance of circumcision as a prerequisite to sharing in the Passover is another Priestly topic (12:44, 48). Propp considers this custom to have originated in clan rites of passage for young adult males at local shrines. He finds that circumcision also can be considered a rite of purification to some degree. (Over time, the Jewish practice changed to circumcising male infants.) As a group rite of passage, circumcision could have become associated with protection rites such as *Pesach*.

As will be mentioned in Answer 60, the Priestly high regard for the special status of firstborn had very ancient pre-Israelite origins. (Eventually in Jewish custom firstborn males came to represent all firstborn.) In Exodus 4:22–23, we should consider all the people of Israel as God's firstborn son, and the dedications in 13:11–16 are presented as acts of gratitude for the final plague and the escape from Egypt.

In his commentary on Exodus, Fretheim reminds us that, at the very point of the deaths, the Hebrew people bowed down and worshipped (12:27). This is the first use of the phrase since 4:31, when Moses and Aaron had first gained the confidence of the people.

God claims all firstborn throughout the world, human and animal, as signs of his loving commitment to life. The image of death in 12:29 is very understated; we can think of a quick, painless demise, passing to almost every house and herd in the manner of an epidemic. In taking the Egyptian firstborn, God was challenging and denying Pharaoh's claim to control all his subjects and slaves; it was an extreme tactic, but the only one that broke this Pharaoh's stubborn defiance. Fretheim rightly reminds us of our duty to recall Passover night not only because the children of Israel were given their freedom, but also because Egyptian children had to pay the price for their ruler's rages.

In summarizing the theology of Exodus 12—13, Childs remarks that over time Christians came to see Passover as simply a model for Christ, the new Paschal Sacrifice, and the new Suffering Servant. However, Christians did not really plumb the depths of what light the Old Testament casts on the New Testament. God did redeem Israel that night in Egypt. How do we Christians accept and cherish that fact?

Childs concludes:

God's redemption is not simply a political liberation from an Egyptian tyrant, but involves the struggle with sin and evil, and the transformation of life. Similarly, the slaughtered lamb becomes a symbol of the cost to God of Israel's redemption, indeed, the redemption of the whole world. 1 Peter makes the move of bringing together the passover lamb with the suffering servant (2:22) which becomes a model for later Christian theology. The Christian testifies to his redemption by sharing in Christ's suffering for the sins of the world. The celebration of the eucharist likewise points to the dimension of new life as an identification with Christ's death and resurrection.

The Christian understanding of the passover has always been dialectical, but all too often the movement from the New Testament back to the Old Testament has been forgotten. The New Testament not only fulfills the Old, but equally important the Old Testament interprets the New. Certainly Melito of Sardis is guilty of this failure when he speaks of the passover once being of value, but "today becoming worthless" (*Paschal Homily 43*). Rather, the New Testament provides adequate warrant for seeking to understand what the redemption in Jesus Christ is by means of the witness of the Old Testament passover. First, the ceremony of passover testifies to the redemptive nature of God's dealings with Israel. The New Testament's insistence that divine deliverance is a spiritual transformation does not abrogate the Old Testament witness that the physical is involved as well. In spite of its ambiguity, the political overtones of Israel's deliverance are part of the whole biblical message. Again, the passover ritual serves as a warning against overlooking the collective nature of God's intervention. He redeemed a people. Israel shared a meal in the night of deliverance as families, and went out of the land together. Individuals were destroyed, but a people was redeemed. Liberation was achieved when God overcame the powers of evil in a struggle and invited his people joyfully to share in the event. Finally, the eschatological dimension of redemption, already found deeply embedded in the passover traditions of Judaism, must not be lost through an overconcentration on the death of Christ. The formal parallelism between the Jewish and Christian hope—both look to the past, both hope for the future—affirms the profound degree of solidarity which unites the two faiths together in a common testimony to God's final victory. (*The Book of Exodus*, 213–14)

Section Nine:
Exodus 13:17—14:31

> This passage is a complex combination of E, J,
> and P, as outlined immediately below.

Introduction

Propp attributes the final verses of chapter 13 to the E and JE levels (verses 17–19 to E; verses 21–22 to JE), with the probability that verse 20 is from a redactor.

Chapter 14 combines two traditions, one from J and E, and the other from P.

> In the opening section verses 1–4 and 8–9 are from P, verses 5–6 from E, and verse 7 from J or P.
>
> Next, as the Israelites panic and then get reassured by Moses, verses 10–14 seem to be from JE and verses 15–18 from P.
>
> The events by which everyone enters the sea are mostly from P, with the exception of the E tradition in verses 19–20 and the middle part of verse 21, which describes the LORD pushing the sea back by a strong east wind and turning the seabed to dry land. Specifically, P includes 21a, "Then Moses stretched out his hand over the sea" and 21c, "and the waters were divided." Next, P includes verses 22–23.
>
> The next section (verses 24–29) describes how the Egyptians were trapped. JE traditions include verses 24–25; the latter part of verse 27, where the sea returns to its place, the Egyptians flee, and the LORD tosses them in the sea; and the very last part of verse 28, where it

mentions that all the Egyptians died. The other verses—all of 26, the start of 27, the start of 28, and all of 29—belong to the P level. Specifically, P includes verses 26, 27a, "So Moses stretched his hand out over the sea," all of verse 28 except for the final phrase, "not one of them remained," and verse 29.

The two concluding verses, 30–31, are from the JE level.

As you prepare to study chapter 14 it would be helpful to highlight these two sets of verses, or to print them in bold or italics if you have access to biblical texts on computer software. It is usually easiest to mark the P level—verses 1–4; 8–9; 15–18; the start and end of 21 as quoted; 22–23; 26; the opening part of 27, as quoted; all of 28 except the final phrase "not one of them remained"; and 29.

There is a word play in 13:17 between God not *leading them* (*naham*, from *nhm*) the nearest way, for God said, "…lest they *change their minds*" (*yinnahem*, from *nwh*).

The body of water is called *yam suph*, which may mean "sea (or lake) of reeds (or weeds)." The location of this sea or lake is not known. Long-standing tradition dictates that we speak of the well-known *Red Sea* in verse 18, because of the intense descriptions in chapter 14.

The smoke and fire (13:21–22; 14:19–20) seem to come from a single miraculous column or pillar. Commentators often mention the ancient practice of having a smoking torch in the lead for armies or caravans on the move.

Later Jewish traditions honored Moses for treating the remains of Joseph properly. Rabbis said that Moses was buried by God himself as repayment for this respect for Joseph (Deut 34:6). The people carried the coffin of Joseph along with the tablets of the covenant all the years of wandering in the wilderness. Joseph's remains were finally buried at Shechem (Josh 24:32). Joseph's wish for reburial (Gen 50:25) was taken as an act of abnegation on his part, a desire to delay the appropriate rites as long as needed for everyone to return to the Promised Land.

English translations vary considerably in their treatment of one phrase in Exodus 14:27. The Hebrew says that the Egyptians were fleeing *to meet it* (*the sea*). This sense is maintained in the RSV (the Egyptians *fled into it* [*the sea*]), in the Jerusalem Bible (the fleeing Egyptians *marched right into it* [*the sea*]), and in the NAB (the Egyptians *were fleeing head on toward the sea*). Some translations, relying on the larger context, freely take it to mean that the Egyptians were going *back to the shore*. Thus the NEB (the Egyptians were *in flight as it* [*the water*] *advanced*), and the NRSV (the Egyptians *fled before it* [*the sea*]).

Questions

63. Try drawing a simple diagram of what happens in chapter 14. At the start you might have in a line from west to east the Egyptian army, the pillar of fire, the Israelites, and the sea. In the next scene in the sea you could draw from west to east the Egyptian army, the Israelites, and the waters forced some distance to the east by the wind. On each side of this axis would be one of the walls of water (that is, to the north and south of the Egyptians and the Israelites). As you finish diagramming the story, what two problems arise? Which verses generate these two problems?

64. What impressions do you gather as you read 13:18–22? How do your reactions fit in with 13:17?

65. How do 14:1–4 and 8–9 contrast with 14:5–7? How can we profile the continuity in the story when we read 14:1–9 as a unit?

66. How seriously should we take the complaints spoken in 14:11–12? Why is Moses so confident in 14:13–14?

67. Look at the P contributions in 14:15–18, the start and end of verse 21 (Moses stretching out his hand, and the dividing of the waters), and verses 22–23. What picture do these verses develop?

68. Now study 14:19–20, the middle part of verse 21, which describes the LORD pushing the sea back with a strong east wind and turning the seabed to dry land, and verses 24–25. What picture do these E and J verses develop?

69. Look at 14:26–29, which is mostly from P, except for the majority of verse 27, starting from "at dawn the sea returned," and the very end of verse 28, "not one of them remained." What do these two layers of tradition have in common?
70. Note the happy ending in 14:30–31. Have you seen such unity of purpose mentioned previously?
71. What are the effects for the reader in having the JE traditions and the P traditions combined into the final form of chapter 14 as we now have it? Why would any editor or redactor choose to blend these two stories together? Why not tell them separately?

Conclusion

Fretheim reminds us that chapter 14 is enclosed by the liturgical regulations and reflections of 13:1–16 and the great hymn of worship in 15:1–21. In much the same way that the final plague was so heavily entwined within the Passover story of chapters 12—13, and changed by that location, the deliverance at the sea is also a foundational story, part of the greater story of the acts of God. In chapter 14 we are reading an impressionistic account about a cosmic victory, in which the Pharaoh and the Egyptian soldiers were the direct target. The victory comes at the point when the Egyptian soldiers say, "Let us flee from the Israelites, for the LORD is fighting for them."

The *deliverance* (*yeshu'h*) promised in 14:13 is for each individual, for the whole people, and for the whole world. When God exposes the pathway of dry land at the bottom of the sea, it is an echo of the original calling up of dry land in Genesis 1:9. Israel then trusts God and walks on the dry land toward redemption, and on the same dry ground the Egyptians pursue their unjust goals and come to stern judgment before the judge of all hearts. Their unjust goals may have grown from a desire to recapture slaves who broke away or from a crazed resolve to slaughter them all (see 15:9).

The cosmic victory is for God alone. He waged the battle (14:13–14) and claimed the honor (14:4), but the honor came not only from the Israelites but also from the Egyptians. Both groups represent the peoples of the world.

In his study of the sea story, Childs points to the consistent mix of miraculous or wondrous elements with natural or ordinary elements and forces. Opening the dry pathway was done at the stroke of the staff in Moses' hand, but a strong wind had blown all night. When the pathway was flooded by the second gesture of Moses, the sea returned to its normal depth at dawn. God sent a panic upon the Egyptians, but the chariots also failed somehow in the mud and sand. Egyptian hearts were hardened, but they also chose to pursue and attack out of greed or revenge.

Therefore, we can see that the editors have combined two earlier traditions, each of which gave God full credit for defeating the Egyptians by use of extraordinary wonders involving natural forces. The final form does the same; it is bigger than the sum of its parts, but consistent in its theology. Childs affirms, "There never was a time when the event was only understood as ordinary, nor was there a time when the supernatural absorbed the natural" (*The Book of Exodus*, 238).

In his commentary on chapter 14, Cassuto seeks to explain the geophysics of it all. He tries to identify the route taken, the shallow lake or tidal basin near the Red Sea where certain sandbars can be fairly dry at low tide, the exact failures of the chariot wheels, and so on. He discounts the high walls of water as a hyperbole, and tries to tie everything else into a smooth overview. One brief passage shows his approach:

We should endeavor to understand how our text pictures the wondrous happening of which it tells, and what is the natural basis of the miracle described, for it is clear that the Torah does not imply that laws of nature were changed, but that a wonderful use was made of those laws. The miracle consisted in the fact that at the very moment when it was necessary, in just the manner conducive to the achievement of the desired goal, and on a scale that was abnormal, there occurred, in accordance with the Lord's will, phenomena that brought about Israel's salvation. (*A Commentary on the Book of Exodus*, 168)

With no desire to minimize Cassuto's scholarship, which is still much respected, I think he misses a lot of the emotional and theological depth of this chapter. Fretheim has a wonderful phrase for scholars getting bogged down in secondary details and points of accuracy. He calls this "retouching Renoir's paintings to make them look like photographs" (*Exodus*, 158).

Section Ten:
Exodus 15:1–21

Scholars generally agree that this victory hymn, elements
of which are shared in both J and E levels elsewhere,
is quite ancient, and has not been significantly reedited.
Exodus 15:1a, 19–20 form a redactional framework,
but 15:21 should be considered as part of the hymn.
Propp cautions that the hymn could be a more
recent imitation of older poetic styles.

Introduction

Commentators have long noted a "blessed fault" in the first
half of the opening verse of this Song of the Sea. We are told,
"Then Moses and the Israelites sang this song to the LORD." If
we were to assume that Moses was the composer of this hymn,
his poetic skills would be quite improved from the claims he
made to God earlier that he was a very poor public speaker.

Propp observes that the more important fact here is not who
composed this, but that all the Israelite men sang it in unison. In
many ancient cultures, victory hymns were normally sung by
women only; here the men humble themselves and take this role
to honor God. (Miriam and the women participate, as will be
mentioned in 15:20–21.)

In 15:20, Miriam is called *Aaron's sister* since he was the
brother most senior to her. The hymn begins with "I will sing…"
The phrase *for he has triumphed gloriously (ki ga'o ga'a)* is much
more compact in Hebrew, and the verb *he has thrown* or *he has
hurled (rmh)* is figurative speech for God's initiative and power.
The verb *rmh* can also mean to *shoot arrows with a bow*; Propp
suggests the additional image of a sling and stones.

Propp notes that ancient lyric Jewish poetry was probably sung or chanted, not simply recited. That poetic style includes complex and unexpected forms, confusing tenses, and a reliance on allusions. He suggests that we "over read" as a method for catching more of the allusions, and that we not go looking for original historical cores of fact beneath the allusions, since these works of art are lyric and not narrative.

Propp points out that in this poem there is little focus on Moses and no mention of the hardening of hearts. Egyptian motivation is described a bit more vividly. Miriam's chant in 15:21 marks the end of a great adventure, which started with her standing guard at the Nile in Exodus 2:4.

Fretheim observes that it is not only the readers of Exodus who share in the excitement and dread of the plagues and the escape through the sea; God himself had never performed such feats before. He demands praise for this victory over sinful forces, not simply as part of his relationship with Israel, but because praise will enhance his attractiveness to other nations. His victory is a victory over sin and injustice, and should be a message and a lesson to all peoples.

We need to see the cosmic level of the entire story. God needs no weapons; his creative forces conquer chaos and sin, and now he reigns in the midst of Israel over the whole world. The Egyptians are identified just in 15:4. The references in 15:14–15 to Philistia, Edom, Moab, and Canaan are even more brief. In a broader sense, all future enemies are defeated in this great showdown. Therefore, we can say that the enthronement of God as cosmic victor has already happened. So, Fretheim argues, it makes sense to use the past tense in 15:13–17. The Israelites have already been guided to the holy mountain; the neighboring states have already been paralyzed; God has already planted his people at his sanctuary.

Some commentators prefer to use present or subjunctive forms in this section, given that for Moses and the people the things spoken of in 15:13–17 have not yet happened. Propp takes this approach (see Answer 84). Both ways to understand the Song of the Sea have their merits.

Questions

72. Hebrew prepositions are quite different from their English counterparts; they are much more interchangeable, giving great leeway to translators. Some English Bibles choose not to use the preposition *to* in both instances of *to the* Lord in 15:1, although that is what we have in the NRSV. Why would translators use alternatives such as *for the* Lord or *of the* Lord? Who is the "I" in verses 1–2?

73. What is the import in verse 2 of the variations *my God* and *my father's God*?

74. Verse 3 is quite brief. Can you find some of the important ideas in this sentence, limiting yourself to the context of 15:1–4?

75. What is the main topic in verses 6–7? Why do these two verses use no images of water or waves?

76. How would you describe the content and purpose of verses 1b–7 as a complete stanza or opening part of this hymn?

77. Can you suggest correspondences between elements of 15:8 and chapter 14?

78. There are six separate sayings by the enemy in 15:9. What do the first three reveal? What do the last three reveal?

79. Is 15:10 a duplicate of 15:8? Explain.

80. What is the purpose or function of 15:11?

81. Does 15:12 go beyond 15:10?

82. If we think of Moses and his people as the first ones to recite this hymn of victory, how should we cast the verbs in their words in 15:13–18?

83. What is the basic image outlined in 15:14–16?

84. The high point of the hymn comes at 15:17–18. Would you want to change the sense or the tense of *you brought* and *you planted* in verse 17? There are several English translations for these two phrases.

85. In 15:18, over whom will the Lord reign? What is the role of verse 19 in this poem?

86. When did the women's singing take place? Why do Miriam's words echo 15:1?

Conclusion

In Propp's comments on the *mountain* of verse 17, he describes in turn the legitimate possibilities that it might refer to Sinai, Zion, Shiloh, Gilgal, Canaan, or northern Israel. He concludes:

> We should experience this ambiguity as a virtue, not as a source of frustration. With its nonspecific language, the Song may teach the oneness of all historical experiences.... Yahweh protected the Israelites from neighboring peoples, just as he saved them from Pharaoh and the Sea. Nations and the elements are equally in his power. Divine succor is ever available to Israel in distress; they can always win through to God's mountain. Indeed, later historical salvations, most notably the return from Babylon, are conceived as recapitulations of the Exodus. (*Exodus 1—18*, 568)

I think we should take Propp's lead and consider many of the ambiguities in this Song of the Sea as virtues. It forms a fitting end to the great sweep of Exodus 1—15.

Review of Exodus 1:1—15:21

Many commentators on Exodus find it helpful to include an essay or excursus to help their readers deal with the hardening of heart references in the plagues. I briefly reviewed Cassuto's remarks at the end of section 6, and would like to go into somewhat greater detail here, summarizing some ideas from Propp, Childs, and Fretheim (in that order), followed by contributions of my own.

Summary of Propp's Remarks

In a brief overview (*Exodus 1—18*, 353–54), Propp notes that "many commentators infer that Pharaoh's intransigence is primarily self-generated. God intervenes only toward the end, to push him over the brink." For Propp, God's influence on Pharaoh is at the heart of this cycle. "The king may bend, at least in E, but he always springs back. Each episode ends where it began, with Pharaoh still defiant and Israel still enslaved. Each time there follows a new, escalated round of punishment. The cycle ends only when Israel has crossed the Sea and Egyptian corpses litter the shore."

Propp argues that the hardening verses in which the *heart of Pharaoh* is the subject may not clearly put the responsibility on Pharaoh; we could instead think of God causing his heart to harden. The six instances are 7:13, 14, 22; 8:19; 9:7, 35. In addition, four verses specifically identify the Pharaoh as responsible. These are found in 8:15, 32; 9:34; 13:15. Finally, ten verses clearly have the Lord as the instigator. These include 4:21; 7:3; 9:12; 10:1, 20, 27; 11:10; 14:4, 8, 17. Thus, the gradual shift from *heart of Pharaoh* formulations to ones identifying Pharaoh's role to ones identifying God's role "reflects, not a change in the relationship between Yahweh and Pharaoh, but our own deepening understanding of why the king resists...."

Propp then goes on to say that many Old Testament passages imply that sin can be brought about as part of God's plans. He lists the following verses, all of which seem to fit his profile: Deuteronomy 2:30; Joshua 11:20; Judges 9:23; 1 Samuel 2:25; 1 Kings 12:15; 18:37; 22:19–23; Isaiah 6:9–10; 29:10; 63:17; 2 Chronicles 25:16; and 2 Samuel 15:31 (fulfilled in 2 Sam 17:14). Propp concludes, "While people are often spontaneously evil, God may encourage or tempt them to err, until they become so wicked that his own attribute of justice compels him to destroy them. In other words, God ensures in advance that the wicked deserve their fated punishment. He may be just, but he is not necessarily fair."

Propp explains further that, in the Bible, images of Satan as a tempter gradually came to substitute in part for God, but never in full. Propp cites Romans 9, wherein Paul struggles with this same topic. The entire chapter is worth reading, especially verses 16–24.

> [16] So it depends not on human will or exertion, but on God who shows mercy. [17] For the scripture says to Pharaoh, "I have raised you up for the very purpose of showing my power in you, so that my name may be proclaimed in all the earth." [18] So then he has mercy on whomever he chooses, and he hardens the heart of whomever he chooses.... [22] What if God, desiring to show his wrath and to make known his power, has endured with much patience the objects of wrath that are made for destruction; [23] and what if he has done so in order to make known the riches of his glory for the objects of mercy, which he has prepared beforehand for glory— [24] including us whom he has called, not from the Jews only but also from the Gentiles?

Propp concludes, "Paul stands squarely in the Old Testament tradition: God himself may lead sinners to sin. But at least Paul acknowledges the attendant moral problem ignored by the Elohist and Priestly Writer.... So far as we know, no one before Paul had thought to question the justice of his (Pharaoh's) plight."

Propp mentions 1 Samuel 6:6, in which the Philistine priests said to their people, "Why should you harden your hearts as the Egyptians and Pharaoh hardened their hearts? After he had made fools of them, did they not let the people go, and they departed?" Propp finds here a wise use of the plagues story, one that reminds us that we could be stubborn like the Pharaoh himself, even within our own smaller empires.

I find Propp's thesis, that God can lead sinners to more sin, much too negative a theological statement for his evidence. I would argue that most of the passages Propp cited about God and sin refer to major concerns for the nation—war, political struggles, idolatry, and false prophecy. The most convincing among those cited are the ones from Isaiah and 1 Kings 22:19–23. However, we can say that all these verses exhibit "final cause" style. Most believers who are monotheists hold that God is just, fair, and merciful. They cannot adequately "explain" suffering and sin, but they do consistently avoid shortcuts that would "blame" God for these elements of life.

Along with Propp, we are trying to understand the justice of Pharaoh's plight. Paul's questions are germane, but are part of a tribute to Christ that is beyond our scope in this study of the Book of Exodus. We cannot close this topic at this point of analysis, but we can revisit the work of the Elohist and Priestly writers. Propp may be wrong in saying that the writers "ignored the attendant moral problem" of who hardened whose heart.

Summary of Childs's Remarks

Childs notes the uniqueness of this Exodus topic of hardening the heart; there are no good parallels elsewhere in the Old Testament. He is skeptical that we can succeed in any attempt to fathom Pharaoh's motives, his inner sinful tendencies, or how he holds on to his free will.

Instead, Childs tries to look more carefully at the intertwined traditions. He notes that for the Yahwist the hardening usually occurs near the end of each episode, or even after the plague has been removed. This pattern implies that for J hardening is not the cause of this or that plague, but rather a reaction to it. (Most of what Childs assigns to J is given to E by Propp.)

Childs notes the consistency of the goals mentioned in these J (or E) accounts. The purpose of these signs was to show Pharaoh how different Yahweh is, and to show the special protections given to the Hebrews during the plagues. Sometimes the goals are mentioned before the plague occurs, sometimes afterward. Below is my list of most of Childs's citations, augmented with some of my own. Note: Childs assigns Exodus 10:20, 27 to J; Propp credits them to P.

Bloodred Nile Water

7:14 introductory hardening reference, influenced by preceding verse

7:17 goal (before plague): for Pharaoh to know that God is the LORD

7:23 Pharaoh leaves, not taking this sign to heart (quite similar to hardening)

Frogs

8:10 goal (after frogs are everywhere): for Pharaoh to know that no one is like the LORD our God

8:15 at the respite, Pharaoh made his heart heavy

Flies

8:22 goal (before plague): for Pharaoh to know that "I the LORD am in this land." Goshen mentioned

8:32 after flies were removed, Pharaoh made his heart heavy

Cattle Disease

9:4   protection for Hebrews' livestock mentioned

9:7   after Egyptian cattle died, Pharaoh's heart became heavy

Hailstorm

9:14,   related goals mentioned: for Pharaoh to see God's
16   power and to know that there is no one like God, whose name is to resound everywhere

9:29   main goal (after the storm has raged): for Pharaoh to know that the earth is the LORD's

9:34   after the storm is over, Pharaoh sinned and made his heart heavy

Locusts

10:20 the LORD strengthens Pharaoh's heart after all locusts are gone

Darkness

10:27 the LORD strengthens Pharaoh's heart, apparently after the darkness is over

Final Plague Announced

11:7   goal (beforehand): for Pharaoh to know that the LORD makes a distinction between Egypt and Israel

Childs concludes that for J (or E) the hardening serves to prevent the proper function of the plagues as a means for knowing Yahweh. Childs says that "the writer attributes the failure of the plagues to produce true knowledge to Pharaoh's being hardened.

Hardness for J is not a state of mind, but a specific negative reaction to the signs from God."

Moving on to the Priestly traditions, Childs calls our attention to 7:3–4. He sees a strict parallelism between 3a, "I will harden Pharaoh's heart," and 4a, "When Pharaoh does not listen to you." Likewise 3b, "I will multiply my signs and wonders," is parallel to 4b, "I will lay my hand upon Egypt...." We should note also 11:9, "The LORD said to Moses, 'Pharaoh will not listen to you, in order that my wonders may be multiplied in the land of Egypt.'" The two themes of hardening Pharaoh's heart and Pharaoh not listening become the stock phrase in the P stories. Childs's list is given here:

7:13 Pharaoh's heart strengthened, and he would not listen
7:22 Pharaoh's heart strengthened, and he would not listen
8:15 he made his heart heavy, and would not listen
8:19 Pharaoh's heart strengthened, and he would not listen
9:12 the LORD strengthened the heart of Pharaoh, and he would not listen
        (Were we to add Propp's 10:20, 27 here, they do not match entirely. Each mentions hardening, but not the point about listening.)
10:20 the LORD strengthened Pharaoh's heart, and he would not let the Israelites go
10:27 the LORD strengthened Pharaoh's heart, and he was unwilling to let them go

Childs cautions that we should not think of the two themes as cause and effect. The texts do not say that Pharaoh will not listen *because* of the hard heart. Rather, we should take the two themes as equal. We could say that both the hardening and the not listening provide the occasion for plagues to be sent, one after another.

Childs then discusses the blending of the two sets of stories into one longer account. He notes that

in both the hardening terminology is closely connected to the giving of the signs. In J hardness prevents the signs from revealing the knowledge of God; in P the hardness results in the multiplication of signs as judgement....The motif of hardening in Exodus stems from a specific interpretation of the function of signs. Again, hardening did not function as a technical means to tie together originally independent plagues. Rather, the motif sought to explain a tradition which contained a series of divine signs but which continued to fail in their purpose. Hardening was the vocabulary used by the biblical writers to describe the resistance which prevented the signs from achieving their assigned task....It is clear that the P source extended the origin of hardening into the plan of God and thus went beyond J. But the polarity between hardening as a decision of Pharaoh and as an effect of God never was seen as a major issue.

Childs points to the presence of the Egyptian priests in several of the P episodes. They matched the signs of the cobra, the water, and the frogs; they spoke of the finger of God after their attempt to conjure gnats; and they were among the first to be afflicted with the boils. In some of those passages, they provide Pharaoh with an excuse to ignore the full meaning of the sign. In the J (or E) passages, a similar diversion for Pharaoh can be seen in his own attempts at negotiation (8:8–10, 25, 28; 9:7, 27–28; 10:8, 10–11, 16–17, 24, 28).

I appreciate Childs's finding patterns to remind us that the sources are blended together in complex ways. His caution about how much we can learn about the Pharaoh's free will is sound. However, one can wonder about the tradition "which contained a series of divine signs but which continued to fail in their purpose." Wouldn't storytellers or redactors have seen the chaos they were inviting when intertwining their own theological motifs into such traditions? Why wasn't "the polarity between hardening as a decision of Pharaoh and as an effect of God" ever seen "as a major issue"? It remains a troubling question for modern readers.

Summary of Fretheim's Remarks

Fretheim takes Pharaoh's oppression as a cruel mindset that is antilife and anticreation. Nature is threatened by him, including even his own body and heart. Each plague is an act of judgment, and also a pointer or an ecological sign toward the Passover and Red Sea climaxes. In the plagues, various natural forces become *hypernatural*; these forces cause suffering for plants and animals as well as humans. So we should not distract ourselves from the story in order to debate definitions of what is miraculous.

The point of the larger story is that Israel and the whole world must learn of Yahweh's desire for justice and love. Thus the plagues have a public character. For example, the "finger of God" scene is a public defeat for the Egyptian priests. The goal in 8:22; 9:14, 16, 29 is for Pharaoh to know in a public forum that God's power and being are unique, that his commitment to justice is for the whole world (see Rom 9:17).

God's purposes span the world. God is acting in such a public way so that God's good news can be proclaimed to everyone.

Fretheim argues for a "limited determinism" by God over Pharaoh's behaviors, one that slowly develops during the series of plagues. As believers from the outset, we can be sure that Pharaoh will fail, or that he is doomed to fail. Therefore, we see his *heavy heart* (*kbd*) as one that is not healthy or sensitive, one that can get into a rut. His *strong heart* (*hzq*) could have been brave, but his bravery can and does turn into a foolish stubbornness. The conflicting insights of the various sources, P, E, and J, are all mixed together and hard to follow, although we can agree that P leans the most toward the Lord causing the hardening.

In some of the plagues (7:22; 8:19; 9:7, 12; 10:27), the hardening seems to occur early on or while the event is in progress; in others (8:15, 32; 9:34–35; 10:20), hardening seems to happen after the plague is ended. In different ways, these two patterns illustrate the connection between the Pharaoh's oppression, a great sin against all creation, and the suffering that oppression brings. Even when one plague is fully over, his stubbornness brings another to the fore.

Fretheim points to the change of heart of Pharaoh's officials in 10:7, even though they had just been described in 9:34 and 10:1 as being of one accord with the Pharaoh. We can say that no one plague lasts forever, and no single case of hardening is final. Yet many acts of stubbornness gradually make one less open to repentance.

Pharaoh does make some decisions within himself, as the dialogues with Moses show. It is also true that he seems to be in charge in 9:34–35, even after God had done the hardening in 9:12. So God did not render Pharaoh a robot as at the end of the plague of the boils. Yet we cannot ignore those verses that give God responsibility for the hardening. Setting aside earlier mentions in 3:19–20; 4:20; and 7:3, the next reference to God as the hardener is 9:12. After 10:1, God is consistently described as the hardener (setting aside the liturgical quotation in 13:15).

To dig further, Fretheim notes the use of the verb *refuse* (*m'n*). It is found six times (4:23; 7:14; 8:2; 9:2; 10:3–4). In three cases (8:2; 9:2; 10:4), it is in the conditional phrase *if you refuse*, in God's speeches to Moses for Pharaoh. In 4:23, the phrase could be conditional, but the Hebrew is capable of two different translations. Thus Propp and RSV have *if you refuse*, but NRSV has *but you refused*. Exodus 8:21 has a similar conditional phrase, *if you will not let my people go*. All of these uses of *if* come after 4:21 and 7:1–3, where God spoke of himself as the hardener (*qshh* and *hzq* respectively). We must assume that 8:2, 21; 9:2 were actually spoken to Pharaoh. The accounts are condensed for the sake of style; the only case where we are clearly told that the *if* was spoken to Pharaoh is 10:3–4.

In 10:1, God hardens Pharaoh's heart, and gives Moses the brief command to go talk to the Pharaoh. In 10:3–6, the quotation of God includes the condition in 10:4. So God must assume Pharaoh could change. The conditional language must be genuine; so Pharaoh could stop refusing at any point. Earlier, in 4:1–9, God had allowed for the possibility that the Hebrews might not believe each sign, as he said to Moses in 4:8–9.

In 6:12 and 6:30, as Moses claims to be too poor a speaker to go to Pharaoh, Moses must imagine that a good speaker might be able to get the Pharaoh to cooperate. Further, God never gets down to details about *when* he will end the plague series, nor about *when* Pharaoh might cave in. So we can imagine a reasonable period of time for possible repentance by the Pharaoh.

In addition, Fretheim suggests that each one of the *as the* LORD *had said* phrases (7:13, 22; 8:15, 19; 9:12) could mean that things are going *as God thought they would*. This hypothesis could help lessen the deterministic tone of the phrases. We could also say that Moses has been acting as a prophet, warning of doom and cajoling toward repentance. If this is so, repentance needs to be possible, and so the image of a bold, prophetlike Moses could be another way for the biblical writers to put the responsibility for disobedience on the Pharaoh.

Yet after 10:1 the consistent claim that God did the hardening shows the drift of the story—Pharaoh has become completely obstinate. See Psalm 81:11–12, where God speaks of his own long-sinning people, and *giving them over to the stubbornness of their own hearts*. Pharaoh is like a boat on a fast-moving river, headed toward a waterfall. He was not always doomed when he was miles away, but now that he has brought himself to only a hundred yards from the falls, his surviving unscathed is no longer realistic.

Fretheim concludes that the glory for God in Exodus is in fighting the furious power of sin, not in smashing puppets. Fretheim says that "God does not rid the world of evil with the flick of a wrist. There will be genuine conflict in moving a people from bondage to freedom; the pharaohs of this world do not give up easily" (*Exodus*, 102).

God does not crush Moses' free will, or anybody else's. Whatever punishments he gave to Pharaoh might be astounding, but deserved, especially if we consider Pharaoh as "an embodiment of the forces of chaos."

I appreciate Fretheim's attention to several motifs in the plague account, and I agree with many of his logical arguments about the Pharaoh's responsibilities. Yet somehow they remain just that—logical, defensive philosophical arguments to lessen the stern image of God's control and his overwhelming punishments. We need to continue to mull over this topic.

Author's Remarks

As I read chapters 7—11, I find the surrealism of the plague stories unsettling, despite the well-known and reassuringly melodramatic dimensions of one or the other episode.

There is little emphasis on the debris of the plagues: few images of mud, dead fish, dead cattle, famine in the villages. The stories are flat; there is little development in the character of the Pharaoh, little insight into the thinking of Moses or of God. The negotiations and explanations about hard hearts are flat, not convincing. The decision by God to stop at ten plagues seems arbitrary, as does the pause at 11:10.

One interesting profile is that the Pharaoh becomes more and more isolated from his own people at time goes by, but in 10:24 and 10:28, as he insists on holding the cattle hostage and then tells Moses to never come back for another audience, his refusal to bend is hardly comprehensible. Something is missing.

In the foundation story of Exodus 12—13 with all its profound liturgical elements, the death of the firstborn (12:29–32) and the immediate following details (12:33–39) still have this flat, "something is missing" quality.

In 13:15, as the Exodus story is recounted to explain the dedication of firstborn animals, we are told that "Pharaoh *stubbornly refused* to let us go." The Hebrew has "Pharaoh *hardened himself* (*qshh*) against sending us away." In 14:4, 8, 17, we have the final three references to the LORD *strengthening* (*hzq*) Pharaoh's heart. These four mentions of the heart contribute to the plot, but do not shed any more light on the story than we have found so far.

In English, the verb *harden* can be transitive or intransitive. I can harden a loaf of bread by baking it too long (more precisely, the heat hardens it). On the other hand, I can describe a loaf *hardening itself* after a few days sitting on a table. Usually we say that the loaf *got hard* or *became hard*. I could also say that the loaf *was hardened*, but that raises the question as to whom or what did the hardening, even if I did not intend to raise the question.

The NRSV uses *harden* for three different Hebrew words, *kbd*, *qshh*, and *hzq*, which respectively mean "get heavy," "get hard," and "get strong." Further, the NRSV often uses the form *was hardened*, which raises the question as to who did the hardening, when in fact the subject was clearly identified in the Hebrew. This confusion occurs in 7:13, 22; 8:19; 9:7, 35. A less certain instance is found in 7:14.

Even if we used separate verbs to reflect the Hebrew, and avoided the ambiguously passive phrase in the six cases just mentioned, the main problem is still there. The NRSV and many other English translations have the merit of highlighting the issue by repetition of the same word, and no translation can clarify something that is missing.

Over the many years I have been sharing the Book of Exodus with students, I always ask them at this point to identify the genre of literature that best describes all of Exodus 1—15. Of course since these chapters represent centuries of oral tradition and several editings by people with different theological insights, the fifteen chapters are not as smoothly woven together as would be one work by one author. Still, the question is thought provoking.

I find the best answer is to call Exodus 1—15 a grand *drama*. The simplest dictionary definition for a drama is that it is a story meant to be presented by actors that involves *conflict* or *contrast of character*. At the start, we can think of God and Moses as the two main characters, but as the plagues intensify the Pharaoh obviously becomes another main character. However, how can we call any conflict between a human and God a fair fight? Won't the Pharaoh always be a puppet by comparison?

The only answer that brings balance to this mismatch is to think of who or what could be standing on Pharaoh's side. Fretheim touches the answer, in his comments on Exodus 15.

> The Egyptian enemy is certainly historical, but just as certainly more is involved. The Egyptians are also represented as metahistorical in that *the chaotic forces of the world are concentrated there.* We have seen throughout the commentary how they represent anticreational forces. The absence of names for the pharaohs is but one small sign of this larger issue. The references to the divine judgment on Egypt's gods show that the enemy and the battle are cosmic in scope (12:12; 15:11). (*Exodus*, 167)

The first reference to gods in Exodus is found in 12:12, "For I will pass through the land of Egypt that night, and I will strike down every firstborn in the land of Egypt, both human beings and animals; on all the gods of Egypt I will execute judgements: I am the LORD." Most readers would take this as flowery language and move on.

The next time gods are mentioned is in 15:11, and possibly 15:12:

> 11 "Who is like you, O LORD, among the gods?
> Who is like you, majestic in holiness,
> awesome in splendor, doing wonders?
> 12 You stretched out your right hand,
> the earth swallowed them."

Propp says that the earth might swallow the gods, rather than swallow the Egyptian soldiers. Propp calls them "minor gods," and gods "who are incomparably inferior to Yahweh." Perhaps he is too quick to see them as weak or insignificant.

Such gods are spoken of in other biblical passages.

In Numbers 33:3–4 we are told:

> ...on the day after the passover the Israelites went out boldly in the sight of all the Egyptians, while the Egyptians were burying all their firstborn, whom the LORD had struck down among them. The LORD executed judgments even against their gods.

In Exodus 18, Jethro, upon visiting Moses and learning of the great help God had given them, praised God and offered sacrifices. The text, 18:10–12, says:

> 10 Jethro said, "Blessed be the LORD, who has delivered you from the Egyptians and from Pharaoh. 11 Now I know that the LORD is greater than all gods, because he delivered the people from the Egyptians, when they dealt arrogantly with them." 12 And Jethro, Moses' father-in-law, brought a burnt offering and sacrifices to God; and Aaron came with all the elders of Israel to eat bread with Moses' father-in-law in the presence of God.

One might expect Jethro, a pagan priest, to speak of gods. Nevertheless, this passage shows how quickly he acknowledged the LORD's power, and participated in worship with Moses and Aaron and the elders. The mention of rival gods seemed to make perfect sense to Jethro.

Finally, Psalm 82 depicts gods who promote injustice; they are expelled from the heavenly council by God, and their immortality is taken away from them.

Therefore, this drama shows the Pharaoh *and the gods of Egypt* losing a great struggle with Yahweh. However, suppose that within this drama these characters are *powerful gods, major forces* of nature, and *guardians* of the destiny of one of the greatest empires in the ancient world. Suppose *they* back Pharaoh from the beginning, hardening his heart and causing him to lash out in spite of great losses to his land. Suppose Pharaoh is *their* puppet, especially in the six cases mentioned above where the NRSV helps us the least. Their backing would explain how the priests matched a few of the early signs, why the Pharaoh would not yield to the mounting claims of Moses for his god, and why the Pharaoh's soldiers made one insane final charge at the sea. The entire conflict then could be considered more of a fair fight. At the end, the gods of Egypt learn a bitter lesson; an empire built on injustice can be beaten. Slaves can be freed, even if they have no weapons or special bravery of their own.

This drama, then, demonstrates a fair *conflict*, a fair *contrast* of the *character* of Yahweh and the *character* of those gods who wanted Egypt to continue to reign unchallenged.

Propp may have oversimplified how God allows sin to penetrate our world, and may have missed the way the writers of Exodus dealt with the concept of the hardening of Pharaoh's heart. He was right in pointing out that in the Old Testament the sources of evil are not consistently and clearly explained; Satan's role, for example, is not a sufficient vehicle for this topic. Within Exodus, I think that considering the role of the gods of Egypt can help us to understand the Pharaoh and the cosmic battle between justice and oppressive empire.

Childs held up many fine details of Exodus 1—15 for our examination, and was right in saying that the main tradition is about a series of great signs from God that did not achieve their purpose in the short run. I think considering the gods of Egypt can help us understand why the signs failed. The gods were no more ready to accept changes than were the Pharaoh and his officials.

Fretheim raised theological questions more frequently. He was concerned to find good qualities in the midwives and in Pharaoh's daughter at the time of Moses' rescue, and in the Egyptian culture that formed some of Moses' own values. He is very open to the idea that Moses and the Israelites came to be sincerely respected by ordinary Egyptians, and that innocent Egyptians also suffered during the plagues. Fretheim may overdraw Pharaoh as a champion of injustice and oppression (he compares him to Hitler at times). Yet Fretheim is on the right track in calling the Egyptians fighting at the sea *metahistorical*, in that they represent forces of anticreation and chaos. He alludes to the power of sin, and to the Pharaoh as an "embodiment of the forces of chaos." Even the image of Pharaoh as a sinner, as one who is in a boat in a fast-flowing stream heading toward a waterfall, calls on us to think of the power pushing the water forward. I think considering the gods of Egypt egging on *their* Pharaoh and *their* officials and *their* soldiers helps make more sense of this drama.

It would be academically and spiritually poor of us to say simply that the Egyptians in Moses' day were bad people and that's that. The Exodus traditions are much more profound. Being freed from Egypt led to the accepting of the covenant at Sinai, a deep relationship with God far beyond freedom from slavery. Being freed from Egypt also led to the Israelites' making of the golden calf, a story showing the addictive power of idolatry.

We must remember that the Egyptians of any era are also God's children, more like us than we realize. We, too, are more like the Egyptians of any era in our opposition to God than we want to admit.

Exodus
15:22—24:18

Section Eleven:
Exodus 15:22–27

Propp considers the entire passage to be from a redactor,
probably reusing E traditions.

Introduction

The next few chapters depict events prior to the great Sinai
covenant story that starts in chapter 19. When the people came
to the oasis at Marah, the water was bitter or brackish; most likely
this had been a long-standing condition, as the place name indicates (*mrh*, "bitterness").

The *complaining* or *murmuring* (*lwn*) at this point seems
appropriate; everyone was troubled by the lack of drinking water.
The phrase is that they complained or murmured *against* Moses.
They will do this a few times in Exodus (and at several points in
the Book of Numbers). So we will be able to learn some dimensions of the stress of the years of wandering in the wilderness.
Fretheim notes that the long journey in the wilderness will be
much more of a challenge than the Israelites might expect (or the
readers, for that matter). During the journey God guides and
assists, but he does not turn the trip into a vacation for his people.
We could consider the people as adolescents in their faith; they
will wind up testing God as much as he tests them.

The Hebrew in 15:25 says that the LORD *taught* Moses about
the use of this special wood; other ancient versions use a similar
verb that means that the LORD *showed* it to Moses (*made him see*
it). The verb *taught* (*yrh*) is the root for the word *torah*, the key
word for teaching and law in Jewish thought. In Jewish custom
the entire Pentateuch is often called *The Torah*. In 4:12, 15, the
LORD promised to *teach* Moses what to say to Pharaoh.

Ancient commentators suggest that the wood might have been oleander, a bitter wood that in folklore was thought to have the power to make water safe to drink.

In verses 25b–26, God (or Moses) *established* regulations and *tested* the people. There will be many more tests in the future, part of the give-and-take of the murmuring traditions. In this brief story, we are not told any details of what the regulations or tests involved; the main point of the story seems to be whether or not the people will wholeheartedly obey Moses as the leader for their journey.

Cassuto assumes that Moses spoke the words of 15:26, but the majority of commentators attribute the verse to God, continuing the train started in verse 25b. The direct statement from God is quite stern, "*If* you will listen...I will not bring upon you any of the diseases...; for I am the LORD who heals you." God had punished the Egyptians for their injustices; he could do the same again if his people disobeyed Moses and became unjust themselves. So God is *healer* and *judge* at the same time.

Propp notes that this negotiation about making water drinkable resembles a miniature covenant. The people are reminded of their duty to obey God, and in turn Moses is able to use this special wood to purify the water. Fretheim agrees that their obedience can rightly be tested; they can be held accountable for observable behavior. He draws a modern parallel to driving safely, so as not to endanger oneself or others. God will be able to see results, and Israel will be able to form good habits that will promote the goals of creation and justice, and strengthen their own social fabric.

Fretheim considers this improving of the water to be an account of an herbal cure, rather than an impressive miracle (see Sir 38:5). Childs sees incidents of simple, realistic needs in the murmuring stories prior to Exodus 32, and incidents involving greater conflict and disobedience later on. Both types of accounts serve to warn against resistance to God's plans. They also show us more about Moses as he intercedes with God and tries to exhort the people to obedience.

Question

87. Why would storytellers combine 15:22–25a (a story about making water drinkable) with 15:25b–26 (remarks about the importance of obeying regulations)?

Conclusion

This brief passage does several things, and it does them well. The first four verses give an example of the harsh realities of desert travel, of the people's reliance on or criticism of Moses, and of Moses' reliance on God for further help.

The editor or redactor who provided verses 25b–26 is setting this event at Marah within a larger picture. Each new experience of relying on Moses and God will also be a point where one could resent the reliance and turn it into criticism or anger. Each day of the journey is another day to live up to the voice of God, to his tests and commandments and statutes. The redactor is talking to later generations, including ourselves. The mention of the more adequate oasis at Elim provides a successful conclusion.

Section Twelve:
Exodus 16:1–36

> Propp assigns 15:27 and 16:1 to redactors, and also the final two verses, 16:35–36. The great majority of the passage is clearly from the Priestly traditions. Propp finds additions from the JE level in verses 4–5 (testing), verses 14–15 (strangeness of manna), verse 21b (manna melting in sun), and verses 28–30 (not collecting manna on the Sabbath). The combined text has some minor repetitions and disjunctures within it.

Introduction

There are several Priestly words in this chapter, including *'edah* (congregation) in 16:2, 9, 10, 22 and *qahal* (assembly) in 16:3. Another is *kbod Yahweh* (the glory of the LORD) in 16:7, 10. The noun *glory* is derived from the verb *kbd* (to be heavy). Priestly writers were of course interested in Sabbath traditions, and with anything to do with the Ark, Tent of Meeting, or Temple. On the Sabbath the people are to rest, enjoy dinners with their families, and find ways to make it a day of holiness (16:23).

Exodus 15:27 mentions twelve springs and seventy date palms; this abundance of water and dates would have been a welcome change from the troubled water at Marah. In 16:1, *Sin* may be a shortened form of *Sinai*, the name of the region. Soon the people complain of a shortage of food (both meat and bread), putting the blame on Moses and Aaron for leading them to this desolate spot. (There is a longer, related story about quails in Num 11.)

God responds by planning to rain down daily amounts of bread from heaven, with twice as much on Fridays to tide them over the Sabbath. Relying on this special food will be a test, to see if they will follow his *torah* (instruction). Moses and Aaron then relay the essentials of this message to the people, but in an oddly defensive style. More important, they do not mention the double amount that will come on Fridays. Propp suggests that in this complex editing process the Priestly writer might have thought that Moses did not understand all that he was told, and that Moses assumed that the larger Friday amounts would be self-evident. *Meat* is mentioned in verse 8, with no explanation.

The next four verses, 9–12, involve Aaron calling on the people to come closer to the LORD, followed by an appearance of the LORD in a bright cloud, and confirming words from the LORD about the provision of meat and bread. Quails are mentioned in verse 13, but not afterward. We could take this passage as a repetition of verses 6–8, or look on verses 6–8 as Moses' and Aaron's assured faith that God would keep his promises. The command to *draw near to* the LORD (verse 9), and the references to having the jar of manna placed *before* the LORD and *before* the covenant in verses 33–34, match phrases in Exodus 27:21 about having the lamp in the Tent of Meeting near the covenant *before* the LORD.

The initial description in 16:14–15a of the mysterious fine flakes follows easily from 16:4, since both are JE passages. In 16:15a, the Hebrew word *man* is a variant form of *mah*, both of which mean the question word *what*. The Hebrew name for the food (*man*) is rendered as manna (English and Greek). Propp mentions other possible linguistic roots for the word *man*.

Ancient peoples thought of dew as falling from the heavens during the night; we now know that dew is simply water vapor that condenses at lower temperatures. The manna is described as something mixed within the dew, and left behind as the dew melts away. Scholars think ancient manna was a sugary product harbored by aphids, especially those partaking of tamarisk tree sap. This scarce natural product could never have been a plentiful, nutritious staple as it is described in Exodus, sustaining a whole nation for forty years.

In 16:19, Moses cautioned them not to save any manna overnight. Disobeying Moses, some found out the hard way that any extra manna decayed and was consumed by worms or ants. The JE tradition was that manna melted in the heat of the day

(16:21b). In fact, the natural substance from the sap is usually carried away by insects to their nests or hives.

In 16:22, the double portion on that first Friday seems to have come as a surprise, so much so that the elders reported this to Moses. Contrary to Propp's theory above, Childs says that Moses *wanted* to surprise the people when they first experienced this weekly bounty, and then used the occasion to issue further Sabbath instructions. Moses explained that the portion saved for Saturday would not spoil, and that neither would any be found in the field on Saturdays. Still, some had to see for themselves, and checked the fields to gather more on the Sabbath. This lead to an angry intervention by God (16:28–30), who again mentions the double supply on Fridays, and the need to stay at home on the Sabbath. These three JE verses do not fit in well with what immediately precedes, but can be tied to the earlier JE verses if we assume that the editor simply used the P reference to disobedience in verse 27 to stand in for some JE act of disobedience, now missing.

Questions

88. In 16:3, why did the people mention dying *by the hand of the* LORD? How does God respond in verses 4–13? How accurate is their reference in verse 3 to dying of hunger?

89. God speaks of *testing* and *instruction* in 16:4. What does he mean?

90. Moses and Aaron relay instructions in verses 6–8. Meat and bread are mentioned, and the complaining of the people is recalled. What is Moses' intention, as he explains these things?

91. What is the effect for the reader as you work through 16:6–12?

92. What are the physical qualities of the manna, as described in 16:13–26?

93. What is done with the manna in 16:32–34? Why?

Conclusion

Childs (280–304) reviews the principal Old Testament cross-references to the story of the manna. In Numbers 11, the people complain about the manna as somehow inadequate or boring; this led to the provision by God of massive amounts of quail to eat, and to stern punishments at the same time. In Deuteronomy 8 and in Psalm 78:17–31, the manna is mentioned as part of a perspective of warnings to rely on God's initiatives. In postbiblical rabbinic writings manna was mostly used in homiletic imagery. Philo, the ancient Jewish commentator most concerned to reach Greek thinkers, relied heavily on allegory; for example, manna was more noble than regular food, and represents philosophy, the discipline more noble than other areas of learning.

Childs then examines the New Testament cross-references in turn. Many of the brief references (Matt 4:1–4; Luke 4:1–4; 1 Cor 10:3; 2 Cor 8:15; Rev 2:17) seem to be in the spirit of Deuteronomy 8 and Psalm 78. The main manna image is found in John 6:25–59. John portrays Jesus as the true manna, the only source of spiritual life now. In this he more closely resembles Philo, moving away from the biblical text and developing spiritual images. By not using Exodus 16 to the fullest, New Testament writers missed an important part of their Jewish roots. Later Christian writers did the same. Childs concludes:

> The danger of selecting in this way emerges in the later history of Christian exegesis where the process of extending the New Testament themes has led to a virtual separation from its Old Testament base. The manna has become the heavenly food confined to the eucharist whose qualities are limited to higher spheres of spiritual attainment. It is an essential function of theological reflection within the canon to continue to sound the full range of notes from both the Old and the New Covenants. Particularly in our modern culture, the Old Testament witness to God's concern to satisfy the physical hunger of his people offers an essential foundation on which the New Testament's testimony to Jesus Christ as the "bread of life" must be built. (*The Book of Exodus*, 303–4)

Section Thirteen:
Exodus 17:1–7

Propp assigns 17:1a to a redactor, and sees the remaining
verses as a combination of J and E verses. He argues
that we cannot recover a complete E or a complete
J version of this story from such a short account.

Introduction

There is a parallel Priestly story in Numbers 20:1–13. The two
accounts form a framework around the Sinai traditions.

In 17:2, the Hebrew verb *ryb* (quarrel) is used twice. This is
the main Old Testament verb for conducting a *lawsuit*, especially
a *covenant lawsuit*.

The people's demand, "[*You* (pl.)], *Give* us water," is actually a
plural form, which could mean that Moses *and Aaron* (Cassuto)
or Moses *and God* (Propp) were being jointly braced. Many
ancient versions changed this to the more likely singular form of
the demand, directed only at Moses. The people do focus on
Moses alone in verse 3 when they say, "Why did you (s.) bring us
out of Egypt?" In verse 3, the phrase "to kill us and our children
and our livestock" actually uses singular forms, "to kill *me* and *my*
children and *my* livestock." Propp notes that the singular forms
could represent collective thinking, or perhaps each householder's
concern for his own family. Many ancient versions changed these
to the expected plural forms, as we have in the NRSV.

The place name *Massah* in verse 7 is associated with a verbal
form of *nsh* (test), used in verse 2. Likewise *Meribah* is derived
from *ryb* (quarrel), used twice in verse 2. The final question in
verse 7, "Is the LORD among us or not?" clearly indicates that this
complaint is also one of unbelief, a direct attack on God's inter-

est in them, as was the dispute over the lack of food in Exodus 16 (see Answer 88).

The individual names Massah and Meribah occur often in the Old Testament. The two names are mentioned together just here and in Deuteronomy 33:8 and Psalm 95:8. In the latter citation, the people are described as *hardening* their hearts (*qshh*) there. In Exodus 32:26–29 and Deuteronomy 33:8–11, there are accounts of Moses calling the Levites into service to stop the sinful activities attending the golden calf incident, which also took place at Horeb. Propp (606–13) has an excellent study of the theological and poetic references to all sources of water in ancient Near Eastern and biblical writings. He is convinced that locating the spring of Massah and Meribah at Mount Horeb had cosmic significance for the authors, allowing them to link God's care for the laws of creation with his care to promulgate moral laws for all people.

Questions

94. The lack of an adequate supply of water at Rephidim led to a lot of exasperation. What methods did the storytellers use to highlight the tensions everyone experienced?
95. Compare and contrast Moses' words in 17:2 and 17:4.
96. Why did God give such detailed instructions in 17:5–6?
97. What do we learn from Moses' naming the location in 17:7?
98. Compare this story about needing water with the one in Exodus 15:22–27.

Conclusion

One could ask why God is allowed to test his people, yet they are not supposed to test God. The biblical authors feel that God wants or needs to learn how we use our free will and our covenant loyalty, as he looks for ways to help us and to judge fairly.

When people do the testing, on the other hand, it could become a searching for rewards for faith, which can compromise our own free will and our ability to trust in each other and in ourselves. We need to respect the boundary between the divine and human realms.

Section Fourteen:
Exodus 17:8–16

> Propp attributes the entire story to the Elohist, except for
> the redactional element in verse 16b, which could be
> the judgment of a much later editor.

Introduction

Amalek (a collective term for the Amalekites) was mentioned
in Genesis 14:7. They were southern Canaanite nomadic raiders,
assumed in Jewish tradition to be of Edomite origin (descendants
of Esau; see Gen 36:12, 16). They are described as constant enemies of God's people in Judges 6:3–6; 7:12. Saul defeated them
later on (1 Sam 15), and an unwise Amalekite took credit for slaying Saul (2 Sam 1:10). In the Book of Esther, Mordecai was from
Saul's tribe, and the villain Haman was an Amalekite (Esth 3:1).
Thus the reference in Exodus 17:16b to war with Amalekites in
later generations covers time down to King David himself.

In Deuteronomy 25:17–19, the Amalekites are described as
preying on the weary exiles at the rear of the throng. Fretheim
notes that in Exodus 17 the Amalekites function as successors of
the relentless forces of Pharaoh and his Egyptian soldiers.

Moses tells Joshua to *choose some men* to defend the people.
The Hebrew text does not have the word *some*, but that might be
implicit in the idea of choosing or selecting. It is a common
theme of holy war traditions that only a portion of all the eligible
soldiers are actually needed by God, who participates in the battle in his own wondrous ways.

In 17:9, the word *tomorrow* might go with what precedes (*go
out, fight tomorrow*), or with what follows (*tomorrow I will stand*).
Propp prefers the former, NRSV and Childs the latter. Hur, men-

tioned in 17:10, 12, is spoken of in Exodus 24:14 where he may be a leader (a Levite?) associated with Aaron. The same name is found again in 31:2, but that may be a different person (a tribal official, but not a Levite). Propp prefers this figure of a tribal leader from chapter 31, so that both a priest and a prince assist Moses equally.

There are disputes over the original meaning of the name *Joshua* (*Yehoshua*), traditionally taken to mean *Yahweh is my ruler*. He is also called *Hoshea* (*salvation* or *he saved*) in Numbers 13:8, 16, and Deuteronomy 32:44. His name is changed by Moses in Numbers 13:16. The reason for the alternate form of his name may be that Priestly editors did not want the *yeho* component of the name used so soon, since it stands for *Yahweh*, the name so recently revealed in Exodus 3 or 6.

Propp argues that the hill upon which Moses stands is a part of Mount Horeb. He imagines that Moses and the elders were ahead of the people at the spring, situated at the head of a wadi (dry streambed, walled in like a small canyon or draw). Joshua had to take his men back toward the rear of the wadi to fight the Amalekites, but Moses could see and be seen from the hill.

The Hebrew word for *hand* (*yad*), used seven times in this story, can also mean *forearm*. The remark that his hands *grew weary* is actually that his hands *became heavy* (*kbd*), a word we have seen many times before. Propp argues that we cannot narrow down the many possibilities for the gestures and intentions of Moses as he raises one or both hands, with or without the staff. He may have been pointing, taking an oath, waving, making a rallying sign, or holding up his arms in prayer. Given the way the Israelites prevailed or faltered as Moses' hands went up or down, it is clear that Moses is miming or imaging God's participation in the battle, but that Moses is not causing all this by his own power.

Fretheim discounts the likelihood that Moses was praying during the battle, and denies that there was any intrinsic power in the staff that Moses held. Rather, he suggests that the sight of Moses making bold gestures reminded the soldiers of God's help and of Moses' confidence in God. Even with God's help, defeating the nomadic raiders was a very difficult task. Childs also does not think that prayer was behind the gestures of Moses, but he is skeptical of seeing the gestures as simply rallying or encouraging the troops. Childs finds the best model to explain the event in the story of Balaam. In that extensive account (Numbers 22—24), Balaam's majestic blessings upon Israel signify God's blessings; God causes Balaam to see the victories to come. Propp suggests that the image of Moses holding his staff and so representing God's initiatives is virtually a modified image of ancient storm gods holding thunderbolts. Moses is not divine, but so much has been delegated to him by the LORD that we have this haunting image to hold in memory.

Early Christians favored the idea of Moses at prayer, and could not resist seeing a type of the cross in Moses' having his arms outstretched.

In 17:15, there is a reference to *nissi* (*my banner* or *my banner pole*), from the noun *nes*. Here the phrase *The LORD is my banner* is the name given to a memorial altar. The dedication gives the credit for the victory to God; perhaps the banner *pole* represents either God's arm or Moses' staff.

Exodus 17:16 speaks of a *kes*, which is customarily derived from *kisse'*, meaning "chair" or "throne." This may allude to the stone upon which Moses sat in verse 12. Scholars are very unsure of this traditional derivation; some offer other possible roots to explain the meaning of *kes*, while some suggest that it is a mistaken form for *nes* in the preceding verse (so NRSV and Childs). Ancient versions don't offer much help.

Questions

99. What information is missing in 17:8–11?
100. What is the logic or purpose in 17:14–16?

Conclusion

Propp calls our attention to a passage in Exodus 23:20–33, in which God speaks of sending an angel to protect the people on their journey from Sinai to the Promised Land. Propp finds earlier parallels for that account in chapter 23 in 15:22—17:16. A brief listing of the parallels might be helpful.

Exodus 23:21	**Parallels in Exodus 15—17**
Do not rebel against	People rebel against
the angel	Moses in 15:24; 16:2–3; 17:2–4
Exodus 23:22	
If they obey, angel will	God fights for them in
battle for them	17:8–16
Exodus 23:25	
God or angel will bless	People are given manna
their bread and	in chapter 16
water,	Spring provided in 17:1–7
and sickness will be taken	Water purified in 15:22–26
away	

The suggested parallels help us to see that between the escape from the sea and Mount Horeb God was caring for his people. Propp also mentions Jethro's assistance to Moses in the next chapter, wherein Jethro pointed out the need for judges for everyday matters, and his ideas were implemented (Exod 18:13–26).

Thus *before* the covenant at Sinai, Israel had a ruler and helper (God), judges and a law code, and an army.

Section Fifteen:
Exodus 18:1–27

> Propp assigns the entire chapter to the Elohist.
> The meeting with Jethro is warm, as was the initial
> meeting with Aaron in Exodus 4:27–30.

Introduction

Exodus 18:2 mentions that Zipporah had been *sent away* at some point, and that her father had *taken* her *back* (*lqh*). The Hebrew speaks of Zipporah after her *dismissal* (using the noun *shilluhim*). This rare noun form can mean "divorce," as in the "sending" of a wife back to her father. It can also mean "marriage gift" or "dowry," as the gift of a father *sending* his daughter to her new husband. It is used in this latter sense in 1 Kings 9:16.

Instead of the NRSV *After Moses had sent away his wife Zipporah*, Propp proposes the completely different phrase *Zipporah, Moses' wife since her marriage gift*. Childs accepts the likelihood of a divorce, arguing that reference to a dowry has no context. He mentions a rabbinic source that accepted the implication of a divorce in the text. Childs suggests that possibly an editor had at hand a tradition that Zipporah and the sons accompanied Jethro on this journey, so the editor spliced that in as well as possible. Cassuto assumes that the sending away was entirely a matter of Moses' concern for safety for her and their sons, and that there was no divorce.

One last complication: In Numbers 12:1, Moses has a Cushite wife. Scholars are divided on whether that ethnic term refers to Zipporah's Midianite origins. One indicator that it might is Habakkuk 3:7, where the locales of Cushan and Midian are in parallel.

Moses' bowing down to Jethro (verse 7) was reversed in some ancient versions to have Jethro bow to Moses instead. After mutual greetings, they entered Moses' tent for their discussion. We can presume that they stayed in the tent until the end of verse 12. Fretheim sees the tent as a quasi sanctuary, not just a shelter.

Questions

101. In 18:1–6, how does the storyteller serve his listeners (readers)? What impressions do you form of Jethro here?
102. As you observe Moses and Jethro in their initial interactions in 18:7–12, how do they represent things greater than themselves?
103. In 18:13–18, as Jethro extends his stay with Moses, he forms opinions about some of the particulars of Moses' role as leader of the Israelites. Does he have any right to do this? Does Moses understand the question in verse 14? Isn't Moses' response in verse 16 a good description of the duties God had given to Moses?
104. Describe the ideas of Jethro in 18:19–23 as best you can. Why does Jethro have so much confidence in his own analysis, given that he is not of Israelite ancestry, and has not had the experiences they have had in Exodus 4–17?
105. Profile the style, tone, and ambience of this chapter.

Conclusion

The course of Jewish history of religious and civil law did not run as smoothly as Jethro imagined. Later kings often tried to restrict freedoms and rights, religious and civil, and laid heavy taxes on the lower classes. When they did so, prophets spoke out forcefully, and some were punished for this protesting.

In Exodus 18:14–26, there are ten uses of the word *dabar*, a very generic Hebrew word that means "word" or "thing" or "matter," or the like. It is such a workhorse of a word in Hebrew that it is often left out in English translations; for example, by using the word *this* instead of the phrase *this thing* or *this matter*. In the following list I indicate by parentheses the three cases where the NRSV simply uses the word *this*, and in the other instances I provide the word the NRSV actually uses.

Exodus 18 verse	NRSV translation
14*	What is *this* (*thing*)
16	When they have a *dispute*
17*	What you are doing is not (*a*) *good* (*thing*)
18	The *task* is too heavy
19	You should bring their *cases*
22	every important *case*/every minor *case*
23*	If you do *this* (*thing*)
26	hard *cases*/any minor *case*

By using the same generic word in all these verses, Jethro is not only talking about the *disputes* or *cases* (18:16, 19, 22, 26); he is also concerned about the *process* and Moses' *workload* (18:14, 17, 18, 23). To put it another way, Moses' own health is another case that should be judged. His own self-care cannot be ignored. We could illustrate the point by paraphrasing, "What is this workload that you are doing?" and "This is not a good workload," and "This workload is too heavy," and "If you do this lighter work-load...then you will be able to endure."

Section Sixteen:
Exodus 19:1–25

Propp assigns just the first two verses to P. Much of the
chapter is from E, except for the J contributions in
19:10–15, 18, 20–23. The Yahwist touches primarily on
purification rites, while E focuses more on Moses and his
interactions with God and the people. Some of the E
material (as in 19:3–8) has Deuteronomistic overtones.

As we begin the story of the covenants at Mount Sinai, it will be
useful to outline the way the narratives and law passages are woven
together. Then we shall return to chapter 19 in detail. The next six
chapters of Exodus can be set in a simple outline as follows.

19:1–2	Introduction
19:3–6	God's proposal, which Moses is to relay to the people
19:7–8	The people agree to this covenant proposal relayed by Moses
19:9	Next step: God's plan for a more public interaction with everyone
19:10–15	Preparations for this interaction
19:16–19	God speaks to Moses in front of the people
19:20–25	Renewed preparations prior to the Ten Commandments (Decalogue)
20:1–17	Ten Commandments
20:18–21	The people ask Moses to be their mediator with God from now on
20:22—23:33	God continues to reveal a mixed collection of laws, usually called the Covenant Code or the Book of the Covenant

24:1–11   Covenant ratification ceremonies, closing the events begun in 19:3 and described mainly in chapter 19, prior to the laws

[24:12–18   Before bringing the tablets down from the mountaintop, Moses receives special revelations about a movable shrine; this planning and designing takes forty days being alone with God]

Introduction

Propp examines the rabbinic calendar and the possible relationship of this Exodus covenant date with the later liturgical spring Festival of Weeks, but cautiously concludes that their both falling in March may be coincidental.

The reference to *eagles'* wings in verse 4 uses the same word that is used for *vultures* elsewhere. The context probably indicates the effortless flight of such birds, which were also acclaimed to be selfless in their parenting roles.

In Exodus 19:10, 14, Moses is to *consecrate* the people (see verse 22). Childs disagrees with this sense, arguing that the context indicates more remote preparation. In verses 10, 14, he freely paraphrases that Moses *had the people prepare themselves.*

There is little consensus on the origin or significance of the refraining from sexual relations at this point (verse 15). Perhaps it was symbolic of a greater unity of purpose among all the people, old and young, married and unmarried.

The priests in verse 22 are not identified; they consecrate themselves (perhaps they are the young laymen in chapter 24?).

The last phrase in verse 25 is ambiguous. It could mean that Moses *told* them or *spoke to* them about what had just happened. However, it could instead mean that he *said* what follows, namely, every word of 20:1–17. The stronger tradition is that God proclaimed the Decalogue directly to everyone.

Questions

106. Exodus 19:1–3 introduces us to these next six chapters, the major story of the entire book. How do these verses help us to get started?

107. In 19:4–6, it is easy enough to see that God wants to draw closer to these people, but there are two questions to be asked here. Is not God's relationship to them—a relationship going all the way back to Abraham in Genesis 12 (and then through Isaac, Jacob, Joseph, and centuries of their living in Egypt)—already close enough? Who could benefit from this additional obeying and covenant keeping?

108. What are the implications of the three sayings by God in 19:5–6, about the Israelites' potential to be his treasured possession out of all the peoples, a priestly kingdom, and a holy nation?

109. In 19:7–8, Moses delivers this message about God's desire for a closer relationship, and the people agree without reservation. Why is this story moving at such a rapid pace? Why should any group make such a commitment before being told what they will need to obey or what constitutes the covenant obligations?

110. Exodus 19:9 indicates the next step planned by God. The event described there takes place in 19:19. Why does God want everyone to listen to him speak to Moses?

111. Taking 19:9–19 as a unit, we see very serious preparations by Moses and the people, and extensive divine control of storm (or possibly volcanic) elements. Why does God bring all this about? Is this a way to establish a closer relationship, or a way to scare the socks off everyone?

112. In 19:20–25, further divine warnings are issued to Moses regarding physical boundary lines for the people (and for the priests!). (An exception is made for Aaron.) How much impact does this passage have within chapter 19? Does it have any other purpose or function within the larger context of chapters 19—24?

Conclusion

In commenting on 19:5–6, Childs puts things in simple, yet solemn perspective.

Israel is God's own people, set apart from the rest of the nations. Israel as a people is also dedicated to God's service among the nations as priests function within a society. Finally, the life of Israel shall be commensurate with the holiness of the covenant God. The covenant responsibility encompasses her whole life, defining her relation to God and to her neighbors, and the quality of her existence. (*The Book of Exodus,* 367)

Section Seventeen:
Exodus 20:1–21

There is a very similar account of the Decalogue
in Deuteronomy 5. Propp assigns Exodus 20:1–17
to redactors and 20:18–21 to E. Most commentators
admit that 20:1–17 does not easily fit into J, E, or P
classifications since it is so much a foundational text,
and probably edited several times.

In order to refresh our minds regarding such a well-known
text, I suggest that individual readers or study groups
listen to Exodus 20:1–17 read aloud once or twice.
Try to pay attention to any noteworthy points of
style as well as to the content.

Note: The Hebrew of 20:13 includes all four verses of the English of 20:13–16. The rest of the English chapter, 20:17–26, is found in the Hebrew as 20:14–23. For simplicity, I will try to use only English verse citations throughout.

Note: The common name for these revelations in chapter 20 is the *Ten Commandments,* but the Hebrew simply calls them the *ten words* or *ten sayings* (*debarim*). I will use *commandments* or *sayings* without distinction. Roman Catholics and some Protestants number the Ten Commandments in one way, while other Protestants follow the Jewish custom. The Jewish system distinguishes two commandments in Exodus 20:2–3, 4–6, and combines all the warnings at the end about coveting into one commandment. The following chart may be helpful. Should I refer to a commandment by number, I will use the Roman Catholic system with which I am familiar.

Catholic Commandments		Jewish Commandments	
(English vv.)		(Hebrew vv.)	
First one God	(2–)3–6	**First** one God	2–3
		Second no images	4–6
Second no swearing	7	**Third** no swearing	7
Third Sabbath	8–11	**Fourth** Sabbath	8–11
Fourth honor parents	12	**Fifth** honor parents	12
Fifth murder	13	**Sixth** murder	13
Sixth adultery	14	**Seventh** adultery	13
Seventh stealing	15	**Eighth** stealing	13
Eighth false witness	16	**Ninth** false witness	13
Ninth coveting wife	17	**Tenth** coveting	14
Tenth coveting goods	17		

Introduction

Before looking at the individual commandments, I would like to include two overviews of the entire passage. Fretheim focuses on the combination of stories (narrative) and laws (code) at many points in Exodus and the Pentateuch. Childs compares the style of the Decalogue with other ancient Near Eastern law materials, looking for similarities and differences.

Stories and Laws Combined

Fretheim reminds us that the Decalogue is community oriented—focusing on the outer limits of conduct needed for the common good. The brief prohibitions should elicit reflection on related virtues. For example, speaking well of a neighbor is as important as not bearing false witness, and preserving and promoting life is as important as not killing. The spectrum of topics in the Decalogue is not complete. There is no mention of subjects such as the poor, women's issues, or self-care. However, the original list was not meant to be complete. It is supplemented in the following chapters of Exodus, as well as in Leviticus, Numbers, and Deuteronomy, and elsewhere. Perhaps it could be thought of as a constitution, which can be supplemented as time goes by. Cassuto argues that the Decalogue was originally no more than a preview of the range of contents in the following laws in 20:22—23:33.

Other ancient cultures developed law codes, but the Old Testament is unique in combining narrative and code into larger units of revelation. God is presented as designing all the laws in some way. Fretheim lists several consequences of this Old Testament system of combining narrative and code (201–7). My abbreviated summary of his remarks follows.

1. God is the principal agent in both narrative and law sections. The stories and laws complement each other and deepen our understanding of how God thinks and acts.
2. As a result of the combining, the laws are more clearly seen as a gift from God, part of his self-revelation. The laws are intended to help build up this community and to keep the people faithful in their relationships to each other and to God.
3. The combination shows that the laws are part of the personal, relational covenant with God. This wider view can help a nation to avoid an impersonal legalism in their daily interactions.
4. As a result of the combining, following the laws is another way to respond to God's saving initiatives. It joins worship ceremonies, prayers, psalms, and so on, as another fitting way to keep in touch with a loving God. Obedience to law is a way of maintaining a relationship that already exists. Obviously, humans will have to act as judges, hear out the witnesses on both sides, and make difficult decisions in each case that comes up. Keeping the narratives and the laws meaningful for the next generation is the best way to train judges and to motivate everyone to lead just lives.
5. God's role as creator is ongoing; he continues to bring order out of chaos, to guide complex natural cycles, and to promote justice in human life. "It needs to be stressed that the bulk of the law belongs to the sphere of creation. In view of the symbiotic relationship between cosmic and

social orders, the law is a means by which the divine order-
ing of chaos at the cosmic level is actualized in the social
sphere, whereby God's will is done on earth as it is in
heaven."

6. God's relationship with Israel shows his mercy to a people
who did not earn such treatment by their own perfection.
Following his generous path, we must exhibit mercy
toward the other peoples of this world. See Exodus 20:2,
6; Deuteronomy 5:15–16, 28–29.

7. Following the law contributes to wisdom and understanding, which can be recognized as such by those who are not
yet part of the community of faith. Fretheim points to resident aliens and the very poor, who are the subjects of
Exodus 22:21–27; 23:9. Teaching the children what all
these things mean is enjoined in Exodus 12:26–27; 13:8,
14–15; and especially in Deuteronomy 6:20–25. In Deuteronomy 4:6–8, all other nations will be able to observe this
system of justice at work.

8. Despite the biblical depiction of divine proclamations, we
know that law develops from experiences in life. See
Exodus 15:25–26 and 18:13–27 for examples of this
before Sinai. In many places in the Pentateuch we will find
changes and modifications in particular laws as they were
applied over the centuries. These changes are normal; no
code endures for millennia without expansion and modification. Unlike modern codes, in the Bible some of the outdated laws were kept in the text.

9. Obeying the laws is a form of witness to God, and this witness is as important as retelling the narratives.

10. In the combination of story and law in the Pentateuch we
have two sources of instruction for life. The laws help us to
live justly. The retelling of the stories maintains our religious identity, helps us to see Israel (and ourselves) both as
holy and as sinners at different times, and gives us some
basic motives and principles for daily life over and above
particular legal disputes.

125

Comparisons with Other Codes

Childs (*The Book of Exodus*, 393–97) examines many characteristics of the Decalogue, looking for what is unusual in grammar, content, or style in comparison with other biblical and ancient Near Eastern texts. I will summarize his findings as briefly as possible.

1. In Exodus 20:1 (Deut 5:5), having God speak these words directly is quite rare. Elsewhere (Exod 20:22a; 34:32; Lev 17:1; Deut 6:1) God speaks to Moses alone.
2. In Exodus 20:2 (Deut 5:6), the self-introduction by God follows normal royal style.
3. The positive laws about Sabbaths and honoring parents mix well with the prohibitions, and such intermixing is a normal feature of other like passages. There is no way to prove that the prohibitions are an older form or subdivision.
4. Decalogue commands vary in length. This is a normal style.
5. The few motivation clauses vary in length and style. This also is normal.
6. The shift from first- to third-person forms for God (as in verses 1–6 contrasted with verses 7–12) is normal.
7. The second-singular command forms throughout are unusual; each individual Israelite adult is being addressed.
8. The count of exactly ten commandments is not self-evident; settling on that number was probably a development in later traditions.
9. The two tablets are mentioned in Exodus 34 and Deuteronomy 5, but not in Exodus 20. There is no firm tradition on how much text was written on each tablet.
10. The order of commands is not entirely logical. The first few focus on God, while the rest concern other humans. The first, worshipping Yahweh alone, seems to be the most important by location.
11. All the Decalogue laws are apodictic (blunt commands), which is somewhat unusual. Elsewhere in the Old Testament, there is usually a mix of apodictic and case laws.

12. Each command has parallels, but the entire list is only paralleled in Deuteronomy 5.
13. The absence of specific sanctions or punishments for disobedience is unusual.
14. Cultic and ethical laws are intermixed. This is a normal style.
15. Human motives for disobeying are hardly mentioned. Coveting may have originally focused on actions rather than on the inner movements of jealousy or envy.
16. The vocabulary and grammatical forms of the Decalogue do not seem to be identified with a time period such as the preexilic or postexilic, nor with a specific sanctuary or with the Temple. The only exception might be the focus on the Sabbath, which could have been expanded in the postexilic era.

In summary, the second-singular command forms, the apodictic style, the lack of sanctions, and especially the presentation of these as direct words of God are notable aspects of the Decalogue.

The passage has a special name, the *ten words* or *ten sayings* (*debarim*). This term is used in Exodus 31:18; Deuteronomy 4:13; 9:9, and elsewhere. The entire set is repeated in Deuteronomy 5, with the solemn concluding remark (5:22) that God "added no more," and then carved all of the words on stone to give to Moses. In Exodus, they are presented to us as the direct wishes of God, even if repeated by Moses. Not only are they God's direct wishes, but given that they form the spine of the covenant, they are a way of profiling God's essential character. Childs points to the response of the people in Exodus 20:18–21; their fear at that point could have stemmed both from the majestic manner of God's speaking and from the very content of the ten sayings. (In Deut 5:23–27, the response of the people is similar, but perhaps a bit more confident.)

Unlike some of the laws in Exodus 21—23, the Decalogue contains no penalties for disobeying; but clearly they are the foundation upon which all other laws and penalties will be set. The two commandments regarding Sabbaths and honoring parents are standards for holiness and joy in living. They are put in a positive style compared to the half dozen prohibitions of sins and crimes that follow. Childs describes the ten sayings as having a "stark simplicity," and each of the longer ones has an "initial thrust" that matches the style of the shorter commandments near the end. I would call it a drumbeat effect, a solemn drumbeat of God's greatest concerns. The sayings of Exodus are portrayed as comprehensive and clear common-ground rules that everyone can understand. However, the only assurance we have of their comprehensiveness is that they were revealed and spoken by God himself. There are hundreds of laws to come in Exodus, Leviticus, Numbers, and Deuteronomy, yet these few in Exodus 20 are the ones up front, the ones that best express who God is.

The laws later in Exodus are not completely timeless in form; there is room for updating. So too we should not classify the Decalogue as utterly timeless, but rather focus on the fact that it is rooted in this ongoing personal covenant with God.

Individual Commandments

Note: Because this section is rather long, questions will be placed at the end of each commandment. The answers will be found as usual at the back of the book.

Exodus 20:1–6: One God

The various parts of the Decalogue seem to have grown independently over a long period, so that the final form of all of it demands reflection and pondering. Childs notes that the sayings in 20:2–17 are identified as the will of God (whether quoted by Moses or spoken directly by God to the people). Propp cites plural or collective forms in Exodus 20:22b; Deuteronomy 4:12–13, 33, 36; 5:4, 22–23 as examples where the tradition is that God spoke directly to the people. He asks if the editors placed 19:25 as a somewhat awkward way to control 20:1, so that Moses becomes the messenger of the ten sayings. They may have done this to have it match Deuteronomy 5:1–5, in which Moses describes himself as the messenger (despite Deut 5:4 taken by itself).

Childs reminds us that Exodus 20:2 serves as a preface to the entire Decalogue, not just as an introduction to the first commandment. The mention of the name Yahweh recaps all of Exodus 1—19. The verse identifies the authority and right of God to make known his will because he has already graciously acted on Israel's behalf.

However, giving laws reveals a new side of God, not part of guiding their escape so far. Instead, the laws will detail how God expects those in covenant with him to act in the future. Childs puts it this way, "In the act of creating a people for himself history and law are not antagonistic, but different sides of the one act of divine self-manifestation" (*The Book of Exodus*, 367).

Questions

113. Assuming that Exodus 20:2–6 was directly addressed to each Jewish adult who was with Moses that day, how is God depicted in these verses? What does he want, and why? The style of the speech should help you form your answers.

114. In Jewish custom, no visual images can be used to represent Yahweh. Can you glean any insights from 20:2–6 to shed light on this custom?

Exodus 20:7: Misuse of the LORD's Name

The Hebrew of Exodus 20:7 says, *You shall not lift up the name of Yahweh your God in vain* (*shw'*). The idiom *lifting up* can be found in Exodus 23:1, "You shall not *lift up* (NRSV *spread*) a false report," and in 2 Kings 9:25, "The LORD *lifted up* (NRSV *uttered*) this oracle against him." The phrase translated *in vain* can mean something that is *needless* or *useless* as well as something *deceitful* or *fraudulent*.

Question

115. Exodus 20:7 prohibits any inappropriate use of God's name (although we may call on his name in sincere worship or when giving honest testimony in court). How should this prohibition affect the daily lives of believers, then or now? What is implied by the latter part of the same verse?

Exodus 20:8–11: Keeping the Sabbath

The saying about the Sabbath contains a prohibition, as did the previous ones, but it is really a call to action. The command to *remember* (*zkr*) the Sabbath can include specific actions in context. (For example, in Exod 23:13 we are told not to *invoke* the names of other gods. The Hebrew says *do not remember* [*zkr*] *another god by name.*) Here one of the actions will be to abstain from all ordinary chores and employment on the Sabbath.

Historians point out that the seven-day week is mostly of Israelite origin. Most ancient cultures worked out lunar and/or solar cycles for the months and the year, but there was no common system of subdivisions of a month. The Hebrew word for Sabbath (*shabbat*) most likely comes from the verb *shbt*, "to cease" or "to rest." The verb is used this way in Exodus 16:30. Most other ancient Near Eastern cultures celebrated a New Year's Day at local shrines, but apparently the Israelites did not. Instead, they commemorated God's creation each seventh day at home. Remember that Rosh Hashanah and the system of synagogues came much later. The eventual obligation to attend the Temple in Jerusalem was for Passover and harvest festivals, not weekly services.

In verse 8, the Sabbath is *to be kept holy* (*qdsh*). At the end of verse 11, we are told that the LORD blessed the Sabbath and *consecrated* it (*made it holy* [another verbal form of *qdsh*]). However, there must be more to this ideal than simply not working.

Thousands of years have passed since the Sabbath system began, and Jewish customs now center on the liturgical year, divided between synagogue and home observances. Jewish people have explained to me that one may work inside the home on the Sabbath (but not for gain), since that is not considered a public activity. In the United States many people need to work on Saturdays; adjustments have to be made. Even in the time between King David and the Common Era, many farmers in Israel had to bend the rules about working on the Sabbath during harvest time. The harvesting process was a major challenge even when everything went well; at certain periods taking a full day off could have resulted in significant or disastrous loss of crops.

Question

116. In Exodus 20:8–11, the people were given basic rules about the Sabbath and reasons for it. How does God's "resting" on the seventh day bring blessing and holiness to the Sabbath day each week? How should we remember the Sabbath and keep it holy, beyond avoiding certain labors and spending some time at worship services? The original setting involved families at home, so the original command did not mean to attend communal worship every week.

Exodus 20:12: Honoring Parents

The Hebrew verb for *honor* is *kbd*, which we have seen so often already in *heavy* hearts and *honoring* God. Most ancient and modern cultures allow the elderly much more influence and grant them much more respect than is apparent in our own country.

There are dozens of references in the Old Testament to honoring the elderly, and to punishing those who rebel against parents or mistreat them in their old age and incapacity. Some of these laws are stark; see Exodus 21:15, 17 or Deuteronomy 21:18–21. As is often the case in such long collections of rules and warnings, the more family harmony is demanded the more we suspect that ancient families may have been as dysfunctional as our own. At times a biblical mention of the death penalty for those who rebel or mistreat parents is so blunt that we might assume that there were frequent executions. This would be a mistake; judges and later rabbis had many ways of minimizing or even outlawing these penalties, and historians find no evidence for any such executions of disobedient offspring.

Question

117. This commandment to value one's parents applies to everyone, of course. How could the obligation change as parent and child journey through life? Does the mention of long life for those who keep this commandment amount to a reward or bribe being offered?

Exodus 20:13: Do Not Kill

Propp notes that all societies prohibit murder as a matter of common sense and justice. In Genesis 9:5–6, we have one of the most solemn sayings that God is in charge of all living things, and that he will require a reckoning for the taking of human life.

In Exodus 20:13, the Hebrew verb is *rzh*, which makes no distinction between premeditated and involuntary killing. We would call the former *murder* and the latter *manslaughter*, and make further legal distinctions in each category.

Propp proposes that we should translate this command "Do not murder." He argues that the traditional English use of *kill* in this verse has too broad a meaning now, although the older translations hardly ever used *murder* anyplace in either Testament. Living languages change over time, so the older sense of *kill* could easily have meant *murder*. The NRSV uses *murder*, but includes *kill* in an official footnote.

Childs retains the usual "You shall not kill." He notes that speaking of *murder* avoids the question about killing in wartime or carrying out capital punishment. Further, one can only translate *rzh* as *murder* some of the time; the verb seems to have changed its meaning over the centuries. Earlier on, it included unintentional or accidental killings, which we would distinguish as varying degrees of manslaughter, reckless negligence, misadventure, and so on. Twice it is used to describe capital punishment (Num 35:27, 30).

Fretheim takes the impact of *rzh* to cover any act of violence against an individual for unworthy motives that might result in death (even if killing was not the intention). He finds the word *murder* inadequate here, and settles for *kill*. He thinks that the breadth of the traditional formula, "You shall not kill,"

> serves the community of faith best, forcing continual reflection on the meaning of the commandment and reminding all that in the taking of human life for any reason *one acts in God's stead*, in the face of which there should be a lengthy pause filled with careful soul-searching and the absence of vengefulness and arrogance. As a result, taking a life should be very rare indeed.

Question

118. The difficult Hebrew verb in the command not to kill covers not only various levels of murder and manslaughter, but also the unauthorized, independent avenging of harm or dishonor done to a family member. It seems to allow self-defense, capital punishment, and ethical soldiering in wartime. Why was such an important point of morality and law stated so briefly and with a verb that has so complex a set of meanings?

Exodus 20:14: Do Not Commit Adultery

Propp notes the ancient Israelite custom of polygamy. In polygamous cultures, adultery was defined as sexual relations between any man and any married or engaged woman, since that woman belonged to another. Any such relations would upset clan and tribal patriarchal stability; specifically, it would dishonor the innocent husband or engaged man. In Deuteronomy 22:22 and Leviticus 20:10, adultery is punishable by death for both parties. A woman who was not a virgin at the time of her first marriage (to a man who had not known her) could also be stoned (Lev 20:21).

Question

119. This commandment condemns certain sins against marriage, but does not address other categories of inappropriate or sinful sexual activity. Why such a narrow focus?

Exodus 20:15: Do Not Steal

Some scholars have theorized that this use of *gnb* (steal) may originally have referred to kidnapping or detaining a person for slavery (Exod 21:16; Deut 21:14; 24:7; 2 Kgs 11:2), or to misuse of spoils in holy war. The verb is used in Exodus 22:12 for stealing an animal. The reason for looking for an important category of stealing was to match the context; the final five or six commands of the Decalogue refer to vital matters for the life of the community. Further, the broader topic of stealing is probably also the point of coveting in 20:17.

However, whatever the possible original focus, here the commandment is without any specific object, and so includes all cases of theft. Most of these cases were settled by fines (see Exod 22:1–15). One exception was if a thief entered a home during the dark of night. In that case, the homeowner had the right to assume the worst and to defend his family to the death (Exod 22:2).

Question

120. Why is stealing mentioned at this point in Exodus 20? Who loses when someone steals a tool, a lamb, or a sack of grain from another villager or clansman?

Exodus 20:16: Do Not Give False Testimony

The Hebrew says *do not answer ('nh) your neighbor (as a) witness of falsehood*. *Answer* can mean to give testimony or to answer questions as a witness in court. Propp argues for a slight change so that the sentence can be translated *do not answer your neighbor (with) a testimony of falsehood*.

Accusations of stealing, as of murder or adultery, were often settled in court. Clearly all witnesses needed to be truthful; anything less would ruin the entire judicial system. Acting as an honest, impartial witness was an important moral responsibility. Capital cases needed two witnesses, as a safeguard against one unjust accuser (see Num 35:30; Deut 17:6; 19:15). First Kings 21 tells of two false witnesses bringing about the death of Naboth. The consequences of false testimony are spoken of in Exodus 23:1–3; Deuteronomy 5:20; 19:16–21.

Question

121. The vocabulary of Exodus 20:16 indicates that it may have originally focused on perjury in serious court cases. Why such a narrow original focus? Assuming that we apply this commandment now to all forms of lying, who loses when someone deliberately puts forth significant falsehoods or constant personal ridicule?

Exodus 20:17: Do Not Covet Anything of Your Neighbor's

The verb *covet* (*hmd*) is used twice: first for the neighbor's house (perhaps meaning *household* or *estate*), and then again for his wife, servants, and so on. In Deuteronomy 5:21, we find the wife moved from second to first in order, and then another verb, *desire* ('*wh*), is used for the rest. These variations and synonyms in Deuteronomy are behind the Roman Catholic tradition of dividing Exodus 20:17 into two commandments. Childs notes that the variations in Exodus 20 and Deuteronomy 5 are both ancient formulae. We cannot use the variations to conclude anything about changes in the status of women over the centuries.

The verb *covet* (*hmd*) is used in Genesis 2:9 (every tree that is *pleasant* to the sight), and in Genesis 3:6 (the tree was to be *desired* to make one wise).

Question

122. The command not to covet is certainly as far-reaching as any of the other commandments in Exodus 20. How does verse 17 epitomize all ten commandments?

Further Questions regarding the entire Decalogue:

123. Given the variety of subjects and style in the Decalogue, what would you call these seventeen verses as a literary unit for the writers and original audiences? They are more than simply God's top ten demands, and too brief to explain an entire moral or ethical code.
124. Given your answer to the previous question, what is the main impact of the Decalogue for us today? What does the passage actually teach us about the larger Exodus story?
125. We believers do try to live by the Ten Commandments, taking them as part of a larger moral or ethical system, and to pass our understanding of them to the next generation. Even so, are there any gaps or serious omissions in Exodus 20:1–17?

Exodus 20:18–21: The People Want Moses Out in Front

This final paragraph, probably from the Elohist, brings us away from the speech by God and back to the story line. The people have been in awe as God boomed out his words, all the while seeing and hearing the forces of nature and supernature accompanying God's presence. Their fear and trembling and standing back are quite understandable. No one should feel worthy to be so close to the divine.

Propp suggests using *recoiled* instead of *trembled* in 20:18. The mention in 20:18 of standing at a distance might mean that the people had not come as close as they were allowed (19:13, 17, 19), but that does not seem to have created any problem for God. The *testing* (*nsh*) of verse 20 is not specified. Some take it to refer to observing the boundary lines at the mountain or, looking ahead to chapter 24, to keeping faith while Moses is gone for the forty days. Propp suggests that the test will be keeping the Decalogue. Perhaps the reference became less specific over time. Some rabbinic commentators took *testing* to mean *instructing*, which is another meaning of the same verb.

The people now ask Moses to be their spokesperson or mediator, to bring God's further words to them. They also say "do not let God speak to us," as though Moses could control the volume or direction of God's voice. Moses agrees to their request, and reassures them of God's intention not to harm but only to test and purify them. Moses then returns to hear more laws, which will be quite different from the Decalogue in content and style.

Childs remarks that before the Decalogue the people had said, "Everything that the LORD has spoken we will do." In 20:19, they pleaded, "[B]ut do not let God speak to us, or we will die." The contrast in these two sayings shows that the people are learning how great a commitment is needed to live out this covenant.

Question

126. In Exodus 20:18–21, the people at first seem to be fearful, although they explain this to Moses and accept his reply before standing at a distance (or letting Moses move closer to God). What does Moses mean in verse 20 when he speaks of God *putting the fear of him upon you so that*

you do not sin? Compare this question and your answer with Question and Answer 112.

Conclusion to the Entire Section

I would like to close this section with a brief remark by Fretheim, who notes:

A multitude of sins are sometimes drawn into the interpretation of one or another commandment, but the fact is that many modern evils are simply not covered or anticipated.... Hence it is of considerable importance that these commandments not be understood as eternally limited in scope or as ethical principles more important than any others that might be formulated. The various canonical expansions of some commandments (see 20:9–11) witness to an ongoing effort by Israel to address changing life situations. This *gives the people of God in every age an innerbiblical warrant to expand on them.* If the Decalogue is understood as Israel's bill of rights, the way for amendment is open. While we probably would not withdraw any one of the ten today, we almost certainly would add a few and expand on others. The canon of the ten commandments is an open canon, and our instruction should recognize this. But the ten words we do have are an indispensable starting point for our ongoing ethical task. (*Exodus*, 222)

Section Eighteen:
Exodus 20:22—23:33
The Covenant Code

> Propp estimates that most of these laws are from
> the Elohist, perhaps displaced from the beginning
> of chapter 20 by the Decalogue.

Introduction

Note: This section will consist of brief comments on many of the
laws, with a few questions placed at appropriate points. Some
readers may wish to skim through these three chapters of Exodus,
but they do present significant aspects of ancient Jewish theology
and jurisprudence.

The final verses of chapter 20 and all of the following three
chapters are presented as a continuation of the great event at the
mountain. They are customarily called the Book of the Covenant
or the Covenant Code. These additional laws, revealed to Moses
and relayed to the people, touch on many different subjects and
situations. Some of the cases refer to the treatment of slaves, farm
animals, and crops, or to details of annual worship ceremonies.
The people with Moses would not encounter some of these situations during their lifetimes. One could imagine that God was
laying down laws for centuries to come, but they are more likely
the traditions of later generations projected back to the time of
Moses. Such projection is a theological claim: All justice and right
worship ceremonies reflect God's will, and are expansions of the
Decalogue. A quick reading of the Covenant Code can have the
same effect as reading Job 38—41. In both cases, the authors

have depicted God as shooting out ideas much like a spectacular display of fireworks. We are hard put to keep up with him.

Propp notes that we are not sure of the purposes of ancient law codes. Local judges tended to follow local customs, without quoting in detail from codes. Public monumental inscriptions and the verbal proclamation of codes may have served as symbols of justice, issued by kings to promote their own administration of justice in general. In all these cultures, kings, princes, and elders performed both executive and judicial functions.

The Covenant Code ignores many matters of trade, inheritance, and marriage. It focuses on complex, ambiguous cases, assuming that basic principles are understood. This code is not attributed to a human monarch, but to Yahweh, the great king. Propp concludes (307), "If the goal of Near Eastern legislation was 'the characterization of the law-giver as just according to internationally recognized standards of law,'...how better to honor God...?"

Those hearing or reading this long passage in Exodus are meant to see it and the Decalogue as the list of stipulations of the covenant between Yahweh and Israel. Therefore, the Decalogue and the code are for everyone. Propp notes (308) that we are all "required to speak truthfully, eschew malice and judge fairly. The court is merely a backup to common decency; disputes that reach formal arbitration represent a failure of the more basic system."

The laws and cases are loosely organized, and not meant to stand as a complete system of jurisprudence. The much larger body of laws in Leviticus, Numbers, and Deuteronomy will fit the same loose pattern of organization, and still leave unexamined many topics that any national system of law would need. One of my teachers jokingly compared the laws mentioned in the Old Testament with wallpaper, saying that editors would reel off a few square feet as needed to be representative, and keep the rest for later use. This selectivity is not a matter of disorganization, but rather a sign of the authors' confidence and familiarity with the law system.

Christians have to be careful not to profile modern Judaism from a few verses here or there in Exodus or Leviticus. These Old Testament laws have been studied for thousands of years and incorporated into Jewish life in a very thorough and competent fashion. As with English law, biblical cases have become precedents, generating a long history of interpretation.

The following brief outline of the Covenant Code is from Childs. The epilogue is quite different in content; some see it as the closing frame of all of the Covenant Code, as the altar law provides the opening frame.

Verses	Topics	Style
A. 20:22–26	altar law	apodictic sayings (*debarim*)
B. 21:1–11	slaves	cases (*mishpatim*)
C. 21:12–17	capital offenses	cases
21:18–36	bodily injuries	cases
D. 22:1–17	property damage	cases
22:18–31	mix of religious and social rules	apodictic sayings
E. 23:1–9	honesty in court	apodictic sayings
23:10–19	liturgical calendar	apodictic sayings
F. 23:20–33	epilogue	

The cases may reflect ancient Near Eastern culture at the time of the settlement and tribal league era prior to the monarchy, and the apodictic statements may reflect covenant theology more specifically. The two forms seem to have been combined earlier rather than later. The Covenant Code in an odd way seems unrelated to the Sinai story of Exodus 19 and 24. It virtually interrupts that sequence.

Childs starts his commentary by looking at the apodictic material. Second-singular forms begin to appear in 20:24. The covenant and the Decalogue are often invoked, as in the altar law, the command not to revile God (22:28), not to lie with animals (22:19), nor to commit idolatry (22:20), nor to oppress resident aliens (as once they were aliens in Egypt, 22:21). Exhortational forms such as 22:31, and the references to coming out of Egypt (23:9, 15), remind us of God's personal involvement in all these sayings. Much of this part of the Covenant Code could be very old (premonarchic), and later joined by editors to the case material. Fretheim notes that the sayings show the personal, intense level of God's concerns, the linkage of obedience to loyalty to God himself, and ties to specific elements in Israel's history and worship. The sayings may have developed in cultic and proclamatory or instructional settings.

On the other hand, the content of the cases points to a settled life long after Sinai. Exodus 20:22 looks like a redactional verse, as does the introduction to the cases in 21:1. The case block is uniform in style except for 21:12–17, which some think was moved there from an original position following 22:20. The cases are not presented as personal concerns of God, accompanied by exhortation and motivational clauses, as were the apodictic sayings.

However, the cases may also be an ancient (premonarchic) tribal Israelite code, since they point to everyday farming and shepherding in the main. Many of the basic principles of justice in the Covenant Code are similar to contemporary ancient Near Eastern codes, though some of the punishments are milder in the biblical passages. Scholars assume that some of these cases underwent later modification, especially in Deuteronomic circles. Fretheim sees the laws shaping community life, based on equality among the male heads of families, given the lower status at the time of women, resident aliens, and slaves. Another basis is the priority of human life over property.

Why were these two different traditions, the cases and the sayings, blended together? Perhaps it was to express the importance of everyday justice and respect for people's rights. It may well also have been to motivate everyone to resist Canaanite culture and religious superstitions. Fretheim notes this respect for others as he explains,

> The issue for Israel is not how it can *become* a holy people but how it can *be* in daily life the holy people it has already become by God's action on their behalf. The pattern for a life of holiness has been provided by the holy God, and that includes a life lived on behalf of the less fortunate. Israel has been set apart by God, not to a life apart from the world, but to a life of service within the world. To serve God is to serve the world. (*Exodus*, 247)

Propp notes that one can read the Covenant Code as commentary on the Decalogue, or perhaps the Decalogue could have been a synopsis of the code. He lists some parallels between the two collections.

Decalogue	Covenant Code
20:3–6 have no other gods	20:22–26 altar law; also 22:20; 23:13; 23:20–33 (epilogue)
20:7 revere the name	22:28 do not revile
20:8–11 Sabbath	23:10–12 Sabbath years and days
20:12 honor parents	21:15, 17 do not hit or curse parents
20:13 do not kill	21:12–36 various cases
20:14 do not commit adultery	22:16–17 the case of seduction
20:15 do not steal	22:1–17 various cases
20:16 false witnessing	23:1–3, 6–8 honesty in court cases
20:17 coveting	22:21–27; 23:9 protect poor

Propp notes that in the Covenant Code the laws are found in small groups, but not organized by content in a modern Western way. Perhaps that is because many of the laws were preserved as oral tradition. Oral traditions are often grouped by similar sounds and the use of key words rather than by content.

I will try to outline these laws as briefly as possible, explaining difficult points and asking a few questions. Any laws that seem clear and logical will be left alone. We can use Childs's subdivisions of the chapters.

A. Exodus 20:22–26: Altar Law

Exodus 20:22 is close in style to Exodus 19:4 and Deuteronomy 29:2, and serves as an introductory framing statement to this brief passage, known as the altar law. The phrase in verse 23, (*gods of silver*) *alongside of me* means *to rank with me*. Altars are to be made of earth or ordinary fieldstones, not hewn or carved.

The altars are to be low enough and small enough so that no steps are needed to reach the top surface.

The remark that steps must not be used to prevent the exposure of nakedness is apparently a stereotypical point of ridicule against priests of other nations. Obviously, Gentiles would not dress inappropriately for their own rites. On the other hand, there were superstitious sexual rites at certain Canaanite shrines for a long period, and in some cultures priests served wearing loincloths only.

These altars were to be used at places or shrines chosen by God (places where he *causes his name to be remembered*). Centuries later, the shrines were closed, and the Temple at Jerusalem became the sole place for the nation to offer sacrifices.

Fretheim notes that 20:22–23 is something of an echo of 20:3–6 and acts as an opening frame for the Covenant Code. In return for their loyalty in worshipping him alone, God freely promises to come and bless the sacrifices they will offer on these altars (20:24).

Question

127. If we take Exodus 20:22–26 as an introduction to the entire Covenant Code, what do we learn about God in these five verses? Do his instructions sound self-centered or fussy? How else could you evaluate God's intentions here?

B. Exodus 21:1–11: Slaves

Worldwide customs regarding slavery eventually were adopted within Israel, and later among Christians. From what we know, most slaves in Israel had sold themselves or been sold into slavery because of extreme poverty or debt. Some were prisoners of war. Male slaves who were of Hebrew ancestry were to be freed in their seventh year of service. Cassuto suggests that here we take the word *Hebrew* not simply as an Israelite clansman, but in its older sense as one from the lowest, ethnically mixed, social classes. The catch comes in 21:4, which notes that if that slave had a wife provided by the master, she and any children would not be freed. This widespread custom, viewing the wife and children as property of the master, endured up to the American Civil War. The only legal solution in those circumstances for the Hebrew slave who was a contented husband and father was to submit to the earlobe-piercing rite (symbolic, not painful) that classified him as a slave for life.

Exodus 21:7–8, 10–11 refers to a female slave, purchased to become eventually a minor wife or concubine. If the master chooses to divorce her, she cannot be sold again. If the master takes other wives, this one loses no rights or status, and must be cared for. If the master fails to support her, she regains her freedom. Some scholars argue that the law implicitly holds that at some point a female slave has a right to be married; the master cannot simply keep her for other labors. Exodus 21:9 concerns a female slave, purchased by a master for marriage to his son. She has the rights of a daughter or daughter-in-law. Apparently, this means that the master may not change his mind and take her for his own wife.

Propp suggests that the term *foreign people* in 21:8 should better be translated *alien kin*, meaning *persons unrelated to the woman*. Thus the master needs to make arrangements with the woman's extended family, or support her himself. The parallel laws in Deuteronomy 15:12–18 dwell on supporting newly freed Hebrew slaves, both men and women, but do not explain marriage regulations.

Question

128. Exodus 21:1–11 describes real but limited rights for native-born slaves in Israel. None of these rules could be used today, and would not now fit any legal, ethical, or moral framework. How does it make any sense to say that these came from God in the first place? Why are these verses in this book?

C. Exodus 21:12–36: Capital Offenses, Bodily Injuries

Question

129. Before looking at the explanations below, it might be good to become law students for a moment. Compare 21:16 (kidnapping for slavery), 21:20–21 (deaths of slaves injured by owners), 21:26–27 (slaves maimed by owners), and 21:32 (slave killed by a notoriously dangerous ox). What legal purpose or logic holds all six verses together?

Two topics are merged in 21:12–14. Murderers (verse 12) must be punished by execution, even if one of them seeks sanctuary and holds on to an altar (verse 14). The case in verse 14 is that of a man who *rages* (*yzd*, from *zyd*, "boiling") against his neighbor. The same verb is used in Genesis 25:29 to describe Jacob *cooking* a stew for Esau.

There is a brief reference to involuntary manslaughter (verse 13), paraphrased in the NRSV by the term *act of God*. The examples of involuntary harm in Numbers 35:22–23 and Deuteronomy 19:4–5 may help a little to explain such involuntary events, but each case will be different. Propp notes the lack of discussion at this point of cases of self-defense, or of crimes of passion and anger, or of violence committed under the influence of alcohol.

The law in 21:13 speaks of a place to which the one who caused the involuntary death may flee. Propp suggests that the original reference could have been to high places or shrines; later, cities of refuge were designated (as replacements for such shrines) when Jerusalem became the sole center of worship.

The next three laws, 21:15–17, and those set in 22:18–20, seem to have been borrowed from another source. They are quite different in style, and their presence here suggests that civil and religious laws are both needed to live God's covenant.

An adult *striking* a parent (not necessarily fatally) or *cursing* a parent is roundly condemned to death, as are those who kidnap people to enslave them. Most scholars argue that the death sentences for dishonoring parents may have been "on the books" but were probably not enforced.

Exodus 21:18–19 obligates a disputant to compensate his injured opponent for loss of work time and costs in convalescence. The reference to the opponent *walking around outside with the help of a staff* means that the injured person must be seen to be on the mend by witnesses.

A slave owner who beats a slave to death with a staff must be punished, according to 21:20. Propp assumes that this counts as murder, and that the punishment will be death. Childs argues that the call for punishment is not the same as a death sentence, although it should be. Fretheim notes that in verses such as 21:20, 26–27 we can see some movement toward humane treatment of slaves. He finds Deuteronomy 15:12–18 to be a later development along this line of compassion.

The proviso in 21:21 that there will be no penalty, *if the slave survives for a day or two*, cannot but shock modern readers. Perhaps there was little understanding of the way internal injuries progress within the body. Propp suggests that the writers considered cruel slave owners to be stupid, since they were damaging their own income-producing slaves.

The next case, in 21:22–24, involves two disputants who unintentionally injure a bystander. Propp notes that having the bystander be a pregnant woman serves as a dramatic example, and so covers less dramatic cases by implication. If the woman suffers a miscarriage but no other harm, a fine must be paid. If she suffers greater injuries, then it will be "life for life, eye for eye," and so on.

This famous formula, called the *lex talionis* in Latin (*law of equal punishment*), appears several times in the Old Testament (see Lev 24:17–22; Deut 19:19–21). At first sight, it appears to enshrine vengeance as an ethical principle.

Propp reviews the history of this formula. Some scholars (such as Cassuto) hold that in reality fines were usually substituted for any physical punishment, except for murder. Therefore, we could say that *life for life* is the only example of the formula at work. Others dismiss the formula as a hackneyed symbolic or philosophical phrase that does not actually foster vengeance.

Propp considers the formula to contain themes of retribution oddly combined with elements of recompense or repayment. Paying life for life, or eye for eye, should deter the rich from buying their way out of cruel interactions with the lower classes. Yet the one who suffered the harm is more in need of recompense than of the satisfaction of seeing his assailant undergo bodily harm. Seeing harm come to one's assailant would be satisfying on one level; it would stress the equal worth of victim and assailant. However, on another level it would not do much for the social fabric of the community or for the long-term alleviation of poverty. The listing of hand for hand, foot for foot, burn for burn, and so on, does not help make anything clearer.

There are several stories in the Old Testament that do exemplify this *lex talionis.* In Judges 1:6–7, the pagan king Adoni-bezek admitted to the irony of suffering physical punishment of the same sort that he used to mete out to other kings whom he defeated in battle. In 2 Samuel 12:10–12, King David is told his wives would be dishonored because he had had Uriah killed. This prediction came true in 2 Samuel 16:21–22. Grim details of King Ahab's death are foretold in 1 Kings 21:19–24, and they come to pass in 1 Kings 22:35–38. In the Book of Esther, Haman prepares a gallows for Mordecai (Esth 5:14), only to be hanged on it himself (Esth 7:9–10). In this very chapter, Exodus 22:22–24, the care of widows and orphans is enjoined, with the threat that ignoring these poor people will lead to the LORD taking matters into his own hands, "and your wives shall become widows, and your children orphans." However, these are examples and anecdotes, not legal formulae.

Therefore, we might understand the *lex talionis* as a way of *controlling* vengeance, limiting it when tempers are high. Propp calls the formula a way of describing the need for court hearings and systems of significant compensation. Childs agrees that the law was meant to hold everyone responsible for criminal actions, and not to have fines be an automatic way out for the privileged. Fretheim reminds us that the formula was to be applied by judges, not individuals acting on their own.

In 21:26–27, there is no *lex talionis* for slaves; their masters do not pay eye for eye or tooth for tooth. Nevertheless, the requirement that the slaves be freed for their injuries can be taken as generous compensation, or at least as some recognition of their dignity as human beings. Propp notes that severely beaten slaves cannot just be put out to the curb. Their owners are bound in justice to care for them as long as necessary.

While I do not normally refer to New Testament passages because that would lengthen this book too much, I note Fretheim's reference to Matthew 5:38–42 where Jesus contrasts the "eye for an eye" standard with his ideal of turning the other cheek and walking the second mile. Fretheim suggests that this reflects a conviction of early Christians that, even if they have been wronged, they ought to settle their differences amicably outside the courtroom. The two passages Fretheim cites, Romans 12:14–21 and 1 Corinthians 6:1–8, lend clear support to this suggestion. When Jesus explained his ideal, he was not rejecting the entire Jewish judicial system.

The next set of laws, 21:28–32, uses a dangerous ox as the dramatic example, again covering other cases by implication. Exodus 21:30 apparently modifies the death penalty of verse 29, allowing the possibility of a fine. Slaves are worth less than ordinary citizens, according to verse 32. Propp notes that 21:20 could well have served as a warning to slave owners, but should an ox (for the first time) fatally injure a slave, there is a sense in which the event may not have been preventable. This might explain the logic of 21:32.

The stoning of the ox in all these cases may not have been simply a matter of prudence. (Sheepherders prudently shoot any pet dogs that attack their flocks, on the conviction that the dogs would do it again.) The stoning may also indicate an older concept—that the animal itself was guilty. Such public legal execution of animals that caused harm lasted into the Middle Ages in Europe. The additional prohibition (21:28) against eating the meat of the ox may also point to this guilt.

D. Exodus 22:1–31: Property Damage, Mix of Religious/Social Rules

Note: The English verses in 22:1–31 are one ahead of the Hebrew verses (21:37–22:30). I will try to use consistently the English system. The NRSV rearranges 22:2–4 in the order 22:3b, 4, 2, 3a because of the logic of the subject matter. Translators rarely rearrange verses, but there are times when it is called for. Childs notes that the original verse order makes sense in itself, encasing verses 2–3a to highlight the principle that thieves should not always be executed. He finds that this leniency for the daytime thief is unique to biblical law among ancient Near Eastern codes.

Question

130. At the start of this chapter it would be a good exercise to hear all of 22:1–17 proclaimed in one reading. What is the tone or impression that you receive from this? Next listen to the second half of the chapter (22:18–31) proclaimed the same way. What is the tone or impression that you receive from this? What results when you think about how both parts of the chapter form one larger picture?

Exodus 22:1 indicates significant restitution rates for stealing oxen or sheep, with a sliding scale for animals that can be recovered. Propp lists some higher rates in other ancient codes. Presumably, the principles of restitution would apply for other real property besides animals.

Exodus 22:3b indicates that a thief who cannot make restitution can be sold into slavery to repay the debt.

Exodus 22:2–3a covers the case of a thief who enters a house, barn, or corral in the dark of night. Because of the greater danger he poses in the dark, he may be killed in self-defense. Should the same break-in occur during daylight hours, he should be fought off or apprehended if possible, since killing under those circumstances would less likely merit the claim of self-defense.

Propp lists similar ancient case law in other cultures with regard to breaking in at night.

The words used to describe grazing and trampling in 22:5 may also include the burning of fields. In some translations, such as the NAB, burning is highlighted.

In 22:9, the text speaks of *disputed ownership* (*pshᶜ*). The Hebrew noun means *rebellion against the community*. It is used in Genesis 31:36 where Jacob excoriates Laban, saying, "What is my *offense?*"

In 22:8–9, one or both parties are *brought before God*. This apparently refers to the taking of oaths, a serious and solemn matter in ancient judicial proceedings. Verse 9 does not explain how one of the two parties is determined to be guilty. Propp notes that we can translate the term *elohim* as *gods* or *God*, but he is very doubtful that we can use the translation *judges*, as some commentators have in the past. Childs agrees with Propp on this.

In 22:14–15, the case involves borrowing an animal for a certain task (plowing, stud, and so on). If the owner of the animal was not a witness to the injury or loss, he has a right to some compensation even if the borrower had acted responsibly. This seems to be a point of honor for the borrower; he should take the lead for the sake of building and maintaining community.

The *bride price* for seducing a virgin (22:16–17) is paid to the woman's father. (Propp notes that the father could in theory arrange a marriage for her with someone else at a later date.) The term is *mohar*, meaning a fee paid to the bride's family. This was an old custom, eventually replaced by the dowry system, in which the bride's family pays a fee to the groom. In Genesis 34, Shechem wanted to pay the bride price for Dinah, and in 1 Samuel 18 Saul allowed David to pay a bride price in kind, since David was not wealthy.

This custom of seducing and then marrying made some sense in a clan culture, where people lived in small groups and women had much less freedom of movement. It was one way to marry outside limited bloodlines. Similar customs survive today in certain regions. Childs observes that this law applies to all virgins not yet engaged, and it could be considered as respecting women in the sense that the man in question should accept full responsibility for his actions, and marry the woman he has taken. While we decry all instances of rape, in some of these cases the seducing may have been planned by both parties, already open to love. The same verb is used in Hosea 2:14, where God speaks of *alluring* Israel and speaking tenderly to her before their marriage.

The prohibition against sorceresses may indicate some cultural or gender biases against them beyond the fact that they claimed to be able to control divine powers or to know the future. The topic arises elsewhere in the Old Testament, leading us to the conclusion that these independent spiritualists always had an audience. Cassuto contends that male sorcerers would also be condemned.

The unconditional condemnation of bestiality is another standard warning, probably meant to caution the unstable or immature. Propp discounts ancient references to such practices at certain pagan shrines.

The next set of exhortations (22:21–27) encourages considerate treatment of the marginalized. *Resident aliens* or *sojourners* never gained full rights, since they were not from the local clan or tribe. Widows without supportive children or close relatives were on their own in times of crisis. Exodus 22:25 speaks of lending *silver* (*money*). Propp claims that the usual interest rate for loans of money was 20 percent, and 33 percent for loans of seed grain.

Holding a cloak in pawn or as collateral was practically symbolic; the poor person pawning it should have it back for keeping warm at night. Similar exhortations to excuse needy Israelites from paying interest on loans can be found in Leviticus 25:35–37 and Deuteronomy 23:19–20. Taking interest on loans to foreigners was allowed.

Exodus 22:29–30 makes reference to ancient practices about which there is still some dispute. The offerings from *harvest* and *presses* might include grain, wine, or oil. The words used are fairly broad in meaning, and might even include newborn animals and people. Exodus 22:29 goes on to mention *giving* firstborn sons to God. The next verse specifies holding firstborn oxen or sheep for seven days before *giving* them to God. The question is what does this *giving* to God involve? Scholars have assumed that firstborn male animals were to be sacrificed, and additional animals used in substitution instead of the sacrifice of firstborn sons. This custom was treated previously in Exodus, in 13:1–2 (most likely a Priestly passage) and 13:11–16 (Elohist). Question 60 was the first time we studied it.

Further passages regarding firstborn include Exodus 34:19–20; Leviticus 27:26–27; Numbers 3:12–13, 40–51; 8:17–18; 18:15–18. There is a P tradition that the priests and their families receive the meat of firstborn animal sacrifices (Num 18:15–18); this is contradicted by the Deuteronomic tradition that the laity offering the sacrifices get to share the meat (Deut 12:6–7, 17–18; 14:23; 15:19–20). In Numbers and elsewhere, an additional tradition is mentioned that the Levites were chosen by God to represent all the firstborn sons of Israel (Num 3:12–13, 40–51; 8:14–18).

Propp sees the offering of firstfruits and firstborn males as an ancient pre-Israelite form of worship, which honored the gods and asked for their blessings of more grain, animals, and children. Propp calls this *preemptive gratitude*, saying that "one relinquishes property in hopes that more will accrue, giving one ever greater cause to be thankful."

Judging from the biblical references, the Israelites heightened the notion to say that all firstborn were *already owned or claimed by* God, and that the humans had to be *redeemed* from that ownership (a modern technical expression is that they had to be *desacralized*). Propp suggests that one older form of redeeming might have had young boys perform temporary service duties at shrines.

However, Propp asks what if Exodus 22:29–30 is older than other biblical passages. Could it refer to an ancient form of human sacrifice that once was legitimate within Israel?

There are several biblical (and ancient secular) condemnations of Canaanites sacrificing infants, of both sexes and any order of birth. These include Leviticus 18:21; 20:2–5; Deuteronomy 12:31; 2 Kings 16:3, and so on.

Some Middle Eastern archaeologists have found the remains of mass cremations of infants at a few Canaanite and Punic sites, and raise the question as to the nature and frequency of those procedures involving infants. Theories abound about the perceived need in time of crisis to offer up a royal or noble child, or greater numbers from the rest of the population, or perhaps some first-born to represent all. But such desperate bargaining in time of crisis is not the same as regular worship in normal times. Further, the possibility remains that the infants died natural deaths before the mass cremations took place.

Propp reviews all the evidence and considers the topic to be mainly a literary theme. My suggestion is that Propp means that it is an "urban legend," something considered factual by everyone even though no one has ever witnessed it. Clearly, some ancient cultures may have resorted to such sacrifices in times of war or famine, but the many literary references to this or that group doing so frequently seem to reflect little more than the prejudices of the authors. Earlier we mentioned a similar point of ridicule regarding improperly dressed priests going up many steps to high altars (Exod 20:26).

Propp (230) states, "I am unconvinced that *firstborn* [human] sacrifice was widespread or even practiced at all. I am equally unconvinced that Exodus 22:29 was ever intended to justify it."

Childs notes that Passover and firstborn traditions in Exodus were originally independent of each other. For example, there is no mention of firstborn in Exodus 12:21–24, and in 13:1–2, 11–16 there is no mention of Passover.

Childs concludes:

The sacrifice of the first-born belongs to the pre-Israelite culture which prescribed special sanctity to the firstlings of animals and dedicated them to the deity as a special token of gratitude. The stipulations regarding the claims on the first-born in the early legal material (Ex. 22.29–30; 34.19) as well as the Deuteronomic (Deut. 15.19–23) and the priestly material (Ex. 13.1) indicate the originally independent character of these laws. The original motivation of the law has long been lost in antiquity.... The much discussed question as to what extent the claim on the first-born reflected a primitive practice of child sacrifice seems incapable of a definitive solution.... The abhorrence of Israel toward the practice at a very early age makes a study of the historical development of any such tradition impossible. (*The Book of Exodus*, 195)

Propp argues that firstborn animals were not all sacrificed on the eighth day, but simply dedicated (set aside) for future sacrifices as needed. Early on, local shrines may have worked well for these animal sacrifices, but when worship was centralized in Jerusalem, it would not have been practical to move so many animals in pilgrimage once or twice a year. Some scholars point out that driving a yearling animal on a long trip to Jerusalem was impractical at best in any era; any injury would have rendered the animal unfit for sacrifice.

Exodus 22:31 refers to carrion, which cannot be drained of blood or used in any correct religious rituals.

E. Exodus 23:1–19: Honesty in Court, Liturgical Calendar

This first section of chapter 23 ranges from matters of justice and compassion to an overview of basic religious obligations.

Exodus 23:1–3, 6–8 focuses on any form of perjury or bribery or injustice brought about by majority or mob rule. The norms certainly apply to the judges as well. Childs notes that in rabbinical courts the custom developed to have the youngest of the judges give his verdict first, so that he would not feel obliged to agree with the older judges on the same panel.

The terms in this passage are broad, and certainly would include malicious gossip. The examples (23:4–5) about what to do with animals that belong to one's hostile neighbor add to the context of the three verses before and after. Exodus 23:5 is hard to translate. Propp considers it to be a warning against looting the goods being carried by the donkey.

Exodus 23:9 is a call to compassion for *sojourners* or *resident aliens*. The phrase *you know the heart* (or *soul, nfsh*) *of an alien* is also found in Proverbs 12:10, "The righteous person *knows the soul* of his animals." The NRSV translates this as "The righteous know *the needs* of their animals."

The next two verses, 23:10–11, mention leaving the fields fallow every seventh year. This custom is mentioned in Leviticus 25:2–7, 20–22, and indirectly in Deuteronomy 15:1–11; 31:10–13. Thus every seventh year is like the seventh day of creation, wherein God enjoyed being with all the good things that he had created. Propp notes the stock question of whether all the fields should be left unplanted in the same year all across the country, or should there be a staggered pattern. The biblical tradition generally favors the same year for all. What is different in Exodus 23 is the emphasis on letting the poor (and even wild animals) forage for what crops grow of their own in the fields without any sowing.

Exodus 23:12 speaks of the whole community, including slaves, resident aliens, and domestic animals, resting on the weekly Sabbath. The exact phrase at the end is that the slave and resident alien may *inhale* or *catch their breath* (*nfsh*). The same word is used in Exodus 31:17 to describe God *catching his breath* on the seventh day of creation.

Exodus 23:14–19 mentions the three annual (agricultural) holy days that the people (at least the adult males) should celebrate by coming together. The first, the pilgrimage of *Unleavened Bread* (*Mazzot*), eventually was joined to Passover ceremonies. The use of new leaven coincided with the start of the barley harvest in late April or early May.

The second, *First Fruits* or *Harvest*, involved the wheat harvest in June, and is also called *Shavuot* (*Weeks*) or *Pentecost*, since it usually took place seven weeks (fifty days) after the start of the barley harvest.

The final celebration, *Ingathering*, celebrated the harvest of all the other crops in late September. It is also called *Succoth* (*Booths*) because of the temporary huts erected for the assembly at that time. The three festivals are mentioned in several other places in the Bible. See Exodus 34:18–23; Leviticus 23; Numbers 28—29; Deuteronomy 16:1–17; Ezekiel 45:18–25.

Originally these harvest festivals were held at local shrines, involving a journey of just a few hours. The exact dates likely varied from year to year as the growing season and harvest time depended on the weather. Centuries later, when all these pilgrimages were made to Jerusalem, calendars had to be developed that could not take local conditions into account. While the biblical passages speak of a solemn obligation to attend all three holy days, the general understanding was that those who had to travel long distances would usually come for just one of the three events.

In a later, secondary process of piety, the harvest festivals have also been historicized, or connected to sacred history. So *Mazzot* has joined *Passover* to celebrate the escape from Egypt; *Weeks* commemorates the law giving at Sinai (Exod 19:1) and covenant renewals such as 2 Chronicles 15:10; and the booths of *Succoth* represent the booths (supposedly) used during the forty years of wandering in the desert (Lev 23:42-43).

The term *Lord* in 23:17 is not the title replacing the name Yahweh, but rather the common noun form (*adon*) from which the title LORD (*Adonai*) was developed. In 23:17, it has some of the root meaning of *master* or *landowner*. Joseph was called *the lord of the land* in Genesis 42:30, and in Leviticus 25:23 God says that "the land is mine; with me you are but aliens and tenants." When the people come to these harvest festivals, they are paying reverence to the real owner of the land from which the harvests came.

Exodus 23:18 speaks of not using anything with leaven in it at sacrifices. Leaven was considered impure and unholy, even though it was needed to make most kinds of bread. The *fat of the festival* refers to fatty coverings over kidney and liver portions of the animals. There are, of course, several instructions in the Bible about the exact preparation, consumption, and disposal of sacrificial animals and the grain, oil, and salt used in offerings.

Exodus 23:19b contains a mysterious prohibition of cooking the meat of a young goat or sheep in its mother's milk. The same law is repeated in a similar context at Exodus 34:26. Propp remarks that such a carefully cooked delicacy would have been a rare part of the average person's diet, and hardly worth a law of its own. Some theorize that the law may simply have been in contradiction to a Canaanite religious custom, perhaps a first milk and yearling animal sacrifice. Another theory is that it is a humane notion, a reaction against the disquieting combination of life-giving milk and a slaughtered young animal. It appears in Deuteronomy 14:21, among a list of clean and unclean foods.

Propp suggests that it may be a proverb. If so, perhaps it is a humanitarian one, an image meant to promote empathy for the lives of animals and people. The context makes some sense for this; the proverb could serve as a motivating finale for all the laws in this chapter that focus on justice and the poor, and on Sabbath rest.

F. Exodus 23:20–33: Epilogue

The final part of chapter 23 is unexpected, following this series of laws. God describes how, with the assistance of a special deputy angel, he intends to gradually have the Israelites overpower the Canaanites in the chosen land. This is accompanied by warnings to hobble Canaanite public religious practices. The style of the passage is very Deuteronomic, and in context this glimpse of God's future plans for his people might serve as an additional motivation for accepting the covenant and the Covenant Code.

The angel is not identified. Some take it to mean a prophet, or a human leader, such as Moses himself. One problem with the image referring to Moses is that Moses did not actually engage in the battles of conquest; he died at the mountain overlooking the Promised Land. The traditional response is that at this point God may have intended Moses to engage in the battles, but changed his divine plans later.

Propp notes that we already have seen angelic or divine presence in the pillar of cloud and fire in Exodus 13—14. An angel will be mentioned in Exodus 33:2, and the cloud and fire of the glory of the LORD will direct the stages of their journey (Exod 40:34–38). Childs notes Genesis 22:15–18 and Judges 6:8–11 as two passages where an angel serves as a very subordinate stand-in for God.

Another possibility is that the angel is related to the *terror* of 23:27, or to the *pestilence* (or *hornets*) of 23:28.

The one thing we are sure of is that in 23:21 God says that "my name is in him." This presence of the name is a common image in Deuteronomy 16:2, 6, 11; 26:2, and so on. In Isaiah 30:27, God's name is virtually personified. God is not fully physically present on earth, nor can he be captured within a representation or idol. Instead, he is represented by his proper name, Yahweh. His name can be used as a hypostasis for his presence.

Propp considers all the references to the angel in chapter 23 as delphic.

> While reassuring the people that, come what may, he will not abandon them, the Deity keeps his options open. He does not specify the form of his guiding Messenger, whether human or divine. He promises only that the divine Name will be in him. (In the composite text, Moses eventually realizes this and objects to Yahweh's equivocations [Exodus 33:2, 12].) (*Exodus 19—40*, 287)

In 23:27 *my terror* means *fear of me*. The same word was used in Exodus 15:16. In 23:28, the word *pestilence* is disputed. It may mean *skin disease*, or *discouragement*. The Septuagint (LXX) used the word *wasp*, which rabbinic commentators accepted. Propp and Childs argue for this tradition that the subject is *hornets* or *bees*, actual swarms of biting insects that would bedevil the Canaanites over many decades. This is the sense in Wisdom of Solomon 12:3–11, especially verse 8.

Propp considers the insects to be similar to the plagues among the Egyptians. There we saw gnats (8:16–19), flies (8:20–29), and locusts (10:3–19) used as weapons against the oppressors. Here too the Canaanites could become discouraged or possibly even sickened by diseases carried by insects. In the passage from Wisdom of Solomon 12, the Canaanites are described as being given *the opportunity to repent*, in that the struggle lasted so long.

In Exodus 23:29, the plan is to turn control of the land over to the Israelites slowly enough so that the farm and grazing land would not revert to wild growth, or so that wild animals would not multiply to the extent of being too dangerous in their numbers. This is a standard explanation for the slowness of the conquest, although it does not match the serenity of nature envisioned in having fields lie fallow each seventh year.

Propp suggests that the boundaries of *Red Sea* and *Sea of the Philistines* (*Mediterranean*), and the (*Arabian*) *Desert* or *Wilderness* to the *Euphrates* paint a grandiose image of the size of God's chosen land. He suggests that the *Jordan* is being glorified as another *Euphrates,* and that we should simply take the bodies of water and the wilderness as a majestic frame for the not-so-large land of the Canaanites.

Questions

131. As you look at the fourteen verses of the epilogue (Exod 23:20–33), can you distinguish firm promises, warnings, and conditional promises? Make a list.
132. Suppose the epilogue is tightly connected to 23:14–19 alone, more than to all of chapters 21—23. In this case, what is the main purpose of the epilogue?
133. As a Christian reader or study group member, what are your reactions to the Covenant Code (20:22–23:33)? Does any of it affect your own faith and moral principles?

Conclusion to the Entire Section

The ordinary Christian, familiar with many of the Old Testament's stories, prophetic passages, hymns, and psalms, usually has had less exposure to the Bible's legal materials and liturgical instructions. These few chapters in Exodus, along with the numbing detail about the Tabernacle, are part of the larger corpus that includes much of Leviticus, Numbers, and Deuteronomy.

Commentators rightly point out that the Old Testament laws are representative of Israel's jurisprudence, but do not present the complete system that must have existed in those times. What is more surprising, perhaps, is that some laws are still in the text long after their period of need. Animal sacrifices have been suspended since the Temple in Jerusalem was destroyed in 70 CE. Polytheism and the use of idols are rare in Western cultures, nor are slavery and polygamy allowed. There are few small farms still dependent on oxen and mules, and few make a living raising sheep and goats. We find no religious significance in the fact that someone is firstborn, nor are we edgy about the microbes in yeast.

Yet it helps to know one's "family history." Christians who look carefully at their own New Testament know that early Christians kept some Jewish customs, did not question slavery or Roman rule, and were very convinced that the Second Coming of Christ would be very soon, perhaps within their lifetimes. Those texts are still there, too, long after their period of need.

The outdated legal materials and liturgical instructions of the Old Testament did more than gather dust. The laws and cases grew into precedents in rabbinic law, much like the precedents in our own (British) legal system, and many of them make just as much sense within a Christian law code. Some of the Temple rites, and rules regarding food and food preparation, have been reworked into ceremonies for synagogue and home. The goals of communal, family, and individual prayer and worship that these ceremonies foster throughout each year are the same goals as those in Christian communities, since they both worship the same LORD.

Section Nineteen:
Exodus 24:1–18

> Most of this chapter may be from E, with the exception
> of the Priestly verses in 15b–18a describing the
> fire, cloud, and glory.

Introduction

Obviously, chapter 24 completes the great events begun in
chapter 19. The three statements of agreement by the people are
dramatic (19:8; 24:3, 7). Moses was called to be the mediator at
the start of chapter 19, further empowered by the people in
20:18–21, and he presides over most of the events of chapter 24.
Childs is struck by God's closeness to the people, as he notes:

> The terrifying God of Ex. 19 who appeared in his theophany
> has not changed. He returns at the end of ch. 24 once again
> in majesty and awe-inspiring terror. What has changed is his
> relation to Israel. This is dramatically portrayed in the
> covenant meal of vv. 9–11. But in the light of God's com-
> plete otherness, the all-encompassing focus of the chapter
> falls on God's mercy and gracious condescension. It is this
> theme which lies at the heart of the witness of the Sinai
> covenant. (*The Book of Exodus*, 508)

Chapter 24 does have subdivisions within it. Fretheim notes
that 24:1–2 interrupts the normal flow or connection between
23:33 and 24:3. The instructions for a meeting on the mountain
will lead to that event in 24:9–11. The intervening ceremonies
(verses 4–8) seem to have been spliced into the first story. Childs
thinks the two stories were combined only when in written form;

162

he suggests that at an earlier time the two events (covenant sacrifices, covenant meal) may have been independent accounts.

At the start of chapter 24, God switches from delivering exhortations and cases to all the people; instead, he gives directives to Moses. He is to bring Aaron, Nadab, Abihu, and seventy elders to a certain place, and then Moses himself is to come higher and closer. It is not clear at the end of Exodus 24:2 how near the ordinary people were allowed to approach. The common tradition is that they remained at the base of the mountain.

Fretheim reminds us that the invitation is to *worship at a distance*. Specific instances of worship have occurred at Exodus 4:31; 12:27; 15:1–21; 18:12. The events in 24:3–8 and 9–11 are worshipful responses to God himself rather than to the laws in and of themselves. The laws are important insofar as they are the words of the God with whom the Israelites are in relationship.

Nadab and Abihu are mentioned elsewhere as sons of Aaron (Exod 6:23; Lev 10:1–2), although in Leviticus they proved themselves unworthy of the priesthood. Perhaps Aaron and these two sons were the unidentified priests of Exodus 19:22.

In 24:3, Moses repeats all the *words* (*debarim*) and *ordinances* (*mishpatim*, also called *cases*) he has heard from the LORD. The *words* could well include the Decalogue and all the sayings within chapters 20—23. The *cases* are from the same chapters. The people immediately and unanimously commit themselves to obey all these. This firmly echoes their agreement in 19:8. In 24:4, we are told that everything was then written down.

In 24:12, what is written on the tablets of stone is not fully identified, being called the *law* (*torah*) and the *commandment* (*mzwh*). Tradition puts the Decalogue on the tablets, but it may be that verses 4 and 12 are meant to refer to the same written texts. Childs notes that in Deuteronomy 5:28–33 God knows that some of these laws will be more relevant when they have settled in Canaan. Childs suggests that in 24:12 the editor simply ignored the final phrase, "which I have written for their instruction," thus not making it clear for us which laws went where. Childs remarks that the fact that Moses wrote the laws down and repeated them again to the people emphasizes the importance of their knowing the exact content of the covenant to which they were committing themselves.

Moses next prepared an altar and twelve pillars for the ceremonies. Stone pillars were very common Canaanite memorials to their gods, and are consistently condemned in the Old Testament (the nearest example is Exod 23:24). Here we are reassured that the pillars represent the twelve tribes rather than gods. Another theory is that the twelve pillars were fitted together to form the altar itself (see the somewhat similar case in 1 Kgs 18:31–32). Propp suggests that the pillars were a vestige of some ancient component of covenant making, such as display markers for blood let from the pierced fingers of the two parties, and had no clear ritual function by the time of Moses.

In addition to the odd mention of the pillars, we next see Moses assign young men to sacrifice the animals needed for whole burnt offerings and well-being offerings. In the latter case, the meat of the animals was to be eaten by the worshippers. Readers often ask why young men are mentioned instead of priests. A rabbinic theory that firstborn were assigned to cultic duties (before the Levites were designated) may be at work here. Propp agrees that firstborn had cultic duties in many ancient religions, although he is open to the idea that the young men are mentioned simply because at this point in the story the elders and priests were waiting for Moses farther up the mountain.

The collecting of the blood of the animals into two sets of bowls may represent the commitment of both parties to the covenant. Sprinkling blood on the altar at this point may sanctify it, so it represents the divine presence. Perhaps holiness or sacramental power was thought to flow from the altar into all the bowls of blood.

Next, Moses read the *book of the covenant*, which may have included the Decalogue and what we have heard in the last three chapters. The people's third response in 24:7, "All that the LORD has spoken we will do, and we will be obedient," looks back at what has just been read to them, and looks forward to whatever else God may ask of them. Then Moses sprinkles the rest of the blood upon the people, signifying their unity with their LORD in this covenant, a unity to which they pledge their lives.

In Exodus 24:9, we return to the leaders approaching God on the mountain. We are told they saw God, but we learn only of the clear blue floor of sapphire (lapis lazuli) beneath the throne. The leaders were not harmed by God, despite their being so near, and they ate and drank in his presence.

Some commentators imagine that the leaders looked up at God through the sapphire panels, or that the blue-colored floor is meant to be the sky itself. In an imaginative sense, climbing the mountain gave the leaders a chance to glimpse the heavenly throne room from what artists call the worm's-eye level.

Propp notes that eating and drinking in a ruler's presence is to acknowledge his authority and beneficence, and conversely one's own dependence and vulnerability (see Gen 43:31–34; 1 Kgs 1:25; Ezek 44:3). Covenants were often closed with a meal (see Gen 26:28–31; 31:44–54; Josh 9:11–15; 2 Sam 3:20–21. So here the leaders at table represent the nation as covenant partners, or vassals. Childs refers to the meal as not only one way to seal the covenant, but as a joyous confirmation of the new relationship.

Fretheim notes that

> God was certainly fully present in the midst of the people during the eating and drinking. It is a communal activity, in which both God and people participate.... *God is committed to a real presence with this people* in all of their journeyings, a deeply personal level of involvement. The God who has made promises will personally see to those promises. This anticipates the discussion between Moses and God in chapters 32—34, where the continuing divine presence with Israel is at issue. (*Exodus*, 260)

Childs points out that, since the covenant meal tradition envelops the ceremonies in 24:3–8, the meal can now be seen as the culmination of one larger event. He notes:

> These verses [9–11] in their present position in the biblical narrative function as a eucharistic festival in which selected witnesses celebrate the covenant sealing of vv. 3–8. The God

of Israel has not become familiar or less awe-inspiring on account of the covenant, but a new avenue of communion has been opened to his people which is in stark contrast to the burning terror of the theophany in ch. 19. (*The Book of Exodus*, 507)

In 24:14 there may be a hint of Aaron's leadership responsibilities, which will become an intolerable pressure for him in chapter 32. Childs notes that setting Aaron and Hur as judges seems to ignore the system set up by Moses and Jethro in chapter 18.

In 24:15, the *glory* (*kabod*) of the LORD *settled* (*shkn*) on the mountain. A noun form of this verb will be used to describe the *tabernacle* (*mishkan*) in 25:9; 26:1, and so on. The glory settled for six days before Moses entered the cloud to hear God. Some suggest that God spent six days making the model of the tabernacle, as he had spent six days in creating the world. Another possibility is that this period was needed to sanctify the place or to purify Moses himself.

Questions

134. At first impression, the covenant at Sinai is a majestic, striking event. One can imagine the days of preparation, the divine voice booming out commandments for hours, and the simple, yet effective, ratification ceremonies, by which the community makes its final commitment. However, a covenant or a treaty should be a mutual pact entered in mutual freedom. Would it have been possible for Moses and the Israelite refugees to decline this arrangement? Could they have walked away at 19:7–8 or 20:18–21 or 24:3?

135. Exodus 24:1–2, 9–11 go well together, while Exodus 24:3–8 seems independent of those five surrounding verses and more connected to 23:33. If we simply looked at the passage 24:1–2, 9–11 by itself, what does it show

us? What do we learn from 24:3–8 as another passage simply taken by itself?

136. In 24:6, some of the blood was dashed upon the base of the altar, and in 24:8, after laws had been read out and the people had proclaimed their obedience (both for the second time), the rest of the blood was sprinkled upon the people. How do you think the blood "works" here? That is, how does it make sense in the minds of the storytellers to use blood in this ritual or sacramental ceremony?

137. Exodus 24:12–18 describes Moses going on another special journey to the mountaintop. We are told that God plans to give him the two stone tablets there. The elders and the people are to remain below; we do not know how much they knew about this special journey. They could see that there was a continuous swirl of cloud and fiery light at the mountaintop (24:15–17). How do you think the people down below should have felt over those next forty days?

Overviews of the Covenant

It is important for us to develop theological overviews of the covenant, given the heightened language of chapters 19 and 24, and the odd collage of commandments, cases, and exhortations in the intervening chapters. I will mention some conclusions from Propp and Fretheim, and then end with remarks of my own.

Propp's Reflections

Propp notes that the covenant united a people into a common society and nation, as part of the more important preexisting relationship between all of Israel and God. The conical shape of Sinai offers an image of a monotheistic nation: many at the base with the one God at the top. In many of the remaining chapters of Exodus, focus will be put on the movable Tabernacle shrine. We can understand the Tabernacle as a portable Sinai; or we could think of Sinai as a stationary Tabernacle. Each image system has gradations of holiness or of proximity to God. At Sinai, Moses can ascend to the summit; Aaron, Joshua, and other elders remain at designated middle-level ledges; the people remain at the lowest level, but can see and hear some of the manifestations of the divine. In the Tabernacle, there will be an inner sanctum for Moses or a high priest, an outer sanctum for the other priests, and a large courtyard for the people. The Tabernacle was designed to support the covenant relationship in the wilderness.

The parallels in style between ancient political treaties and the covenant at Sinai impress some commentators more than others. Propp notes that scholars have found interesting covenant parallels with components of ancient treaties, but they disagree as to how far the parallels can be assuredly drawn. Propp admits that we do not have a complete treaty text in Exodus 19 and 24, but we can be comfortable with the general parallels. He then (301) goes on to remark,"Nowhere does the Bible actually represent the text of the Covenant between Yahweh and Israel. The important thing is that a Covenant exists.... [I]ts contents may be imagined, and even discovered by experience, as specific actions on Israel's part seem to provoke divine responses."

Fretheim is less interested in the parallels with ancient Near Eastern treaties. He notes that some treaty components are missing in Exodus, that the content of the treaties we have are completely secular, and that "the relationship between God and people is too personally oriented for contractual language to do it justice."

Another perennial question is why this covenant was offered in the first place, since the covenant with Abraham was always in effect. Propp considers this the second stage of God's plans.

Why must Israel and Yahweh enter into a new covenant?... [A]t Sinai, Israel learns that the promise of land has strings attached, and great amounts of fine print. Like any solid compact, the Covenant entails specific obligations, as well as specific consequences for compliance and noncompliance. At Sinai, Yahweh begins to disclose to Moses and Israel what he apparently concealed from the Patriarchs: Israel's continued residence in Canaan will be contingent upon their adherence to a legal and cultic standard that will set them apart from the indigenous peoples. Nevertheless, God is not yet fully candid.... Yahweh does not spell out the drastic consequences for disobedience. Later, Leviticus 26 and Deuteronomy 27—30 will explicitly announce that the gift of land is conditional. Apostasy's ultimate price will be loss of the land, i.e., exile. (*Exodus 1—18*, 301)

I would argue that Propp is thinking mainly of the burdens here, the *legal and cultic standard that will set them apart from the indigenous peoples*. God might have concealed these burdens from the Patriarchs, but a second stage of disclosure might not be the only theological explanation available for us for the Exodus events. Concealing or withholding important provisos of a treaty could be misunderstood as a paternalistic tactic, and as unjust in itself.

Fretheim's Reflections

Fretheim seems uncomfortable with the way the covenant was imposed, but gropes for a positive understanding of its import. He remarks (257) that "God made the covenant, that is, set its terms (23:22) and invited Israel to become a participant. While one might speak of a certain democratization evident in the opportunity given the people to respond, they are given no options to choose from. Yet the absence of coercion is important."

Fretheim searches for this absence of coercion by noting the many divine promises in 20:24 and 23:20–33. He points to 23:22, the first of the promises in that speech. There God sets the condition "if you *listen attentively* (*shmᶜ*) to his [the angel's] voice and *do* all that I say, then I will be an enemy to your enemies...." In 24:7, the people say, "All that the LORD has spoken we will *do*, and we will *listen*." (For *listen*, NRSV has *we will be obedient*.) Fretheim (257) concludes, "Thus the people's commitment to God does not stand isolated from God's own commitment to them. Their commitment entails a high level of confidence in God himself that God will see to what God has promised. Their obedience will always be undergirded by the constancy of the divine will and word on their behalf."

Fretheim is also moved by the acts of worship in chapter 24. The sacrifices, blood sprinkling, and assenting, along with the vision and the shared meal for Moses and the elders, were foundational worship experiences, not just one-time events. Not only was God truly present to them; he allowed them to worship him and dedicate themselves to him. Fretheim reminds us to hold 24:12–18 as an equally important part of the story. Moses' ascending to receive the stone tablets and his obedient attendance in front of the cloud and the glory were further acts of worship, in which the other leaders and the people participated, even if from a safe distance.

Fretheim concludes:

Verses 12–18 are parallel to the two parts of verses 1–11, with emphasis on (1) the divine authority that lies behind the "instruction" given to the people and (2) the theophanic context for the tabernacle instructions, which provide a worship complex in which the presence of God is the central reality. *This ties law closely together with worship.* Worship grounds the ins and outs of daily life in God. Obedience to the task set for the people is in need of the sustenance provided by the ongoing experience of the promised presence of God in worship. Without the presence of God, there would be no point in Israel's continuing journey (so chaps. 33–34). *Worship must inform and undergird obedience.* (*Exodus*, 260)

Therefore, Fretheim sees this covenant in Exodus 24 as a "less comprehensive creative act…within an already existing relationship…a *closer specification* of what is entailed in that relationship in view of what Israel has become *as a people* and in the light of their recent experience. *The Sinai covenant is a matter, not of the people's status, but of their vocation.*" Their vocation is to be a holy nation, a kingdom of priests, prepared to advance God's purposes throughout the world. So they are being ordained, set apart for a task that involves their loyalty, faithfulness, and obedience.

Additional Reflections by the Author

As we try to imagine what the covenant meant and continues to mean for Jewish and Christian people, we must remember that ancient Israelites stressed the communal dimension of things much more than we, who reflexively think first of the individual dimension, even in our relationships with God.

As the storytellers weave the images of chapter 19, with clouds, thunder, lightning, boundaries around the mountain where trespassers would die, tremors, and the like, we need to understand their intentions. They are groping to describe the indescribable: a divine being coming to meet humans.

I have always challenged students to think of chapters 19—24 as a nearly overwhelming but positive encounter, not a show of deadly force. As I will mention at the end of Answer 112, I use the example of the movie *Close Encounters of the Third Kind*, where the large alien spaceship casts sequenced beams of light and musical sounds to a dazed audience of humans. The goal of the moviemakers was to portray how fascinating and unusual any such experience would have to be, even when the aliens have peaceful intentions.

So too in chapters 20—23, as the Decalogue, exhortations, and cases are sent across the divide from God to us, the encounter is still positive, obviously blending human notions of right and wrong with God's. The vision given to Moses and the elders in chapter 24 is serene; they are not harmed at this extraordinary time. The fiery cloud of 24:15–18 gives God and Moses a private place and time for further revelations, but modern readers are not afraid of what is coming, nor should the ancient Israelites have been anxious at the foot of the mountain.

In ancient Near Eastern treaties, where one nation was much more powerful than the other, the text consists of first-person statements by the greater ruler. He briefly reviews the past history of the two nations, and sets down conditions that the other nation must follow. All this is done in a noble, polite style meant to encourage peace and good order. The covenant at Sinai maintains this noble tone.

I think Fretheim reacts too quickly to the impersonal, contractual language of these treaties, and Propp focuses too much on the strings, fine print, and penalties for noncompliance. Using the secular treaty form is a legitimate way to express the communal nature of our relationship with each other and with God. The fine print is an odd jumble to be sure. Worshipping one God, honoring your parents, having unleavened bread for a week each spring, and helping your neighbor retrieve lost animals may seem to be a disjointed set of divine obligations, but that is the way God is, and it all leads to justice and faith.

Even today we use an impersonal, contractual form for the most momentous personal event in the lives of most people: marriage. Both bride and groom (let's call them Jane and John) are asked individually if she or he is entering the marriage willingly, and each one individually says "I do." Later, licenses are signed and sent off to civil registrars. This contractual form persists because it works; it expresses the core of marriage—that each partner freely commits to the exclusive relationship.

Finally, I think we should look at Deuteronomy 26:16–19. In that passage, Moses celebrates the very day the covenant was made. He says to the people "Today you *have obtained the* LORD's *agreement* to be your God; and for you to walk in his ways.... Today the LORD *has obtained your agreement* to be his treasured people, as he promised you, and to keep his commandments; for him to set you high above all nations that he has made, in praise and in fame and in honor; and for you to be a people holy to the LORD, as he promised."

The NRSV phrase *to obtain agreement* translates a causative form of the verb *'mr*, literally meaning *to cause someone to say* something. Therefore, the people *have caused God to say* that he will be their God, and God *has caused the people to say* that they will be his people. Causative forms are very common in Biblical Hebrew, but in the entire Old Testament this is the only time we find the causative of the verb *to say*, which is found in all its other forms over five thousand times. Many English translations approximate this causative sense with verbs such as *affirm* (NJPS) or *declare* (RSV) or *recognize* (NEB). The NAB comes closer with *making this agreement*. I think the NRSV is the most helpful translation.

What is the writer in Deuteronomy trying to explain in these words of Moses? I think it is that *each party trusts the other.* Returning to the marriage example, we could report that (Jane's love for) John *caused Jane to say* that she would be his wife, and that (John's love for) Jane *caused John to say* that he would be her husband. There is no coercion here; the great covenant at Sinai, and the little covenant of Jane and John, are built on trust and love.

Exodus
25:1—40:38

Section Twenty:
Exodus 25:1—31:18

This passage is from the Priestly traditions.

Introduction

This large block of verses shows us God's instructions to Moses about building a shrine. The actual construction of the shrine does not begin until Exodus 35:1. At this point at the end of chapter 24, the people waiting at the bottom of the mountain have no idea that these instructions are being relayed to Moses.

These six chapters describe a unique, portable shrine for worship ceremonies in God's special presence. The whole design is often called the Tabernacle, which is the name for the chapel-like tent set at one end of the courtyard. Some of the shrine's elements seem to have been similar to some other ancient Near Eastern cultures (tent sanctuaries, animal sacrifices, incense, and so on) while others were more specifically Israelite (hereditary priesthood, Sabbath system, and so on). The writers certainly felt that all the structures should be made of fine materials, and maintained in spotless condition. Propp notes that the verbal descriptions of some elements of the Tabernacle are complex, and quite difficult to replicate in drawings or in metal and wood. He speculates that this complexity may have been deliberate, to prevent opponents from making a full replica.

The authors did not feel the need to explain the inner logic of whole burnt or shared sacrifices, the use of incense and oils, or the belief that sins can be forgiven or priests ordained. For example, we might speculate that the destruction of an animal by fire turns it to smoke and gases—translucent, intangible, gravity-defying vapors—perhaps accessible by spirits. While God does not need earthly food, perhaps he accepted it as a sign of good will. Some sacrificed portions of meat not destined for destruction were reserved for the priests; the majority of sacrificed animals were returned to the donors to celebrate meals with family and friends. Gentiles often noted with wonder that the Israelites had as many whole burnt sacrifices as they did. Such sacrifices were less common in other cultures. None of these customs is explained in Exodus.

Childs notes that for P the form of the Tabernacle is inseparable from its spiritual meaning.

> Every detail of the structure reflects the one divine will and nothing rests on the *ad hoc* decision of human builders. There is no tension between form and content, symbol and reality throughout the tabernacle chapters. Moreover, the tabernacle is not conceived of as a temporary measure for a limited time, but one in which the permanent priesthood of Aaron serves throughout all their generations. (*The Book of Exodus*, 540)

In Numbers 7:6–7, mention is made of six wagons, each pulled by two oxen, which were used for transporting much of the Tabernacle and courtyard structures, pedestals, and fabrics. Many of the more sacred objects were to be carried by teams of Levites, following specific rules for wrapping each item and using carrying poles and rings. Some scholars doubt that such a shrine ever existed; they point out that nomadic groups would have been hard put to spare the manpower to move all these things each leg of a journey. Propp is willing to allow for a real structure, unless we find proof otherwise. Childs is interested in the final form of the text, with its religious meanings, and is not concerned with the question of historicity.

Fretheim reminds us that Priestly authors may have written these chapters during the period of Exile in Babylon. P imagines every last detail coming from God, since the subject is so important, and humans are prone to error and syncretism. Their thinking may have been that we had a Tabernacle (and then a Temple) in the past; maybe God will give us one again.

Fretheim concludes:

On their journey through the wilderness, God gives Israel two basic institutions, *the law and the tabernacle.* These gifts are alike in that both are portable, both are designed to bring some order out of the disorder, both give shape to life when the center has trouble holding. They provide *an ethical shape and a liturgical shape.* And it is just such formfulness to life that is sufficient for the journey through wildernesses that never seem to end. (*Exodus*, 277)

Questions

138. What roles does God play in this opening paragraph (25:1–9)? Is there anything improbable or striking in the details?

139. As the Ark and its cover are described in Exodus 25:10–22, what are their purposes? What do the *cherubim* represent?

140. The table and lamp stand (25:23–40) may not be remarkable in themselves, but they are described in great detail. What religious symbolism could you suggest for the bread (verse 30) and the lamps (verse 37)?

141. Without getting lost in the obscurities of this chapter (26:1–37), what is the basic shape, floor plan, and purpose for the Tabernacle?

142. Exodus 27:1–21 mentions the main altar (a safe distance in front of the Tabernacle), and the outer courtyard curtains that surrounded the entire arrangement. In Genesis, altars were made of earth or fieldstones. Why the switch now to one of bronze? Why is the courtyard curtain wall a bit over seven feet tall? Would not a three-foot-high curtain fence have made it easier for everyone to watch the sacrifices?

143. In chapter 28, the vestments for Aaron are glorious and complex. He wears two onyx stones at his shoulders, each inscribed with the names of six tribes. He has a breast-

plate with twelve valuable stones, each inscribed with the name of one tribe, and a gold plate with an inscription mounted on his turban. Two more special stones were kept in a pouch (verse 30). As you work your way through chapter 28, what do you learn about why vestments were used and what their purposes were?

144. The ordination ceremony in chapter 29 is equally complex, calling for seven days of special sacrifices and sanctification of the altar, anointing the ordinands with blood and oil, and the eating of holy portions of certain sacrificed animals by the ordinands alone. In 29:38–46, mention is made of the two daily sacrifices to be made for all time, and the passage ends with a solemn proclamation by God. As you work your way through chapter 29, what do you learn about the role of Moses in these ceremonies?

145. Chapter 30 describes the incense altar, the annual tax for supporting the Tabernacle, the large bronze water basin near the main altar, and the formulae for making the anointing oils and incense. What are the advantages of the annual tax? Why are the formulas for the oil and incense restricted to these ceremonies alone? They were not to be prepared for any other purpose.

146. What is the point of God's speech in 31:1–11? Why is the Sabbath mentioned in 31:12–17?

Conclusion

Given the material presented in this book, a fair amount of detail about the plagues, the Ten Commandments and the Covenant Code, and these encyclopedic speeches about the Tabernacle plans and rituals have already been covered.

These six chapters, 25—31, put us in the position of a captive audience, as the Priestly authors measure every cubit, tassel, and stitch. We should reflect on Moses, the first captive audience, so to speak. We can imagine how astounding it must have been for him to be tutored by God in this crash course in architecture, to be given diagrams, floor plans, formulas for oils and incense, and so on. Moses the mediator and lawgiver must also become Moses the building-project coordinator and liturgical authority. God is willing to spend as long as he needs to give Moses all this training.

The entire Tabernacle and all its furnishings, with its inner rooms approachable only by priests, have now been shown to everyone who hears or reads these chapters. If anything else were to be added later, fellow Israelites would have the right to protest. This Tabernacle was meant to keep any hint of polytheism or idolatry miles away.

The irony, of course, is that those for whom the Tabernacle with all its features was being designed were down below in the camp, unaware of the existence of these plans. Not only were they unaware; they had started down a path that would make them unworthy of God's presence in their lives.

Readers who wish to learn more about Jewish liturgical concepts can find good overviews in the following books. The first section of Walter Brueggemann's *Theology of the Old Testament* explains the theology of Old Testament liturgy well. E. P. Sanders's *Judaism: Practice and Belief, 63 BCE–66 CE* is a very thorough history of the worship during that era. Chaim Raphael's *Festival Days: A History of Jewish Celebrations* catches the emotions and the mutual support found in the yearly cycle of current synagogue services, and explains those well for non-Jewish readers.

Section Twenty-one:
Exodus 32:1–35

Most of this chapter seems to be from E, with some
Deuteronomistic overtones in 32:7–14. The story appears
in a modified form in Deuteronomy 9:8–29. In 1 Kings
12:25–33, gold calves were installed at two shrines by King
Jeroboam after the northern kingdom broke away. Most
scholars assume that the events in 1 Kings 12 have
contributed to the Exodus account in some way.

Introduction

The irony and shock of this story of the golden calf is all the
greater in light of God and Moses going over Tabernacle blue-
prints and worship instructions for the past forty days. Fretheim
calls 32:1 a blast of cold air—the people taking the future into
their own hands and compromising their loyalty to Yahweh. He
calls it the story of Israel's fall, comparable to that of Adam and
Eve. He notes that the question of the divine presence is a key
theme, which will keep chapters 32—34 in context with the two
groups of chapters that describe the Tabernacle.

Childs credits the redactors with skillful editing of chapters
32—34; the work is much more polished than chapters 19—24.
In chapter 32, the sequence of contrasting scenes hampers any
strict chronological order, but that cannot be avoided. For example, God first knows of the rebellion below and Moses intercedes
for the people right away; later Moses sees the camp for himself
and gets quite angry. Readers are in the same situation; by 32:25
we cannot help but imagine new dimensions of the spontaneous
or reckless events taking place.

The plural term *gods* is used in verses 1, 4, 8, 23, and 31, even though there is only one calf statue in the story and no divine name is used except that of Yahweh.

The Hebrew word for *gods* (*elohim*) in certain contexts can also mean one *god* or *God*. Propp suggests that in these odd uses of plural verbs and nouns there is a pattern not previously understood. The biblical writers always have polytheists make plural references to gods, and have monotheists make singular references (even when using the plural *elohim* for their God). Thus in 1 Kings 12:25–33 we read of Jeroboam, who set up two rival shrines, including two gold calves. In 1 Kings 12:28, he used the same formula, "Here are your gods, O Israel, who brought you up out of the land of Egypt." Yet Propp argues that Jeroboam was basically a Yahweh worshipper, not a purveyor of new polytheistic cults. Also in Isaiah 42:17 the prophet has God speak of those who say to a carved image (*pesel*) or to a cast image (*masseka*) "you are *our gods.*" See 1 Samuel 4:7–8, where Philistine soldiers speak of the Ark of the Covenant, and the "power of these mighty gods...the gods who struck the Egyptians with every sort of plague."

Propp concludes:

> In the Bible's imagined world, how one uses the word *elohim* is a cultural code. The monotheist always uses it as a singular, in defiance of grammar; the polytheist always uses it as a plural, even in defiance of logic. The polytheist cannot conceive of a single deity; the Yahwist cannot conceive of pluriform deities. (*Exodus 19—40*, 552)

The chapter is full of sharp contrasts. God and Moses are at a creative task, while the people and Aaron allow themselves to get agitated. The devout, precise planning at the mountaintop of everything needed for worship contrasts with the rapid, emotional manufacture of the calf and impromptu preparations for the extralegal festival. Each scene involves two characters, the cast of six including God, Moses, Joshua, Aaron, the people, and the Levites. Moses ties all the scenes together, serving as leader, mediator, prophet-punisher, or spiritual guide.

Questions

147. In Question 133 you were asked how you thought that the people at the base of the mountain *should* have felt during the forty days Moses was with God. The correct answer (mine!) was that they *should* have been experiencing a spiritual "honeymoon period." However, it is quite clear in 32:1–6 that things are going badly. How many sins do the people commit here? How many does Aaron commit?

148. In Exodus 32:21–25, Moses interrogates Aaron. In 32:21, Moses says, *What has this people done to you that you have caused a great sin to come upon them?* In 32:25, we are told that Moses watched the people running wild *(for Aaron had let them run wild...)*. Is Moses being fair to Aaron in these two verses? Why does he not hold any dialogue with Aaron regarding the remarks Aaron made in 32:22–24?

149. How many human (anthropomorphic) qualities can you find in God's words in 32:7–10? He could have punished or destroyed the people instantly from afar, and spent his time counseling Moses instead, but he does not do this.

150. In each of the three verses in Exodus 32:11–13, Moses offers a different reason why God should calm down. Which reason seems to be the weakest? Which reason seems to be the strongest? Does 32:14 indicate complete forgiveness?

151. In 32:15–18, what effects are created for readers as you learn several details about the tablets and about Moses' reply to Joshua's puzzlement?

152. In Exodus 32:19–25, what do you learn about Moses himself?

153. In Exodus 32:25–29, what do you learn about Moses himself?

154. Exodus 32:30–35 wraps up this chapter, but not the larger story. What do we learn about God, Moses, and the people in these verses?

Conclusion

I imagine most readers find the executions, the plague, and the continued hard feelings of God (speaking of coming days for more punishment) to be gruesome and unsettling. Hopefully these are bombastic legends, but the consequences of idolatry for one who is in a monotheistic covenant is soul-ruining and self-destructive.

Fretheim reminds us that the story is not complete at the end of chapter 32, although things look bleak. God is here represented as one who is sorting out possibilities with Moses. It is an amazing picture of God, a God who enters into genuine dialogue with chosen leaders and takes their contribution to the discussion with utmost seriousness. It is a God who works at the level of possibility, who chooses not to act alone in such matters for the sake of the integrity of relationships established. The final determinations should be the best for as many as possible.

Fretheim concludes:

> This text lifts up the extraordinary importance of human speaking and acting in the shaping of the future. Simply to leave the future in the hands of God is something other than what God desires. Simply to leave the future in the hands of the people is not a divine desire either. That leaves chosen leaders in an uncomfortable position—between God and people, but to such they are called. Moses' way is to be preferred to Aaron's. (*Exodus*, 292)

Propp concludes his study of chapter 32 with this overview:

> Like a melodrama, the Bible's plot is propelled by alternating scenes of alienation and reconciliation between a faithful and irascible God and a fickle Israel. This is a difficult relationship for both parties. God interprets the people's repeated backslidings as plain stubbornness.... A more sympathetic assessment would describe Israel, after centuries of enslavement, as pathologically insecure. Between humans, at least, such a relationship would be dysfunctional. It appears, however, to be the best that Israel and Yahweh can sustain,

if only by the continual, soothing intermediation of Moses. No wonder the prophets will compare the Covenant with a bad marriage! God and his people cannot live together and yet cannot live apart. (*Exodus 19—40*, 566)

In one way, this chapter is addressed to later generations. If the people with Moses had so much trouble trusting the LORD, how much more do we today have the same problem? This chapter calls us all to obedience, but also to patience and faith.

Appendix on Priesthood Genealogies

Much of the following brief summary is based on Propp's remarks on chapter 32 (see *Exodus 19—40*, 567–74).

In the Pentateuch, Historical Books, and Prophets there are indirect references to serious competition among priestly families or lines. Since the office was customarily inherited, one way to compete would be to exalt one's own genealogy or question another group's genealogy. Kings at times demoted individual priests or appointed certain ones to high office, thus contributing to the competition.

Our best current estimate is that early on men called *Levites* (possibly from a root verb meaning "attached" or "hired") held priestly positions at various shrines. These were men from certain villages or small clans where priestly skills were developed and handed down. In later tradition they were understood to be the descendants of Jacob's son Levi. There are various biblical traditions as to how Levites got selected for the priesthood by God. The Elohist has this one about executing some of the idolaters at the golden calf festival.

Centuries later, as local shrines were closed by King David, Levites were offered roles (at least part-time) in Jerusalem in compensation. The northern shrine at Shiloh housed the Ark. When David brought the Ark to Jerusalem, he installed co–high priests, Abiathar (a northerner) and Zadok (a southerner). Solomon had disputes with Abiathar and eventually banished him, so the Zadokites grew more powerful.

When the northern tribes seceded and took the name Israel, they chose to reestablish some shrines and add new priests. Jeremiah had bones to pick with some of their choices, but was also anti-Zadokite. After 597 BCE, Ezekiel favored the Zadokites and argued that the rest of the Levites should be assistants at the Temple, ineligible for the highest priestly duties.

Finally, the Zadokite line was edged out by the line from Aaron and Phineas, his grandson (Exod 6:25). Priestly editors generally favored this development. The Deuteronomists were anti-Aaron, favoring the older traditions about the Levites. (In Deut 9:20, Moses describes God as so upset with Aaron that he wished to destroy him, but Moses pleaded for Aaron's life.) The Elohist also seems to be anti-Aaron; he wrote of Jethro conducting ceremonies with Aaron present (Exod 18:12).

The biblical redactors learned to live with all these conflicting claims. They accepted the final Aaronide supremacy, but retained as many favorable stories about the older Levitical families as possible. They felt no need to whitewash Aaron himself, even though he was of the tribe of Levi and was the patron of the current prevailing group of priests. As Childs notes, in chapter 32 the story of the Levites executing the idolaters is set alongside traditions unfavorable to Aaron, who appears to be an awkward and ludicrous figure.

Appendix regarding King Jeroboam

I am also indebted to Propp's research in chapter 32 for this overview of Jeroboam's shrines (see *Exodus 19—40*, 574–82).

Jeroboam, the most important of the early rulers of the breakaway northern kingdom of Israel, set up key shrines at Bethel and Dan with a golden calf at each place, and appointed non-Levites as priests. This is recounted in 1 Kings 12. The same term *great sin* is used for this in 2 Kings 17:21 and Exodus 32:21, 30, 31.

An older rabbinic explanation was to say that Jeroboam duplicated Aaron's sin to spite Yahweh and the southern kingdom of Judah. More recently, scholars take Exodus 32 as a polemic against Jeroboam. Exodus is likely the older of the two accounts of Jeroboam's actions.

Jeroboam may have revived old but not forgotten Yahweh images. In the ancient Near East, three-year-old bulls were common religious symbols of strength, and were related to various gods. Jeroboam and the northerners may have considered themselves true Yahwists using legitimate images. In Exodus 32, the Elohist disapproved of Jeroboam's use of the calves, but he also was against the Aaronide priests, so he included negative traditions about Aaron. The Elohist may have used Aaron to represent the northern priests in general. Propp (578) concludes, "We may at least say that, just as Exodus 32 must be read in the context of ancient debates over who was a priest, so it also addresses the question of whether a gold calf is an appropriate Yahweh symbol and perhaps whether Jeroboam's secession from Davidic hegemony was legitimate."

In general, biblical authors do not distinguish clearly between polytheism and idolatry. The moment one makes a statue, even in the service of Yahweh, one is worshipping "other gods." Most scholars would doubt that Jeroboam intended the calves to represent other gods, or even Yahweh himself. They now propose that each calf represents an angel or semidivine force as a mount or pedestal for Yahweh, or as a throne support for him. Propp notes how overlapping purposes were common in polytheistic imagery:

> In the end I do not think that we can or should choose among these interpretations. Cross...reasonably comments "The young bulls were no doubt conceived as pedestals for the same god in the two national shrines [Bethel, Dan]. However, there were, we suspect, grounds for the accusation in Exodus 32:4 = 1 Kings 12:28 that the bulls of Dan and Bethel were worshipped. A god and his animal 'participate in each other,' and while the god may be conceived as enthroned or standing on the bull in Canaanite mythology and iconography, he also is immanent in his animal so that the two may be confused." Part of the perennial appeal of religious iconography—and its non-appeal for certain monotheistic religions—is the ease with which it sustains multiple interpretations. (*Exodus 19—40*, 582–83)

Childs agrees that the editor in Exodus adapted the story about Jeroboam's statues. The later editors of Deuteronomy may have been glad to have the Exodus account available as they commented further on Jeroboam. Perhaps Aaron did not see the festival and the calf as apostasy from Yahweh, yet he may have allowed others to head in that direction. Therefore, Aaron remains in this awkward and compromising position, allowing syncretism in the use of an image.

Childs notes that the editor in Exodus is "reporting and interpreting at the same time. He is reporting the events of the great apostasy, but in a manner that makes it representative of all subsequent idolatry. The theological aims of the author, far from being a disturbing secondary element, form the warp and woof of the entire narrative" (*The Book of Exodus*, 565).

The story is representative of religious disloyalty and rebellion for any generation of believers. The threat of apostasy did not end with Aaron and the people with him.

Childs concludes:

> What gives the story such a cutting edge is its penetrating insight that religion itself can be the means to disobedience. Aaron, who is the representative of the cult, is left to squirm as a dubious ally. He has no word from God and yet he tries to adjust to the situation by throwing the mantle of religion over their program for change....
>
> Then again, the story of the golden calf has found a place in scripture as a testimony to God's forgiveness. Israel and the church have their existence because God picked up the pieces. There was no golden period of unblemished saintliness. Rather, the people of God are from the outset the forgiven and restored community. There is a covenant—and a new covenant—because it was maintained from God's side. If there was ever a danger of understanding Sinai as a pact between partners, the rupture of the golden calf made crystal clear that the foundation of the covenant was, above all, divine mercy and forgiveness. (*The Book of Exodus*, 580)

Section Twenty-two:
Exodus 33:1–23

> Propp finds this chapter to be mainly from the Elohist, who seems to have blended several disparate themes into this complex meeting between Moses and God. For Childs, the various sections of this chapter have been so thoroughly edited into the main theme of reconciliation that searching for sources is in vain.

Introduction

If by the closing verses of chapter 32 God had been more lenient, it would be possible to imagine moving right from 32:32 to 33:17 or to 34:1. But that is not the case (God is still upset in 32:33–35), and we are fortunate that it is not. Otherwise we would have missed the high point of the entire Book of Exodus, the plea of Moses in 33:12–17. We can look on the first three paragraphs of this chapter—God's reluctance to go with them, the people's removal of ornaments, and the description of the tent outside the camp—as small steps that lead up to 33:12.

Fretheim assumes that the angel simply stands for God, who is the one in verse 2 who says, "I will drive out the Canaanites...." Childs sees a unity between verses 1 and 3, and judges that verse 2 has been added for continuity.

The verb in verse 6 for *stripping themselves* (*nzl*) of their ornaments was used in Exodus 3:22; 12:36 to describe the Israelites *plundering* the Egyptians of their jewelry. The people with Aaron also gave some of their jewelry as metal for the golden calf, although a different verb was used in that account.

The reference in verse 11 to Joshua praying or serving at the tent may be an indirect criticism of Aaron. Joshua was an Ephraimite, not a Levite, yet he had more important religious duties here than Aaron did. Fretheim suggests that 33:7–11 may preserve something of a pre-Sinai tent tradition. He suggests Exodus 16:10, 33–34; 18:7, 12, 19; 23:19 as hints of how such a tent may have been used in the past. Clearer references are found in Numbers 3:5–8; 11:16, 24, 26; 12:4, 10; Deuteronomy 31:14–15.

This initial command (33:1–3) to move the campsite will not be carried out until Numbers 10:27, because of the story line and the large number of laws mentioned in Leviticus and Numbers.

Questions

155. What do you learn about God in 33:1–3?
156. What do you learn about the people and about God in 33:4–6?
157. In 33:7–11, how are the people portrayed?
158. In 33:12–17, describe as simply as you can how Moses steered the negotiations. God is not a co-steerer here. He just tags along with Moses.
159. Why does Moses ignore the angel in 33:12?
160. Why is the topic of *favor* mentioned in verse 12 and twice in verse 13?
161. What does *show me your ways* mean in verse 13?
162. How bold is the remark in verse 15, "If your presence will not go, do not carry us up from here"? In 33:16, why does Moses want the Israelites to be so *distinct* from all other nations?
163. Why in 33:18 does Moses ask to see God's *glory* (*kbod*)? Is this related to 33:1–17 or not?
164. Looking at God's response in 33:19 by itself (skimming 33:20—34:8, which describe the response being carried out), how is God now steering Moses?

Conclusion

These interchanges between Moses and God in chapter 33 are striking, told in the most human terms. It will be worth reviewing some of Propp's comments here, at the risk of repetition. Propp speaks of Moses' initiatives this way:

> To my ear, at least, there is a tone of overfamiliarity in Moses' words, even disrespect. Such freedom is the sign and consequence of intimacy, and in this context a rhetorical strategy. Moses is establishing his right to hector Yahweh. Although he appears to speak querulously on his own behalf, he is really exploiting his grace with God to obtain a favor for Israel. (*Exodus 19—40*, 602)

Later, Propp describes Moses as wheedling, even bullying Yahweh into reconciliation with Israel. Moses wants God with them, not an angel. He has the audacity (Propp's term) to complain that God knows more about him than he does about God.

Propp calls God's agreement in 33:14 a capitulation; Moses wore him down. The phrase in verse 14, *I will give you rest* (*nwh*), could mean *I will appease you* (*give you rest from your pleading*) or *I will give you guidance and protection*. In 32:10, it was the verb for an offended God to say *let me alone*; here by contrast God is more forgiving, and more ready to help his people.

When Moses replies *do not carry us up from here* Propp sees it as a statement that "risks the entire people's fate."

Moses wants them to be guided by God himself, so that they can be *distinct* (*plh*) from all other peoples. This is the same verb used to describe the *setting apart* of Goshen so that flies would not go there in Exodus 8:22, and the *distinction* of the livestock of Israel (Exod 9:4) and of the firstborn of Israel (Exod 11:7). Moses is describing their unique relationship with God, which he considers the essential component of what it means to be an Israelite. They have a role to play in the salvation of the world, but first they need to try to restore their own relationship with God himself.

I think all of Propp's sharp terms for Moses—hectoring, exploiting his favor, wheedling, bullying, having the audacity to complain, risking the entire people's fate—make sense as over-statements to dramatize 33:15–16. Moses may be desperate, but he is on the right track. God's presence with them is what makes them a people; nothing else is worth fighting for, but this is worth their lives.

Fretheim notes that the final preparations (having Moses stand within a rock cleft, with God's hand shielding him until he can safely see God's form from the back) still preserve God's mystery. He concludes:

> For God to be fully present would be coercive; faith would be turned into sight, and humankind could not but believe. God's presence cannot be obvious; there must be an element of ambiguity, such that disbelief remains possible. A sense of God's mystery must be preserved. This text shows that even for Moses there is an essential mystery in the confrontation with God. (*Exodus*, 301)

Section Twenty-three:
Exodus 34:1–35

> This chapter contains mostly Yahwist and some redactional
> elements in verses 1–10, and Deuteronomistic style
> regulations in verses 11–26. These cultic regulations now
> serve as part of the Yahwist's main covenant story.
> The Decalogue is assumed to be included, as mentioned in
> the editorial remark at the end of verse 28. The final part,
> 34:29–35, is often taken as a Priestly tradition, but it
> may be the work of a final non-Priestly redactor.

Introduction

Chapter 34 continues the story from 33:17, at which point God
agreed in principle to Moses' request that God himself should lead
them up from the wilderness to the Promised Land. In this chapter, God will proclaim his name, which was part of what he agreed
to do in 33:19, but he will also solemnly agree to a covenant in
34:10. Additional covenant laws follow, and another set of tablets
is inscribed. The final story, about Moses wearing a veil, touches
on other aspects of his roles and relationships.

The command in verse 2 to *be ready in the morning* might refer
to Moses abstaining from relations with his wife, as was ordered
for all in Exodus 19:15.

In the Hebrew text of 34:5, Moses may be the subject of *stood
with him* (meaning *stood with God*) and either Moses or the LORD
could have *proclaimed the name*, although tradition holds that the
LORD did the proclaiming.

Propp takes the entire quotation in verses 6–7 to function as the
full, proper name of God. He finds a shorter example of such a
name in Isaiah 9:6. The word *name* (*shem*) in verse 5 can also mean

"nature" or "reputation." The double invocation at the beginning of verse 6, *The* LORD, *the* LORD, adds to the solemnity.

The Hebrew for *slow to anger* is that God is *long-faced*. Proverbs 14:17 has the opposite idiom, *short-faced*, meaning "impatient."

In 34:29, 30, 35, mention is made of the *skin* (ʿwr) of Moses' face *shining* (qrn). The noun *qeren* from which this verb seems to be derived usually means *horn*. The only other use of the verb in the Bible is at Psalm 69:31, which speaks of a bull *having horns*. The one use of the noun which might possibly tie these two meanings together is in Habakkuk 3:4, which speaks of the *brightness* of God's glory, and of *rays* (*horns*) coming from his hand. Rabbinic commentators also took advantage of similarities in sound between the Hebrew word for *skin* (ʿwr=ywr) and for *light/brightness* (ʿwr=awr) to try to explain why the verb means *shining* in chapter 34. Their argument from the similar sounds is not convincing to scholars. The rabbinic tradition that rays of light could have looked like horns was actually used by Michelangelo when he placed two small horns on the forehead of his statue of Moses, which is in St. Peter's Basilica in Rome.

So Propp argues that one may better translate that Moses' skin *became hornlike*; that is, that it was damaged by coming so near to God, and so had a darkened, ridged, or cracked surface that was so upsetting to others that Moses wore the veil to spare them the painful vision. Moses had been very close to God for the forty days in 24:16–18 and here for a second time in 34:28. The disfigured skin shows the price he paid to mediate the divine presence to Israel. Or it may represent the symbolic wound of a rite of passage. Propp also notes that the Priestly authors tended to slight Moses and exalt Aaron whenever they could.

While there is some justification for Propp's analysis, it will be simpler for us to stay with the traditional translation of *shining*.

St. Paul's use of 34:29–35 in 2 Corinthians 3:7–18 is extremely complex, and would not be helpful to our study of Exodus. See Childs (620–24) for a thorough analysis. Jan Lambrecht comments at length (49–63) on the passage in his *Second Corinthians* (Sacra Pagina series). Lambrecht speaks of "the sad and pained attitude on Paul's part toward unconverted Jews," which influences his use of this story from Exodus.

Questions

165. In 34:1–5, are there any new or notable details?
166. Compare the proclamation in 34:6–7 to the sayings in 20:5–6, and to the brief hint in 33:19.
167. Look at 34:8–10. Why does Moses continue to negotiate in 34:9, given what God had said in 33:14, 17?
168. Comment on the style of God's remarks in 34:10. Why are there no ratification ceremonies such as we saw in 24:1–11?
169. Why is God so pessimistic in 34:11–16? Why doesn't he urge his people to be evangelizing witnesses of the good news of monotheism? Why can't they try to convert the Canaanites from their polytheism?
170. Exodus 34:29–35 has an odd story about Moses' shining facial features and his use of a veil. In this story do we learn anything about God? Why did Moses use the veil? How do you think Moses understood this experience as he wore the veil most of the time over many years?

Conclusion

A few comments on the laws in chapter 34 may be in order. The covenant regulations in 34:17–26 have much in common with those in chapters 13 and 23. Exodus 34:19 is somewhat like 13:12, but not exactly. Exodus 34:20 is close to 13:13. Exodus 34:26 is an exact copy of 23:19. Exodus 34:25 seems to expand on 23:18. The whole collection reflects the needs of the same era when the Israelites first settled in Canaan. The caution in 34:20 not to appear *empty-handed* refers to bringing offerings at the major holy days, but the customary minimum offerings would not have been a burden on even the poorest members of the community.

The command in 34:27 to *write these words* is actually *write for yourself these words* in the Hebrew. Propp takes *for yourself* as another instance of God being miffed, as in 34:1. What was written down here were all the instructions in 34:11–26. Propp points out that in the saying in the latter half of verse 28 *he wrote on the tablets the words of the covenant, the ten words (commandments)*, the subject is God, who reconfirmed the original Ten Commandments from chapter 20 (see Deut 10:1–4).

Childs speculates that whatever laws may have been originally in chapter 34 could have been supplemented by editors working on chapters 32—34 as a larger unit. A reference to the Decalogue could have come last. In any case, there is no evolutionary scheme of higher ethics in these laws as compared to those in chapters 21—23.

However, perhaps in chapter 34 there is an emphasis on Moses' office as ongoing mediator. Earlier references to Moses' role are in Exodus 20:18–21; 33:7–11. At this point we have 34:27–28, where Moses alone has had this experience and spends another forty days with God, and then 34:29–35, which will tell us about the veil Moses used to hide his shining face. Additional passages that honor Moses are in Deuteronomy 5:28–31; 18:15–19.

At this point Moses' work is by no means completed. He will oversee the actual construction of the Tabernacle, transmit many more laws, and act as judge for several more decades.

Editing of the
Covenant Stories

By the end of chapter 34 we have seen the great reconciliation (34:10), the restoration or renewal of the covenant, and have been told that Moses continued to receive additional commandments or laws after that point. The plans for the Tabernacle have not yet been turned into actual structures, but Moses takes on that task at the start of chapter 35.

This would be a good point to review some of the theories about how the various covenant traditions have been combined over the span of chapters 19—34. I will use the analyses of Childs and Propp as guides.

Childs's Review

Childs notes that one point that has concerned many people over the years is the fact that the Decalogue of chapter 20 (and Deut 5) is not found in the text of chapter 34. Given its importance and primary position in chapter 20, and the fact that Moses smashed the original tablets, one might expect to see the Decalogue repeated at 34:11, instead of the warnings about living with the Canaanites. Further, the laws that are mentioned in 34:11–26 are then carved on the tablets (34:27–28), although they are not identical to any one block of text seen earlier in the book.

One response to this observation is to remember that chapter 34 is the Yahwist's (J) parallel account of the covenant, while the description of the covenant in chapters 19 and 24 is from the Elohist (E). In the past, some speculated that the J account was older and more primitive in content (focusing on cultic matters), and that the E account was newer and more advanced, focusing on ethical conduct. That approach, scholars dividing cultic from ethical and being more interested in the latter, is now considered to be wrongheaded. Old Testament authors never made those distinctions.

It is true that the two covenant traditions are not identical. The heart of the first covenant was the Decalogue. The Elohist version involves the people not only as witnesses, seeing and hearing from a distance, but also as active participants who confer with Moses at several key points (Exod 19:8; 20:18–21; 24:3, 7), and who freely ratify the covenant in the ceremonies of chapter 24. The one variation regarding this participation of the people comes in Deuteronomy 5:30, where Moses alone receives the additional laws we have called the Covenant Code (Exod 20:22—23:33). Scholars point to the covenant renewal ceremonies in Joshua 24 as close in spirit to the profile E has given us of the people accepting the covenant.

The Yahwist version in chapter 34 seems much simpler. Moses alone meets with God and accepts the covenant; the people meet Moses when he returns to the camp (34:30). The cultic regulations (34:17–26) are brief in comparison with the much larger body of the Decalogue and laws in 20:1—23:33. There are no ratification ceremonies in chapter 34, although one may assume that Moses (34:28) and the people (34:32) appreciate God's mercy. Childs argues that the references in 34:27–28a to writing *the words* should be taken in the broadest sense, and would include whatever creeds, commands, or case laws that make sense as part of a covenant.

A later Deuteronomistic redactor seems to have added the very last phrase in 34:28, *the ten words (commandments)*. The same person may be responsible for 34:11–13, 15–16. It is possible that the Deuteronomistic redactor was responding to some current problems with idolatry. These added fine points make the original regulations in 34:17–26 seem less original to chapter 34 than they actually were, and may contribute to the longing many readers have had to see the Decalogue repeated at this point.

Childs next brings up the subject of redaction. As centuries went by and various oral traditions were written down and assembled into larger sequences, editors or redactors would add connecting elements for the sake of continuity. These later editors or redactors generally tried to save almost everything, but they did have to make choices at times, and they had their own theological insights. So we have some early editing of J and E stories, some editing from the Deuteronomic school of thinking, some from the Priestly school, and so on.

The current prevailing theory is that the Jahwist and Elohist Exodus stories were fused together early on, prior to Deuteronomic or Priestly levels of editing. So we will speak of an early redactor of the J and E levels, and call that person RJE.

This same RJE moved 20:18–21 to its present location in order to join the Covenant Code (20:22—23:33) to the Decalogue. RJE added references to these cases to 24:3 and 24:12, as further connectors to the Decalogue.

Childs sees unity within chapter 32, assigning it mostly to J, with verses 7–14 as a Deuteronomistic unit sensibly attached to the story of verses 1–6, and an independent unit in verses 25–29 regarding the executions of the revelers. Thus Childs allows for J to have some version of the gold calf story, and some account of the loyalty of the Levites, with later additions.

Childs assigns much of chapter 33 to RJE, especially the great plea in 33:12–17. RJE also modified chapter 34 to connect it closely to chapters 32—33, even though chapter 34 had originally been an independent tradition. One way to link the chapters was to mention the blank tablets in 34:1, 4, 28a. These were then used in the restoration or renewal of the covenant. There was no need to mention the Decalogue again, since RJE had no problem with the way J's few laws in 34 assumed the validity of all of 20—24. Childs remarks that "the golden calf story follow[s] the Exodus narrative after it had received its shaping by the JE redactor [RJE]." A later Deuteronomic editor reworked the golden calf story into a polemic against Jeroboam.

However, RJE produced a larger story far beyond the individual elements of the earlier sources. He provided a theological interpretation of the meaning of the Sinai covenant that affects the entire Old Testament. For example, having the proclamation of God's name occur during chapter 34 shifts it from being a theophany just for Moses alone to being a confirmation of God's covenant relation with all Israel. The God who calls himself merciful proves it by forgiving his people for their idolatry (34:9–10). The community that treasures the proclamation is not the naïve people who say 19:8 and 24:7, but a people who know the history of their idolatry, which lasted for centuries.

Childs then looks at the veil story, allowing that it might not be from P. In some way it was meant to help explain Moses' special office as a divine mediator. The veil story emphasizes that Moses' shining face was only a reflection of God's glory. By placing the story in this form in its present position, the author has given an interpretation of how he wants the entire Sinai tradition to be understood. God and the revelation of his will stand at the center. However, Sinai is also the story of Moses, the mediator between God and Israel, who continued to function as a mortal man and yet who in his office bridged the enormous gap between the awesome, holy, and zealous God of Sinai and the fearful, sinful, and repentant people of the covenant.

Propp's Review

Propp pays attention to the final form and flow of the covenant chapters, in addition to identifying sources. He notes that the Elohist's covenant in 19—24 was first offered or "negotiated" orally, then put into written drafts (24:4, 12), and finally ratified. The trip made to the upper mountain by Moses and Joshua (24:13–14, 18b) prepares the reader for the gold calf story, at least in indicating the forty days the people waited below.

Propp provisionally assigns the gold calf story to E (not J, as Childs), and sees more of E in 33:1–6, 7–11. He agrees that chapter 34 contains the original Yahwist version of the covenant, and that RJE has edited it to be the renewed or restored covenant after the sinful gold calf incident.

Propp then asks two questions. Should we assign 33:12–23 to E, along with what precedes; or could it belong to J and what follows in chapter 34? And, secondly, could E's version of the covenant have ended with the gold calf story? One solution to both questions would be to assign all of chapter 32 and much of chapter 33 to RJE.

Let us assume for a moment that this solution is sound, and that RJE has modified J's original covenant in chapter 34 to be now a renewal of the first, broken covenant.

Propp notes that E's covenant story is much longer. Propp starts it back in chapter 17 where Moses is summoned, followed by the people. They fight the battle, with Moses holding out his arms. Then at Horeb Jethro visits and gives advice. Then we have 19—24 and the gold calf story up to 33:11, the description of the tent of meeting.

If RJE worked with these traditions after the destruction of the northern kingdom, he would have wanted to condemn any northern tolerance for calf images but otherwise support northern sensitivities. So he made two successive covenants into a drama of concord, rebellion, and reconciliation. The merger of two covenant accounts adds overlays and tensions, such as who sees how much of God how directly and when, but in general it flows well. In the combined version, the brevity of J's covenant helps it to fit well into second place in the sequence. The renewal does not need to be as elaborate as the first. Propp notes Cassuto's analogy to the ceremony of remarriage to one's own divorced, previously unfaithful, wife. That second ceremony would be kept quite simple.

We could take chapters 25—31 and 35—40 as an alternative or quasi covenant. Propp notes that the Priestly covenant traditions are almost entirely focused on the Tabernacle. The setting in 24:15–17 and the shining face story may be the only other Priestly covenant paragraphs, with brief additional references in 25:16, 21 and 40:3, 20. At times, Priestly thinking is different from that of both J and E. The P traditions discount or tone down direct, close contact between God and nonpriests, including Moses. They ignore priestly roles for Jethro or Joshua, or any criticisms of Aaron. The shining face story might be an indirect diminution of Moses (if we consider his face damaged); another slight might be that he cannot enter the Tabernacle once God's glory filled it (40:35).

At the end of the process of collecting the Exodus traditions, a final redactor (we will designate that person as RF) had to combine J and E with P. Propp speculates that RF started by inserting 19:2, which was an attempt to distance chapters 17—18 with the honors to Joshua and Jethro from the covenant starting in chapter 19. RF may have inserted the Decalogue in 20, and left 19:25 ambiguous as to who spoke the Decalogue. RF may have added the phrase *the ten words* in 34:28b, for clarification. If we consider the shining face story an honor for Moses, risking so much to see the limited vision of God from the back, that would be an argument for assigning the story to RF. Finally, RF could have split 25—31 and 35—40 by inserting the gold calf and second covenant material within.

In the end, Moses, with great effort, gets God to reconcile with Israel after the great sin of the golden calf, and in the future expiation for the people can be sought by the high priest within the Tabernacle. Exodus 34:11–26 is thus a preface to the building of the Tabernacle as well as a warning for future centuries.

In an appendix on the validity of studying theories about sources such as J, E, P, and D, and levels of redaction such as RJE or RF, Propp reviews his findings on Exodus. He works forward from the oldest material. Segments of lyric poetry, especially chapter 15, are probably very old (twelfth–eleventh century BCE). Codes, compilations, and lengthy instructions can be studied for their style, but their antiquity may vary. Some of the law cases could be much older than others. The Priestly writers could have imagined details of the Tabernacle. The Decalogue as we have it here is not as ancient as its setting.

Propp is firmly convinced of the chance that many of the Exodus stories are from the Elohist. He mentions recent scholarly uncertainties about the Yahwist levels and the greater doubts about the existence of an E level altogether, but he argues that these doubts work well for Genesis, but not for Exodus. In Exodus, Propp finds clear strata of J, E, and P, although he admits that he plays the devil's advocate for E whenever he can. Propp sets the J materials in the tenth century BCE, and E in the eighth century or earlier.

After the fall of the north, RJE blended J and E to create a national history supportive of northern Israel refugees as well as the Judeans of the southern kingdom, structuring the Sinai covenant traditions into a beginning, rupture, and renewal, in order to articulate his hope for a full national restoration. This reunion never came about; the northern tribes lost their cultural roots over the next few centuries.

Propp is quite cautious in assessing recent attempts to find various levels within the P traditions, admitting that such attempts may eventually prove themselves, but not wishing to discard the practicalities of the present system in getting everyone started in biblical study. In general, Exodus P traditions ignore the Temple of Solomon and the monarchy altogether. Propp dates P to a late monarchic or exilic time, and guesses that the priests involved may have been from one of the family lines no longer in favor.

Propp notes that J, E, P, RJE, and RF remain totally anonymous. They may well have been scribes, supported by palace or Temple authorities. Thus, much of the Old Testament was committed to writing by elites for elites (those who could read), but the texts very often criticize kings, priests, prophets, and other wealthy and influential classes. The texts appear to speak for the common man (who was illiterate). The biblical stories are populist, even if only a few had access to the written versions. Many Jewish adults had a good grasp of most major Jewish theological traditions; they felt included—they were the children of Abraham, the followers of Moses, the citizens of David's kingdom.

It is important for us to remember that redactors such as RJE and RF (sixth–fourth century BCE) had the final say. We have no other sources; all our reconstructions of J, E, and P are hypothetical. However, many contemporaries of the Redactors (people who felt included) would have been aware of the various and conflicting sources and stories. Redacting longer and longer written collections under these conditions would have been a public venture; we could call it a voluntary, sporting endeavor to assemble larger blocks of tradition, smoothing out some wrinkles but not all of them. Contemporaries would have been the first critics of any new collection, arrangement, or edition too far from the mainstream.

Those who study the Old Testament now inherit the same task of smoothing out some wrinkles but not all of them. We cannot simply atomize the biblical text as linguists or archaeologists. As fellow believers, we should try to appreciate the spiritual value of the final text, and transmit our appreciation to others. The source hypotheses can get us started. As long as we have a sense of the limitations of our hypotheses and linguistic tools, we can use them to celebrate the faith that underlies all these texts, the faith that has come down as a gift also to us.

Section Twenty-four:
Exodus 35:1—40:38

This passage is from the Priestly traditions.

Introduction

This account of the actual construction of the Tabernacle and all its furnishings differs in small ways from the original designs in chapters 25—31. We will note significant touches, but not the several small inconsistencies or changes.

Moses begins with another reminder of the importance of observing Sabbaths. Then he announces the freewill collection of metals, fabrics, oils, and so on. Those who do contribute are called *generous* (*nadib*) *of heart*. The term refers to the purely voluntary giving of gifts. In 35:10, he also calls on *skillful* Israelites to come forward to help fashion all the items. The Hebrew term for these men and women is that they are *wise of heart.*

In 38:21–31, the separate weights (in *talents* and *shekels*) of all the donated gold, silver, and bronze is recorded. A talent is equal to seventy-five pounds. In this report, the silver is from the annual tax, and that weight represents the 603,550 adult males of the camp. Most scholars find all these weights and the calculation of the population to be much exaggerated. The number of adult men matches the results of the census in Numbers 1:46, which is also subject to question by experts in ancient populations (demographers).

I recall a statistic that at the height of the Roman Empire Jewish people comprised about 10 percent of the empire, but this account of the wandering in the wilderness describes a period fifteen hundred years earlier, when the Jewish people were an insignificant fraction of the Egyptian population (and of those within its sphere of influence).

Questions

171. Exodus 35:1—36:7 serves as a long introduction to the construction of the Tabernacle, all the plans having been imparted to Moses in chapters 25—31. What do we learn about the ordinary Israelites in 35:20—36:7?
172. Exodus 39:32–43 describes the gathering of the finished materials. Do the opening and closing verses of this paragraph remind you of any other biblical scene?
173. In Exodus 40:34–38 we come to the climax of the Tabernacle account, which started back in 24:15–18. Why is this final account so brief? What do you make of the remark about Moses in 40:35?

Conclusion

Fretheim attempts to describe the belief that God chose to dwell among his people in the inner sanctuary of the Tabernacle. Christians might use terms like *real presence* or *sacramental presence* to (inadequately) explain the same mystery. Fretheim concludes:

When all is ready, God comes to dwell among the people in the completed tabernacle. The sanctuary is not simply a symbol of the divine presence, it is *an actual vehicle for divine immanence*, in and through which the transcendent God dwells. The concern for consecration and an appropriate setting for the Holy One makes it clear that *the tabernacle does not collapse presence into immanence*. The God who is present is present as the transcendent one. It is *as* the Holy One that God is present. God remains transcendent in immanence and related in transcendence.... Israel's God now dwells, with intensity and at close range, in Israel's very midst. God actually takes up space in Israel's world. At the same time the God who "fills" the tabernacle also "fills" the cosmos.... On the one hand this makes it clear that Israel's place of worship is not the only place in the world where

God's presence can be found. God cannot be so confined; God is both near and far. Yet there is no other *specific place* in creation that is said to be filled up with God; the focused choice of place by God provides for an intensity of presence that is not true of the creation generally. (*Exodus*, 315)

Answers

Section One: Exodus 1:1–22

1. The storyteller or editor is echoing some of the details from Genesis 46:8–27, perhaps to provide continuity between the two books. The point is that some centuries have passed since Jacob's family arrived in Egypt, and now the families are no longer households but tribes. They comprise a large group of people (Israelites) who could become an independent nation, as God had promised Abraham, Isaac, and Jacob.

   Verse 7 clearly echoes the blessings in Genesis to Adam and Eve, to Noah, and to the patriarchs. The Israelites are filling the land because God is blessing them, not because of their own merits.

   We have no reliable way to confirm or challenge the optimistic claim of great numbers of births in verse 7. (Demographers are certain that Hebrews then living in Egypt were at best a fairly small part of the entire population.) At this point, we should simply take the mention of high numbers as part of the vivid folkloric style of Exodus.

2. This king does not recall Joseph; he does not consider the history, talents, or other positive attributes of this subject ethnic group. He wants to have tighter control over these Israelites, even if that control entails cruelty, so that they may never join in rebellions or invasions in order to break free and emigrate. The king is being cast as the opposite of the loving God of verse 7, who is the Lord of life and fertility.

   The whole passage describes some or most Egyptians as obeying or agreeing with these policies of oppression. As with the reference in verse 7, we have no way to confirm or challenge the claims of excessive and cruel forced labor. The image of oppression is vivid, and the mention of many newborn in the midst of such travail can point only to God's design.

211

3. One could doubt that any great ancient Near Eastern king would ever have had a private conversation with two ordinary subjects, whether they were Egyptian or Israelite. It is also not clear that cutting down the number of male infants, even if it could be done this way, will have the desired effect, except perhaps in the very long run. Why not periodically sell off the surplus of slaves? Why not focus on the female infants, or on the women of childbearing age, or on the adult males, rather than the infant boys?

   The midwives' explanation, that they cannot get to the women in labor in time to carry out the king's orders, seems far-fetched (or even humorously untruthful, to us). Perhaps the story intends us to imagine that the king is naïve enough to believe them, or just fed up with their lack of cooperation, but too impatient, restless, or indecisive to punish them for their resistance.

   The storyteller approves of the midwives' love of life and their backbone; they were rewarded by God with children of their own.

4. The names of the midwives and of the buildings or cities are hardly enough to set any accurate time frame for the story. (The names of the cities vary in ancient manuscripts.) The style of this chapter is vivid but folkloric. It shows us forces of blessing and life being confronted by powers of an empire that wants to stay on top.

   Chapter 1 has important themes within it, but its main purpose is to serve as a background for the story of the early life of Moses. It has little independent weight as a set of verifiable facts about early Israelites, even if we could come close to the right century for the setting of the story. We have not any right or need to hold this chapter under the harsh light of our own penchant for accuracy or precision. The story has just begun, and we should simply follow where it leads.

Section Two: Exodus 2:1–25

5. It is most likely a mark of honor in the tradition to note that Moses was from priestly family lines through both parents. We can admire the mother for caring for Moses under dangerous circumstances, hiding the child as safely as she could and setting his sister nearby as a lookout (or perhaps the sister acted on her own).

   However, readers may still have questions. The references to the tribe of Levi may be idealizations or anachronisms, and, more importantly, there is an element of danger for Moses confined in the basket among the reeds. The river itself or soldiers or vigilantes or some animal could become a threat, and Moses' sister might not have been able to assist him adequately.

6. Most commentators agree that the traditions give credit to the princess for choosing to save this endangered child. She could have ignored the basket at the outset, or handed the Hebrew infant off to servants or soldiers for disposal. She did not need to bring him under her own care after he was weaned, nor pay for that period of nursing; nor can we ignore the possible risk to her own standing in going against the clear royal commands regarding these male infants.

   Moses' sister offers to find a Hebrew wet nurse at just the right point and in just the right way. Moses' mother successfully hides the fact that she is the child's biological mother, and later judges that he can be entrusted to the princess for a privileged upbringing within the palace. These three women, and the two midwives before them, go about protecting life while many men were enabling the king to commit greater and greater injustices.

7. One could see the princess as a wild card, helping this Hebrew child only on a whim. We could imagine her idle curiosity at the finding of the covered basket, and her instinctive, merely humanitarian pity for the baby, mainly because it began to cry. Perhaps we can say that she was

quite undecided as to her next move, and that Moses' sister did her thinking for her by the deferential suggestion in the form of a question that needed only a simple yes in reply.

The pronoun in the opening of the statement "*I* will give you your wages," in verse 9 can be translated *I myself* or *I, even I.* These forms could well point to a haughty, privileged person used to being obeyed. One could judge the nursing wages as mere petty cash in the princess's scheme of things. Perhaps she enjoyed ignoring her father's edicts or felt that they did not apply to her.

Finally, giving the child the Hebrew name *Mosheh* (rescuer) which sounded to her like *Mashah* (I rescued) might be a story that spoofs her shaky knowledge of Hebrew. Having the name *the rescuer* certainly indicates the true destiny God had in mind for Moses. The princess may well have been a crooked line that God used to write something straight, as the saying goes.

This catalogue of shortcomings is purely conjectural. There are just a few hints in the text that partially support this profile. For instance, verse 6 mentions in order opening the basket, seeing the child, the child crying, and her taking pity; there are no words to indicate that she took pity *because* the child cried, but the child's cries are artfully mentioned *before* the fact of her pity. Nevertheless, this is a good example of how complex a tapestry four or five verses can display. Whether the princess was brave and caring, or merely a headstrong wild card, she assisted in the divine plan by sparing this child and raising him as her own.

8. Despite commentators who consider this killing an overreaction in a good cause, I think that killing one cruel Egyptian in secret could hardly be part of a master plan to improve the lot of the Hebrews or to promote eventual freedom for them to leave Egypt. More likely, Moses reacted wrongly in the heat of the moment. If it had been a case of self-defense, Moses could have explained his actions publicly. Verse 12 clearly indicates premeditation and intention to deny after the fact. No matter how sincere his desire to stop the cruel

Egyptian from further injuring the unfortunate Hebrew, the violent outburst by Moses was a second wrong, which cannot become something right.

The aggressive Hebrew who responded to Moses' intervention on the next day may well have been indignant at Moses' crime, and rightly dismissive of his posture as a peacemaker or friend to the Hebrew people. It makes little difference at this point in the story whether or not any of the Hebrews knew of Moses' true ethnic roots.

Another motive may lie behind the rebuke. Should word continue to spread about the killing, Moses would soon be found out by the authorities; they might then assume that some Hebrews were in conspiracy with Moses to rebel or to resist in other dangerous ways. So having any contact with Moses now is a great risk, even if Moses is not yet aware of all this. Thus the aggressive Hebrew may well have wanted to get away from Moses as soon as possible for his own safety.

Moses then realized that his outburst and covering up had destroyed his standing in Egyptian society. Siding with subject peoples within an empire is treasonous in the eyes of the establishment. Escape to the land of Midian was the only way to survive, but it is also a stark reminder to us that violence, even when in response to great injustice, is never a cure. Moses has lost everything, the Hebrews have gained nothing, and the Egyptians have learned no lessons.

9. When Moses defended the women and their flocks, he apparently acted in a less violent manner than he had in 2:12. He was therefore not a risk to the family of the priest in any way. The priest took the opportunity to recruit Moses as a prospective son-in-law, and mention is even made of Moses' and Zipporah's first child, *Gershom*.

These events in the life of Moses did not directly benefit the Hebrews still living in Egypt, except insofar as they seem to depict Moses maturing, settling down but still longing to be with his own people. Naming his first son with a word related to *ger* (sojourner or alien) represents

Moses' own situation, living in a foreign land. Joseph had had similar sad musings on his own situation when he named his two sons (Gen 41:50–52).

10. As we come to this solemn summary of the story about the Hebrews serving in Egypt and the early years of Moses' life, the writer sounds a note of destiny, but it is centered entirely on God. God hears the cries of suffering, even if those crying out have no idea that any god is listening. Their cries may not have been prayers of petition but rather the audible fears and angers of ordinary humans (of any religion or none). Yet God honors these cries as prayers.

   The mention of God recalling his covenant with Abraham, Isaac, and Jacob is significant for believers who know the great stories of Genesis, but Exodus 1—2 has not shown us any details of the faith of the Hebrews in Moses' time, nor of Moses himself. The midwives feared God in the sense that they had the ethical and moral integrity to refuse to suffocate male infants at birth, but we do not know anything of their own personal religious concepts.

   At the end of chapter 2 no one seems ready for the call from the burning bush. The Hebrew people are locked into the lowest economic level of a massive empire. Moses himself has entered his third cultural experience, taking into account his Hebrew roots in early childhood and his shattered attempt to help the Hebrews after many years of living among the ruling class of Egypt. His days in Midian are busy, caring for his wife and son and tending to flocks of sheep.

   All this is about to change. Covenants will be honored. People will be called soon, and God's directives will change their lives.

11. There is certainly the possibility that Moses had some Egyptian roots and upbringing. Various scholars theorize that Moses may have had an Egyptian father, and that his mother may have been freely married, or perhaps a slave wife or not married at all. Another suggestion is that Moses was actually abandoned by his parents and raised by gener-

ous Egyptians. The details of Levitical ancestry, rescue by a princess, and life in a palace could be more legendary, perhaps driven by discomfort about Egyptian origins.

The story of Moses slaying a cruel Egyptian is striking. Some scholars express respect for the fact that this sinful outburst was not lost or covered over in the traditions, and that Moses was not thereby turned into a flawless saint or savior. Others do not consider the slaying sinful at all, assuming that Moses' caution in 2:12 was appropriate for that emergency.

It would be hard to prove that Moses actually fled to Midian to avoid arrest, but there is general confidence that there were early cooperative contacts between Hebrew and Midianite groups. Moses' Midianite wife and sons seem to play little part in later Jewish traditions. In scripture there are several stories about a man and a woman meeting for the first time at a well, and the watering of flocks is often a part of these tales.

Working back to chapter 1, most scholars doubt the historicity of this profile of a Pharaoh who was so cruel as to demand the death of newborn Hebrew males. The peasants, serfs, and slaves in Egypt all had to contribute to a well-run system of corvée (mandatory service on national building projects), but these assessments and required work periods were usually scheduled so that they did not interfere with agricultural and shepherding tasks. Most of Egypt's great projects were built by her own citizens, not slaves, and the stereotypical image of slave drivers cracking whips and driving unfortunates to exhaustion and dehydration can hamper our understanding of much of the Book of Exodus.

We should think of Egypt as an empire; it was the greatest power in the Near East for centuries, and had highly skilled civil servants and judges. Like all ancient empires, it was devoted to self-preservation, and the Pharaoh and the ruling class kept everyone else in line. It is certainly easy to imagine the thinking behind early Hebrew traditions—all Pharaohs were absolute monarchs; any one of them could have developed or intensified prejudices or fears regarding one ethnic minority among the lowest classes. (Note the casual disregard for life or justice in Esth 3:8–15.) Any ruler so determined had the power of the empire behind him to cause suffering and death. There would be no appeal, no chance to change public opinion. Therefore, in chapter 1 a nameless, representative Pharaoh turns cruel, and Moses' parents in desperation hide the child in the basket. The ensuing dangers and discovery by the princess were completely out of their control.

One of the purposes of chapter 1 is understandable. It *justifies* or *explains* the abandonment of Moses; it casts the Egyptian upbringing of Moses as an honorable event. The adoption is depicted as willed by God, or at least arranged by God, and there is no blame or question about his parents or lineage.

As in the answer to Question 4, we should not be concerned about historical accuracy or precision here; interest in factual details is part of our culture, not theirs. The first two chapters of Exodus serve as a background for the great story of God intervening and bringing his people out of Egypt. That story has just begun, and we should simply follow where it leads.

Section Three: Exodus 3:1–22

12. Moses seems to be very curious about the burning bush, but we might also imagine that he is drawn to the presence of spiritual forces in this unusual event. He answers when his name is called, and removes his shoes when told, as a sign of obedience or respect. His fear is understandable. Such interaction at a holy place or during special contact with divine powers is at once exciting and dangerous. Contact with the holy should induce both fear and fascination.

God takes the initiative in this approach to Moses. The mention of the presence of an angel standing in for God, the bright fire, the warning to not come any closer, and the focus on the spoken word describe divine intervention in ways that are appropriate for human comprehension. Unmediated contact would be overwhelming, and is reserved for time beyond earthly life.

13. If you read 3:7–10 aloud, it becomes quite clear that the deputizing or commissioning of Moses in verse 10 was not likely expected by him. The task given to Moses does not follow logically from verses 7–9; it is not self-evident that God would need or would wish Moses or anyone else to represent him.

    Moses' reply "Who am I..." may indicate his surprise and his humility, or it may reveal his lack of self-confidence for this responsibility. Verse 12 confirms that God will be overseeing the task, and that he wishes the Israelites to return to this same holy ground after they are freed. Verse 12 refers to this return as a sign of God's authority or power to save, but verse 10 is still in effect a directive.

    Verse 10 can hardly be called an invitation or a vocational prompting. It is a direct command, a revelation of decisions and plans already made. Moses' cautious responses in 3:11; 3:13; 4:1; 4:10; 4:13 do not bring God to any reconsideration of his original plan. Moses is going to be in the front lines in this struggle with the mighty empire that is Egypt, no matter how Moses feels about it. Childs reminds us that the pattern of the call to Moses to be a prophet or messenger is so strong in chapter 3 that we cannot simply ignore the pattern and fill in biographical details or guess at the inner psychology of Moses. For example, some have suggested that Moses was a sensitive refugee who gradually followed the promptings of his heart and decided to return to try to bring freedom to his fellow Israelites. Such ad hoc musings do not always help us to understand the faith or the thought processes of the biblical authors.

14. In 3:13, it seems that Moses (and apparently the other Israelites) does not know either God's true or correct name, or that he is asking for more understanding of who God is. These gaps in Moses' comprehension are not held

against him—it is fair to assume that the centuries of servitude have eroded some of the religious identity of these people. In ancient Near Eastern cultures, knowing someone's name was considered essential for intercommunion, and for any possibility of influence with that person. (Adam was given some of these powers of control when he named the animals in Gen 2:19–20.)

At this point (3:15) according to E traditions God reveals his personal name, *Yahweh*. (In most English translations, it is customary to replace this name with the title LORD, usually printed with small capital letters after the larger capital letter *L*. The custom developed in respect to Jewish sensitivity that the name Yahweh was best revered when not pronounced aloud.) We are assured that Yahweh is indeed the same God who made the covenant with Abraham, and who is now calling his people to new freedom.

There is a different J tradition in Genesis 4:26 that the name Yahweh was revealed to humanity before the Flood. There is no need to attempt to harmonize the two claims.

In 3:14, the name Yahweh is related to the verb *to be*. This is another popular tradition not likely to be accurate according to the standards of the modern discipline of linguistics. The verb form *'ehyeh* can mean *I am* or *I will be*, so the phrase "I am who I am," or "I will be who I will be," has a solemn, formal, even majestic resonance to it, but it still needs to be examined.

Most scholars find the Exodus context not lending itself to classical Jewish and Christian philosophical considerations of God as the source of all creation, or as the ground of the existence of all other beings. Rather, it seems that the phrase with the repetition of the verb is simply meant to be a way of reassuring Moses of God's intention to help.

Some readers will feel that the saying remains very brief, even mysterious, vague, or tangential. This might be a way to insure God's own freedom to act according to his will, perhaps to improvise as events unfold. Any further revelation of his true name could leave God open to undue influence or control by others, given the ancient cultural convictions about the essential power and vulnerability that names have in themselves.

However, in the larger context God wishes to encourage Moses and the Israelites in some way, acknowledging the honesty and humility of Moses' question in 3:13. Other reassurances appear in 3:17, 18; 4:12, 15; 6:1–8 as well as in the signs in chapter 4.

15. These instructions by God have a matter-of-fact tone to them. It sounds so simple—Moses will recount God's message for the Israelites, and then Moses and the elders will explain to Pharaoh that special worship services for the LORD need to be held in a desert area at the far edge of Egypt's borders.

The logic of the formal request to make a one-time major religious pilgrimage may be that such worship should not be held near polytheistic centers within Egypt, but the underlying plot element is that the pilgrimage will easily become a one-way march to freedom, an exodus from slavery. This request to worship will continue to be a plot element (cover story) for several chapters, even though everyone in the story and all the readers of the book know that the freedom to worship and the freedom to emigrate are one and the same within this series of arguments and miraculous signs and wonders.

16. The declaration that the Pharaoh will not cooperate, and that God will wage battle with great confidence in the outcome, does in some sense reveal the plot. Clearly, the editors do not consider this great story, ranging over fifteen chapters, to be a suspense story or an adventure that needs a surprise ending. The considerable length of the account with its emphasis on the varying emotions of the many participants will allow these two verses to be part of the artistry of the whole, and they should be judged on that basis. The next two verses also give away the outcome of the story, even though they focus on just one specific detail about acquiring Egyptian jewelry and fine clothing. This too must be under-

stood as part of the artistry of the entire first fifteen chapters. In fact, God will refer to the future often in his remarks to Moses.

17. At first impression one could feel uneasy about this reference to asking for jewelry and fine clothing. As this battle for freedom from slavery intensifies, we can think of the suffering of many ordinary Egyptians, and can imagine that their favor towards the Israelites was founded in fear. So the gifts or loans will in reality be bribes or payoffs. It should be difficult for modern readers to justify such extorting or plundering, even if commanded by God.

However, there are other literary, logical, and legal ways to approach these donations or loans. The alternatives challenge us to think corporately—to think of all the Egyptians as of one accord with the Pharaoh and the nation's policies. If we consider all Egyptians to want their empire to stay dominant, then they all supported slavery and the elimination of Hebrew infant boys. They all, men, women, and children, deserve the punishments.

So the gifts could be thought of as some sort of long-overdue back wages for the years of servitude. Alternatively, they could be seen as booty, the traditional, even legitimate spoils of war, the war that God will help his people win against their Egyptian masters. Another image is that the valuables serve as a bonus, especially useful by slaves when they are freed. (See Deut 15:13–15 for the biblical exhortation.)

Fretheim considers the favor or honor shown by the Egyptians to be genuine. He suggests that the Pharaoh's daughter and many other Egyptians did sympathize with the lot of the oppressed Hebrews, and looked for ways to end the injustices. Childs admits that such favor would be unusual, but he can imagine it as something brought about by God within this story. Cassuto considers the jewelry and clothing as showy distractions, glitz to be enjoyed by very poor people, especially the children; he does not consider the total amount of precious metal or fine cloth a true recompense or a substantial bonus.

Section Four: Exodus 4:1–31

18. Some may take this response by Moses in 4:1 (which in a way includes his prior questions in 3:11 and 3:13) as a fair question, indicating a realistic understanding of how the ordinary Israelites might feel after hearing his message. Others might see it as a statement of legitimate humility regarding his own abilities. Commentators note a pattern of undue reluctance starting to develop within Moses, as will be seen in the next few chapters. At first God does not seem offended by these questions.

As we read about the turning of the staff into a snake, we could appreciate God's power over nature, or we might find the miracle to be too small for the task. Even as believers, we do not rely much on the impact of this one demonstration for a proof of the significance of God's activity in our lives. In verses 1 and 5, *belief* is mentioned. In context, this belief must involve trust and obedience, since Moses is at the very start of his journey to meet his own people. He will not be able to carry out God's plans without their enthusiasm.

Propp calls these three demonstrations minor magic tricks, which will not lend Moses massive credibility. The first two, handling the snake and having the hand whitened with disease, pose dangers to Moses himself.

Fretheim sees God himself as unsure of how the people will react, as he gives further instructions to Moses in verses 8–9. The giving of the signs seems to go against the simple prediction in 3:18 that the people would listen to Moses. Such signs, even if respected as possible contacts with divine powers, cannot always persuade.

Childs takes the signs as confirming Moses' prophetic office, but they are not to be overused. Strictly speaking, the three were used briefly in 4:30 (perhaps only for the elders), and then the staff and snake sign was used in 7:8–12, at the Pharaoh's court. From then on, all the great plagues were each used one time, including the bloodred water in 7:15–25. Childs argues that the Egyptians are part of the focus all the way along; they are the ones who continue not to believe, the ones who defy sign after sign.

19. In verses 8–9, *belief* is spoken of three more times. Unlike 3:18 where God spoke of everyone following Moses, here God seems to expect that it will take several signs to get the people going. Changing (or defiling) some of the water of the Nile is a sign of God's power over the nature gods of Egypt, who were so closely identified with this river, the unique resource for Egypt's life and prosperity. At the end of verse 9, God completes his instructions, apparently presuming that Moses has no more doubts or need for assistance at this time.

20. The Book of Exodus depicts God developing complex relationships with everyone. God prepares Moses and Aaron for their roles, but does not need to make them sinless or superhuman. He tries to move the hearts of the Hebrew elders and of all the chosen people, with mixed results. When he gets them to start out of Egypt, others tag along (the multitude of 12:38). The public spectacle of all the plagues against the Pharaoh and the Egyptian people is meant to have life-giving effects on the Egyptians and on all the nations of the earth. God does not wipe out opposition or eradicate human imperfection; he struggles with our sins as he promised he would in Genesis 8:21—9:17.

God's reply in verse 11 is majestic and shows his determination. In verse 12 he renews his command; in the reassuring phrase, *I will be with your mouth*, we have the explicit Hebrew use of *I will be*. In the same way the verb *I will be* is used once in verse 15, along with the mention of Moses' *mouth* and Aaron's *mouth*.

Fretheim takes the greater part of verse 12 as a possible admission by God that Moses does have an impediment,

224

but the point is that God is not worried about any effects of this condition. In verse 15, God simply looks to the future, where things will go well. Cassuto is skeptical that Moses has a physical impediment, and sees God simply promising to help as needed. In any case, God responds quickly in verse 14. The mention of the LORD's anger glowing at Moses leaves no doubt that God is getting impatient with Moses' chain of hesitations.

Choosing Aaron as Moses' special, almost coequal, assistant brings honor and responsibility to Aaron and at the same time reminds Moses of his own foot dragging. God seems to have no worries about Aaron in 4:14–16. The phrase in verse 16 about Moses serving *as God* (or *as a god*) to Aaron may seem dramatic, but it makes sense. In the same way in 7:1, Moses will be described as being made *like God* (or *like a god*) for Pharaoh. These are additional examples of how much God is trying to encourage Moses to accept his role as the leader.

Given God's impatience, it is reasonable to see the choice of Aaron as a compromise, a change in plans meant to satisfy Moses, but still a compromise with its own risks. Aaron can speak effectively, and cooperates with Moses in the next few chapters, but the focus of the larger story eventually returns to Moses alone. In chapter 32, Aaron will be responsible for the disastrous incident with the golden calf. Some argue that Moses was cured of his impediment at some point, or learned how to compensate for it and became a better public speaker as time went on.

In 4:27–30, Aaron willingly went to meet Moses, kissed him, listened to all the details, and helped convince the elders of all that had happened. In a way, Aaron seems more eager to go to work than does Moses himself.

21. This brief passage shows Moses starting the trip, apparently without any more questions or self-doubts. He is told not to worry about those who had sought to punish him for the slaying of so long ago, and he feels sure enough to take his wife and children with him. The command of God in

verse 19 might be meant to stand for the entire call story so far. Certainly one might wonder how Moses felt at the start of this trip. Did he fully trust God? Was he pinning his hopes on the strength of Aaron? Was he fatalistic?

In verse 18, Moses asks Jethro for permission to take his family to visit his kindred (*brothers*, in the Hebrew text). Some commentators take this as a misleading request; Moses does not tell Jethro of his commission to unite his people and to confront the Pharaoh. Had he done so, perhaps Jethro would have been worried for the safety of his daughter and grandsons. (Two sons are mentioned in 4:20.) For all we know, Jethro may have thought that Moses was of Egyptian ancestry. Rabbinic sources imagined Jethro as very reluctant to give permission, only conceding after rounds of courteous diplomacy with Moses.

Fretheim notices the phrase that Moses wishes to see if his kindred *are still living*. Could this indicate that Moses mistrusts God, or hopes that he may not have to do all this if his kindred are long dead or gone away? John Calvin wondered if Moses was embarrassed to speak of having received this revelation and commission. Fretheim notes that Moses' taking of the staff (4:20) may indicate that he intends to cooperate with God's wishes, but we do not know Moses' inner thoughts at this point.

22. God's words in 4:21–23 jump ahead to the last plague (announced in chapter 11, brought to pass in 12:29–32). The mention of Israel as God's *firstborn son* (*bn bkr*) is a metaphor, a symbol for the entire nation. A similar image is found in Leviticus 25:39–55. The *firstborn son* of Pharaoh is a specific individual. Childs remarks that putting the metaphor and the individual next to each other is not simply a literary parallel. It is a way of highlighting the rivalry between God and Pharaoh over who has the power of life. God identifies himself as the executioner in verse 23. In Exodus 12:23b, the subordinate power who slays is called the *destroyer*. This passage in chapter 4 is a bit more detailed than the one in 3:18–20. In 3:19, God referred to

his own *strong* hand, using an adjectival form of the verb *hzq*. In 4:21, God speaks of *hardening* the heart of Pharaoh, using the same verb *hzq*. This will be a key word in the larger story of the plagues. See Deuteronomy 2:30; Joshua 11:20; Ezekiel 2:4; 3:7; 36:26; Zechariah 7:12 for close parallels beyond the Book of Exodus.

23. This brief passage throws most readers for a loop when they first read it. It seems that suddenly God is offended and decides to end Moses' life! Moses' wife, Zipporah, intervenes by circumcising their oldest son, Gershom, and touching some of the blood to Moses' genitals (*feet* is a euphemism). She calls Moses *a bridegroom of blood*, and then expands the formula to *a bridegroom of blood by circumcision*. At this point God spares Moses, and the main story continues.

    Readers might consider this episode as a reminder that circumcision was of vital importance, and imagine that Moses was at fault for neglecting to circumcise his son. Zipporah, who was not of Hebrew origin, seems to know what to do at the right time, although there is no explanation as to how she had come to this knowledge. I have heard teachers say that Zipporah might have been guessing about what to do! One teacher of mine explained the passage as an ancient advertisement for circumcision that an editor did not want to leave out, so he put it here even though he knew it would disrupt the progress of the larger story.

    Cassuto assumes that Zipporah had learned about the importance of circumcision from Moses. He points to Joshua 5:2–7, which describes the apparently uncontested delay of circumcision during the years wandering in the wilderness. He suggests that during this crisis Zipporah decided to observe the custom more strictly. She performed the ceremony on her son, committing him to the covenant, and also put some of that blood on Moses as a way of reconsecrating him to his covenantal mission. Letting the blood of the son pay for the father's sin is the logic behind verse 23, the stern warning to the Pharaoh. In verse 25, the blood of the son in some sense atones for Moses' failure to observe the custom. Therefore, Zipporah calls Moses her bridegroom again, in that his life was spared. In verse 26, the same title of bridegroom may refer to the infant, following Jewish honorific uses of this word. Fretheim applauds the initiative of Zipporah in this story, reminding us that she joins the heroic women of Exodus 1—2 (the midwives, Moses' mother and sister, Pharaoh's daughter), all of whom bravely carried out God's plans.

Childs doubts that anyone can find the underlying cause of this puzzling fragment of a story, although he admits that in some way Moses was assumed to be at fault. Childs sees verse 26b, "It was then she said, 'A bridegroom of blood by circumcision,'" as the remark of an editor regarding verse 25. Childs feels that the editor did not understand much of the detail of Zipporah's words or deeds, and in verse 26b simply classified verses 24–25 as a story related to circumcision. This editor was not trying to explain the origin or meaning of the phrase *bridegroom of blood*.

Propp takes another approach. He admits that P or P redactors might have been interested in circumcision traditions, but feels that J (our source here) was less likely to focus on circumcision. Propp returns to the fact that Moses had killed the Egyptian, and had never formally atoned for that act of violence. In Exodus 2:15; 4:19; and 4:24, the same verb *seek* (*bksh*) is used; the first two times Egyptians seek his life for that slaying, and here God seeks it. Now that Moses has been instructed to return to Egypt, some atonement must be made.

Propp is interested in the topic of *bloodguilt* for murder, as can be found in Genesis 4:10–11, which uses the plural form *bloods*, hinting at *bloodguilt*. So too in Exodus 22:1–2 and Leviticus 20:9, 11, 12. At various points in Exodus 21 and Numbers 35, the death penalty is invoked for first-degree murder, but cases are mentioned with the option of having cities of refuge to hold those guilty in quarantine or protection from vengeance by relatives of the one who died. Someone living in a city of refuge was to stay there until the death of the current high priest (see Num 35:25, 38). In some way, the death of the high priest brought about atonement or amnesty. In our story, Zipporah symbolically circumcises Moses or brings about atonement with the blood of Gershom's circumcision. In context, she may have called Moses *a bridegroom of bloodguilt*, referring to his earlier slaying of the Egyptian.

Propp also reviews evidence that ancient circumcision rites were reserved to older teens attaining manhood and marriageable rank within their clans. Only later did the custom move to the period of infancy, and become a domestic rite initiating one into the faith of the nation (rather than into the clan). Some of the older terms for adults in these ceremonies may have been retained even when the rite was later used for infants. So in 4:25–26 the term *bridegroom of blood* could refer to either Moses or Gershom. At the time when circumcision was a premarriage ceremony a title such as *bridegroom of blood* might have meant something like *a bridegroom now protected by the blood vengeance code of the family*, or *an adult now responsible for any future bloodguilt*. In any case, in our brief account of Moses and Zipporah the blood of Gershom, like the blood of the Paschal lambs, expiates and fends off destruction.

The same verb *to touch* (*ngy*) is used in 4:25 and in 12:22 (for putting the blood of the Passover lambs on the doorposts). Exodus 12:44, 48 and Joshua 25:2–11 require all men to undergo circumcision in order to share in the Passover meal.

While Propp's ideas raise more questions than answers, the advantage of his focus on the need for expiation for the killing by Moses is that it seems to fit the larger context. Moses has to learn the self-discipline and humility needed for his pioneering role as leader and lawgiver. Expiation for violence seems a weightier element of the story than the ritual need for circumcising one individual infant.

24. Assuming that everyone needed the signs, the initial reaction to the message of Moses and Aaron must have been

one of caution and doubt. So we see in Exodus 6:9. At 4:30, the storyteller (E) glosses over this point and speaks of everyone believing and worshipping. The belief spoken of is trust, not academic, theological expertise. Fretheim finds the heart of their trust in verse 31 in the conviction that God knows how much they are suffering as slaves (rather than in the small signs of his power). The next use of the verb *to worship* (*shhh*) will come in Exodus 12:27, and of the verb *to believe* (*'mn*) in Exodus 14:31. Another word play may be between the Pharaoh *refusing* (*m'n*) to let Israel go (verse 23), and the people *believing* (*'mn*) God.

The tone of these closing verses is quite optimistic. Moses and Aaron are able to persuade the elders and the people, who respond with sincere worship and hope. Exodus 4:31 is a "happy ending."

Section Five: Exodus 5:1—6:1

25. The Pharaoh's mocking response is understandable, insofar as he may have had little or no knowledge of Israelite history or religion, nor of the background or merits of Moses and Aaron, and may well have been turned off by the abrupt style of the quotation from Yahweh, with his blunt command. After 5:2, the Pharaoh will not use the word *Israel* again until 12:31; he may have avoided the title out of contempt.

Moses and Aaron backpedal a bit in 5:3. They explain that the *God of the Hebrews* had *met* them (*qrh*, as in 3:18), and this time they ask for permission (exactly as commanded in 3:18). They then add that, if the people do not get the chance to offer these sacrifices, Yahweh will strike them with epidemic or sword. This death threat seems to be a wild exaggeration; it may have been intended as a devious bluff on their part. Moses and Aaron could be hinting at the wrath of their God, a wrath that could result in the death of many of Pharaoh's Hebrew slaves, or of Pharaoh's own people during such an epidemic or outburst.

The backpedaling and bluffing were of little use. This Pharaoh does not want any time lost on building projects for his empire. He does not want Moses and Aaron *taking away* or *releasing* (*pr^c*) people from their work. This verb could easily be a play on the word *Pharaoh* itself (*pr^{c}h*).

His remark about going back to their *labors* seems to include the obligations of Moses and Aaron themselves as well as the other Hebrews; time is money, and this unusual request is simply a waste of time. This Pharaoh is not like the one in chapter 1, who feared the growing number of Hebrews.

The normal pattern of ancient Near Eastern worship ceremonies involved the adult males in good health coming to a local shrine or temple. Women, children, and the elderly would not have been under the same obligation to attend. Ceremonies often lasted just one day, with most of the meat of sacrificed animals consumed by the assembled worshippers.

26. If the distinction is correct that the *supervisors* were Hebrews, the plan of the Pharaoh is easy enough to follow. He sets the supervisors in the middle of the conflict; the supervisors have to push their own people to the breaking point, and the supervisors are beaten when the quotas are not met. Propp gives credit to the Pharaoh for being a clever strikebreaker, for setting up the supervisors as something on the order of noncommissioned officers or warrant officers with the thankless task of carrying out his plan. Pharaoh calls the people *lazy*, in verses 8 and 17, and accuses them of listening to *deceptive words*, in verse 9. Such insults put the blame on the people. So everyone's anger will be diverted toward Moses and Aaron, and perhaps also to Yahweh, the one misleading Moses and Aaron into this confrontation. Eventually God will become a strikebreaker, too. He will drive a wedge between Pharaoh and his own people, as we shall see in 9:20; 10:7; 11:3, 8; 12:33.

27. These verses repeat the essentials of the Pharaoh's commands, most likely to heighten the sense of despair being

experienced. The phrase, "Thus says Pharaoh," in verse 10 is a deliberate parody of Moses' use of "Thus says the LORD" in verse 1.

The Hebrew people are addressed directly or indirectly in verses 10, 11, 13, 15, and referred to in verse 12, but the feelings of the ordinary Hebrew people are not described. Fretheim suggests that their silence in the midst of this account is a good indicator of their suffering. The Pharaoh's sarcastic portrayal of them as lazy upstarts who want to distract themselves with an odd religious festival is not borne out here. The people do the extra tasks as best they can, even though production quotas suffered.

28. At the end of verse 16 the Hebrew has *but the fault/sin* (*ht't*) *is your people.* The NRSV has "You are unjust to your own people," following some of the paraphrases in ancient translations. Propp suggests that the meaning was *your officials are causing the decline in brick making.* (Propp imagines that they wanted to say to Pharaoh, "You are the fault.") Although the supervisors were not courageous enough to brace the Pharaoh, they have more diplomatically pointed out that the end result is less production because everyone is under stress. They call themselves the *servants* of Pharaoh three times in verses 15–16; so it is easy to imagine them calling themselves Pharaoh's *own people.* The term *servant* in this context is an honorable one, or at least not demeaning. Moses, however, never uses this term to describe his own relationship with the Pharaoh. By any reckoning, the Pharaoh is winning this struggle in the short term.

29. In verse 19, the supervisors saw that they were in *trouble* or in a *bad situation* (*r'*). In verse 21, they accuse Moses and Aaron in very vivid terms of *getting them into a bad odor* with the Pharaoh, and of *putting a sword* in the hands of the Egyptians. The same word for *sword* was found in 5:3. Clearly, verse 21 is quite emotional; the supervisors are near panic at their situation. In verse 20, the verb for their *com-*

ing upon (*pg‹*) Moses and Aaron is the same as Moses' speaking of God *falling upon* them in verse 3. In their stress they pass the blame to Moses, just as the Pharaoh had planned. Even as late as Exodus 14:12 the fearful attitude this Pharaoh put into the hearts of the Hebrews can be found.

30. Moses' plea to God is as emotional as was that of the supervisors to himself and Aaron. He asks why God has *mistreated* (*r‹*) the people, and notes that the Pharaoh has *mistreated* them also. Moses twice speaks of the Hebrews as *this* people, and at the end says, "You have done nothing at all to deliver *your* people." Moses reminds God of his own revelations when he says, "I first came to Pharaoh to speak in *your* name." Moses is obviously passing the blame to God for this mess. He probably also felt humiliated or frustrated, as evidenced by his question, "Why did you ever send me?" Perhaps Moses expected that this whole task would be a piece of cake. The resistance of this Pharaoh is in stark contrast to the happy ending of chapter 4.

    We should remember the Jewish insight that complaining to God is a valid form of prayer, even if the complaints are impolitely phrased. This emotional outburst could testify to Moses' own sincere commitment, even though at other times he had self-doubts.

31. In 6:1, God looks ahead to Pharaoh letting the people go, perhaps even driving them out of his land. Pharaoh will do this *by a mighty hand*. It is not clear if this refers to Pharaoh acting on his own or acting because he is forced by God's mighty hand. Propp favors the first possibility, although he concludes that both Pharaoh and God are involved. He notes the previous mention of a mighty hand in 3:19, which by itself could refer to Pharaoh. In 3:20, God's role is indicated. The other passage that should be consulted is Exodus 12:31–39, which seems to support the notion that in some sense the Hebrews were driven out in haste by the Egyptians. The reply of 6:1 is meant to be encouraging, even if God did not answer any of the particulars in Moses' complaint.

Throughout chapter 5 God is spoken of frequently. Moses and Aaron relay his message, and the Pharaoh scoffs at his name and his wishes. In verses 8, 9, 17, Pharaoh belittles the desire of the people for time off to worship this god. The supervisors in verse 21 call on God to judge Moses and Aaron for misleading the people; and Moses complained to God at the end. In all of this God remains silent.

We readers are outside observers, so to speak, but surely we should empathize with the ordinary Hebrew people, with their supervisors, and with Moses and Aaron, as they crumble so completely before this strong-willed Pharaoh.

Section Six: Exodus 6:2—7:7

32. A quick look at Exodus 6:2—7:7 shows many Priestly parallels and repetitions from 3:1–12 (E, J). Priestly traditions do have their own vocabulary and interests. For instance, the P title *God Almighty* (*El Shaddai*) in 6:3 echoes its use in Genesis 17:1. This is an old Semitic title often used by P writers to refer to God in their Genesis patriarchal stories, because the P tradition is that the name Yahweh was first revealed at this point in Exodus 6:2–8.

In Exodus 6:4, 5, 7, 8, the covenant with Abraham (Genesis 17, all P) is recalled, the covenant in which God promised that Abraham's descendants would someday have a land of their own. He will be their God, and they will be his people.

The P word for *groaning* (*n'qh*) in Exodus 6:5 is found in Exodus 2:24. In 6:6, the word for *slavery* is the same as in 2:23. The verb *holding as slaves* in 6:5 is used in nearly the same form, *imposing tasks*, in the P verse, Exodus 1:13. Clearly P stresses the continuity of God's relationship with the patriarchs and with their descendants up to Moses' day, as well as his intention to now free them from Egypt.

The four *I am the LORD* statements (6:2, 6, 7, 8) not only reveal Yahweh's name, but they do so in a solemn, affirming way. The repetitions amount to an oath to give the people their freedom now. Propp calls this phrase an acoustic icon; I take that to mean a holy (verbal) image blessed with spiritual or sacramental power.

33. In 6:9, the Hebrew says that the people have a *shortness of spirit*. This same idiom is found in Numbers 21:4 (describing the Israelites), Judges 10:16 (describing God), and in Judges 16:16 (describing Samson).

    The term *uncircumcised* (*yrl*) can be used in an extended sense to refer to religious sensitivity. So we find it in Jeremiah 6:10 to describe those who are spiritually deaf. In Leviticus 26:41, Jeremiah 9:25–26, and Ezekiel 44:4 it points to the spiritually heartless or faithless. In Exodus 6, Moses may be describing himself as spiritually mute, or unskilled as a speaker. The notion of a physical impediment may also be in the mix. Propp speculates that P writers may be slighting Moses to some extent by using this phrase, perhaps for not observing the custom of circumcision either for himself or for his son.

    The story of the appointment of Aaron in 6:13 is not identical with that of 4:13–16. In 6:13, there is no hint that choosing Aaron was a compromise or change in plans due to Moses' hesitations. Readers keeping the earlier account in mind might assume that Moses' hesitations are still significant, because of the immediately preceding remark about being a poor speaker, in 6:12. In this passage, God simply moves forward, firmly guiding Moses and Aaron.

34. This genealogy follows Levi (verse 16) through his son Kohath (18) to his son Amram (20). Amram married Jochebed, a paternal aunt, and they had Aaron and Moses. Aaron married Elisheba (23) and they had several sons, including Eleazar. Eleazar became the father of Phinehas (25). There is no mention here of Moses' wife or his two sons, nor of his sister Miriam or other possible sisters. The focus is entirely on the legitimate Levitical lineage of Aaron, the first high priest, and of his successors Eleazar and Phinehas. The importance of descent from Aaron is

mentioned in Numbers 3:10, and Phinehas is honored in Numbers 25, especially verses 11–13. He is considered to be the founder of the Zadokite line, one of the main priestly lines in later centuries.

35. In Exodus 4:14–16, God, who was irritated by Moses, chooses Aaron; Aaron will be an assistant or quasi replacement for Moses. Moses is to relay messages to Aaron, and Aaron will be his spokesperson (mouth). Both will be guided by God. Moses is to be *as God for Aaron*, that is, to issue the directives.

In 6:13, God appoints Moses and Aaron as a team, and there is no mention of God being irritated or impatient. They also seem to work together in 6:26–27.

In 7:1, the words are changed; now Moses will be *like God to Pharaoh*, and Aaron will be Moses' *prophet*. In 7:2, Aaron is charged to tell Pharaoh to let the Israelites go. Commentators wonder if in 7:1 P considers the priestly role superior to that of prophet, or if P is legitimating the prophetic role by so naming Aaron. Moses and Aaron obey this new set of instructions fully (7:6), in the closing summary of this section. Given the complaint of Moses in 6:30 that he is still a poor speaker, one could consider Aaron as a more important member of the team now, no longer just an assistant. Fretheim sees the charges given to Moses and Aaron in chapter 7 as an example of authentic, extensive delegation from God, and a form of self-effacement on God's part.

36. In this sequel the signs of 4:30 to the people (snake, white hand, bloodred water, as described in 4:1–9) will now be reused for Pharaoh. The demonstration using the snake is found in 7:8–13. Then the bloodred water as the first major plague will occur in 7:14–25. Propp argues that the sign of the whitened hand may have been transferred to the sixth plague (9:8–12), but we will come to that later.

We could look on all of this sequel (minus the genealogy) as a time for God to give Moses and the Israelites more encouragement. The people are still down (6:9).

Moreover, the sequel could simply be looked on as adding to the suspense or the solemnity of the story. The Pharaoh is riding high at the end of chapter 5. He and his people need to be confronted more forcefully. In this sequel, God speaks more plainly about getting the Hebrews out of Egypt (see 6:6, 8, 11, 13, 26, 27; 7:2, 3, and especially 4). God's instructions to Moses and Aaron (6:13; 7:2) are now *commands* (*zwh*), and are to be fully obeyed (7:6).

One thing that almost gets lost in this editing process of putting the P traditions after the story of the bricks and straw is the P tradition that the name Yahweh was revealed for the first time in Egypt. Set in this sequence, the story of the burning bush predominates, and the revelation of the name in chapter 6 seems to be no more than a reminder.

In this sequel, 6:12 and 6:30 are not simply echoes of 4:10. The two pleas, in spite of the greater involvement by God and his stronger confirmations of Aaron's role, make Moses appear all the more weak-willed or cowardly.

37. In the next several chapters three key words describe the Pharaoh's stubbornness. One is that God will *harden* (*hzq*) his heart (4:21). Propp suggests that it would be better to translate *strengthen* for *hzq*, although the NRSV does not. Propp argues that *hzq* means to "embolden," but not to make someone "more cruel."

Another Hebrew verb for *harden* (*qshh*) is found in 7:3 and 13:15. A third verb, *kbd*, will also be used in these chapters. Propp suggests using *made firm* for *kbd*, although the NRSV does not. (The NRSV uses the same word *harden* in all these cases). The root meaning of *kbd* is to "be heavy" or to "make heavy," as Moses used it in 4:10 to say that he was heavy of lips and tongue.

The reason for so many different words is partially due to the different sources. J uses *kbd*, while P and E use *hzq* frequently. P and E each use *qshh* once, in 7:3 and 13:15 respectively.

While it is too early in our study to analyze this stubbornness, we should indicate briefly the basic ideas, since the topic is so essential to the story. In 3:19, God foresees that Pharaoh will not let them go, and in 4:21 (E, E redactor), God said he would *harden* (*hzq*) Pharaoh's heart and make his firstborn son suffer the consequences. P continues this theme of God *hardening* Pharaoh's heart in 7:3 (*qshh*). The thrust of 7:3–5 is that because of God's coming victory the Egyptians shall know that *I am the* LORD.

Fretheim indicates that God's public rescue of the Hebrews will be a demonstration of his creational purposes for the entire world. These mighty acts will be public acts of justice, worldwide moral object lessons. Childs sees the Egyptians' coming to know of the LORD as an extension of the Hebrews' coming to know him. The mighty acts are a great act of revelation, showing God's purpose for all humanity for all time.

Propp takes a darker view of God's role, that he pushes Pharaoh over the brink. Propp notes that "while people are often spontaneously evil, God may encourage or tempt them to err, until they become so wicked that his own attribute of justice compels him to destroy them. In other words, God ensures in advance that the wicked deserve their fated punishment. He may be just, but he is not necessarily fair" (354).

I think 7:1–5 describes God as wanting a great, even protracted, public showdown. His reasons are not explained at this point. For that matter the character and motives of the Pharaoh are not yet fully developed. We do not know in what sense he may represent forces beyond the collective will of his own people, or beyond his own personal will to survive and dominate. We need not agree with Propp at this early point in our study.

Section Seven: Exodus 7:8—11:10

38. Relying on these six verses alone, we do not have enough to judge the story of how miraculous or nonmiraculous the Egyptian staves and cobras were. As believers in one God,

we assume that no Egyptian could have done anything identical to the sign by Aaron, but what they did was enough to satisfy the Pharaoh. We have to leave the question open for now. Moses and Aaron had taken the initiative, and the Egyptian priests had to try to match the sign, as their Pharaoh wished. To us, when Aaron's cobra consumed the rest of them, the greater power of Yahweh is striking. Yet the Pharaoh did not accept this display of force, although it is much too early in this account to understand clearly his motives. It is fair to note that even for believers any one sign from God can be of limited effect as a motivator. The signs of 4:2–9 helped the Hebrew people, but only for a while. By the end of chapter 5, the people and Moses were wailing in panic, and completely unsure of God's concern for them.

39. Apparently the priests are satisfied that duplicating the sign by turning more water bloodred, as Aaron had done, cancels the religious significance of the power of the Hebrew god. Now all the Nile water has become red and unusable; the result is that ordinary Egyptians have to scrounge all the more for clean water. Rabbinic traditions mocked the priests' production of more unusable water as counterproductive.

    The Pharaoh may share the satisfaction of his priests, or he may feel humiliated and frustrated, or he may have simply retired to the security and luxury of the palace and ignored his own subjects. The storytellers do not speculate on what the Pharaoh was thinking at this point.

40. Pharaoh makes his heart heavy amid great piles of stinking, dead frogs. His own priests had brought some (perhaps half) of the frogs on the scene by their own interest in duplicating another sign. Ancient rabbis could not resist the opportunity to make fun of this pointless way of competing. During this entire episode, we have had several vivid images of myriads of frogs in ovens, bowls, courtyards, and bedrooms. Pharaoh had asked Moses and Aaron to pray to Yahweh to remove the frogs, and had agreed to

let the people make their sacrifices. Pharaoh's request for mediation by Moses and Aaron and for mercy from God seems believable and realistic—Egypt had just experienced a second severe disruption of the life-giving processes of the Nile. We can presume that the dangers to public health, and the discomfort caused by the frogs, were as serious as the previous discoloration and fouling of the water and aquatic life.

As that next step was taken by Moses, and by God, we read of the orderly details concerning the times for the frogs to retreat, and for many of them to die. This lulls readers into assuming that Pharaoh will keep his part of the bargain.

Again, we see the Pharaoh revert to an unyielding stance. Pharaoh's request for mediation was either totally insincere, or so short-lived as to be useless. The Pharaoh seems to have considered the *respite* to be a cessation of hostilities, but we know that the next plague is close at hand. (The word for *respite* is rare, only occurring elsewhere in Lam 3:56.) Perhaps the Pharaoh thought that his priests were breaking even, in some sense, in these contests with Moses.

41. At the end of this story about the plague of gnats, the priests are willing to admit that Yahweh is more powerful than the forces they serve, or that Yahweh can thwart their spells in this case. Reading between the lines, the priests were counseling the Pharaoh to yield or to negotiate, but the heart of Pharaoh *hardened* (*hzq*) again. The NRSV continues to translate that "Pharaoh's heart was hardened." The story continues to shed no light on the motives for Pharaoh's decisions beyond these standard phrases about his hard or heavy heart. He remains stubbornly independent, despite the anxieties of his priests.

42. This episode is told in fits and starts. The opening speech is long and slow, describing how the flies will come, where they will invade, whom they will horrify, and how the

Hebrews will be spared all this. There is no mention of the Pharaoh's initial reaction nor of any dialog with Moses. Suddenly the flies are everywhere. Under this stress, the Pharaoh suddenly gives a limited permission to have sacrifices, but Moses has a new objection about Egyptian persecution for offensive rites. Again, the Pharaoh concedes and listens to a warning not to renege at the end. His final refusal, after the flies have been removed, seems nearly incomprehensible in the larger context.

In this episode, the Pharaoh did not get much beyond reacting to events; he made reluctant last-minute concessions instead of designing serious negotiations. He made no move to grant protection or immunity for the Hebrews against the bald claim of Moses that his people would be stoned if they worshipped within the land.

43. At first glance, one might consider that the bloodred Nile water, and the frogs, gnats, and flies were in effect nuisances or inconveniences. However, they were more than that; the fish in the Nile died, and the millions of frogs and insects must have stressed the health of many Egyptians and their livestock.

    The Pharaoh has been beating his head against this wall, and in 9:1–7 he continues to be madly defiant. This time Moses' message is that all Egyptian livestock will be laid low. The only new detail—that the Pharaoh investigated to verify the safety of all Hebrew livestock—confirms for the readers what the Pharaoh knew and when he knew it, but sheds no light on his refusal to budge. In this episode, the Pharaoh does not even try to renew the negotiations held at the plague of flies (8:25–28).

44. The storytellers may have found some of the details humorous, and they ignored some logical points. Here, for example, the animals that developed the boils could not have been the same ones who died in 9:6.

    The plague of boils focuses mainly on the suffering of the Egyptian people. This brief account gives us information but no insights. Even if a modern culture had such a plague story about Nazi soldiers in World War II or about more recent terrorists, it seems inhumane to image such disease falling upon children, the elderly, and infirm, or other innocent civilians. As we admit to our discomfort with such a passage, we must withhold judgment as to the intentions of the ancient storytellers. A theological analysis should only be proposed when the entire Book of Exodus has been fully studied as a statement of faith.

45. As we read these stories of disease and boils upon people and animals, and of a furious hailstorm that endangers human, animal, and plant life, the Hebrew word *eretz* has multiple meanings. Ideally, the *ground* sustains life, but it can also be made into an arena of death as God pounds this great empire, while sparing his people and flocks in Goshen. Yet the same God speaks of no one like himself in any *land* (verse 14), and of showing his power and name in every *land* (16), and of all the *land* everywhere (29) being his.

So the Creator of all that is good, the one who brings life-giving rain and life-bearing plant seeds, and all birds and animals and fish for food, must want a world of harmony with nature for all of his creatures. Showing his power and battling sin, injustice, and oppression must somehow lead to life-giving benefits in the long run for the whole world.

46. When Pharaoh says he is in the wrong *this time* (verse 27) it could be an indicator that he is waking up to the impact of all his stubbornness. Or it might mean that he is in denial about all the previous episodes, but is now terrified at the hailstorm.

Likewise, he admits, "I *and my people* are in the wrong." This could indicate an appropriate sense of unity on the part of the Pharaoh (or in the mind of the storyteller). However, mentioning his people might rather be Pharaoh's way of spreading the blame. He has not spent much time worrying about the suffering of his people in these last few chapters.

47. The three verses in 9:34—10:1 come from two different sources. The first and last, using *kbd*, to *make heavy* are from E, while the intervening 9:35 is from P, using *hzq*, to *harden*. Exodus 9:34–35 clearly places the blame on Pharaoh and some of his officials; they renege the moment the hail stops, and they will not let the Hebrews leave. However, at the end of 9:35 we are reminded once again that God had spoken beforehand through Moses about this very level of defiance by Pharaoh, and in 10:1 God says, "I have made his heart heavy, and those of his officials, in order that I may show these signs of mine among them." These two elements completely contradict what had just been said.

As we try to learn more about God's plans for the world, we cannot ignore the topic of the Pharaoh's free will, nor can we ignore the fact that we are puzzled by God's drumroll of catastrophes for the Egyptians, their animals, crops, and land. The writers and editors of these three verses, and of the several prior references to the hardening of the heart, must be working toward another way of explaining God to us, and they have not yet completed the task.

48. This is a very easy question to answer. Everyone is getting more melodramatic! God speaks of the Hebrews' grandchildren one day hearing the stories of how he *made fools* of the Egyptians so that everyone can learn that he is Yahweh. He berates the Pharaoh for not *humbling himself*. He promises so many locusts that *no one will be able to see the land*.

Moses defiantly demands that everyone go on the pilgrimage, *young and old, sons and daughters, flocks and herds*. The Pharaoh does not give the broad permission he had briefly offered and taken back in 9:28. Here he asks *which ones are to go?* Then he drops any pretext of full cooperation by his remarks in verses 10–11 about holding the little ones as hostages, and letting only the men go. He mutters about their having an evil purpose in mind. His firm "No, never!" in verse 11 dissolves into special pleading in verses 16–17, where he talks about doing wrong

(sinning) against God and against Moses. He begs for forgiveness from Moses as well as from God.

The Pharaoh's advisors go much further than the priests
who spoke of the finger of God, or than those who quietly
sheltered their servants and livestock in 9:20. The advisors
declare Moses to be a trap or snare, and boldly ask the
Pharaoh, "Do you not yet understand that Egypt is
ruined?" By implication, the Pharaoh may be giving in to
their demands when he has Moses and Aaron brought back
to talk to him in 10:8.

The storytellers lavishly portray hordes of locusts, black-
ening the land in their mass, eating every plant leaf, fruit,
and tree. At the end, the wind that took them away took
every last locust.

49. Pharaoh obviously wants to hold the flocks as hostage to
ensure that the Hebrews would return after their pilgrimage. In most Near Eastern religions, the animals needed for
sacrifice would only be an insignificant percentage of the
total cared for by a shepherding tribe or clan. This attempt
on Pharaoh's part to negotiate is selfish, but it is also a reasonable perception of what the ceremonies should require.
His earlier assumption that only the men needed to go was
equally reasonable.

Moses could have agreed to take just a few animals, but
we know that the pilgrimage will really be the escape or
emigration long hoped for. His excuse, that the animals for
sacrifice can only be selected at the last minute, is a bluff,
as were his ploys in 8:26–27 and 10:9.

50. The variations and repeating pattern of the introductions to
each plague do not have any significant effect on the stories
of the plagues themselves, and most readers would likely not
even notice them. They did have a purpose long ago, when
most of these stories were part of an oral culture. Preserving
lengthy oral traditions demands high art forms, complex
poetry, and other rhyming and memorization schemes, in
order to maintain the integrity of small units of tradition

and, even more, to connect small units into larger sequences. Many of the Genesis and Exodus stories were preserved in oral form for centuries before any of them were written down. One easy example to note is the mention of the female slave in Exodus 11:5 and the prisoner in the dungeon in Exodus 12:29. Each verse has preserved a saying that was originally poetic or dramatic; such vivid phrases are easier to memorize and to pass on to the next generation.

51. The pairs, and their sequence, may also have developed as aids to memorizing oral traditions. The five pairs follow a simple logic: The first two plagues involve the Nile, the next two cover the whole land, the next two involve cattle (and people for the boils), the hail and locusts destroy mostly plant life, and the darkness could be easily associated with the deaths of the firstborn.

    We could also see the second in each pair as a more intense instance of God's power. The frogs could be seen as more invasive than the bloodred water; the flies more dangerous than the gnats, the boils more stressful to people than the suffering of the cattle, the locusts destroying any plant life that survived the hailstorm, and, of course, the deaths of the firstborn worse than any sandstorm or darkness. Note Exodus 9:31–32; 10:5, 15, which specifically mention that some vegetation survived the hailstorm but not the locust invasion.

52. The four accounts of plagues in the Priestly tradition (and the contest of the cobras) seem to be low-keyed. None of the effects were insignificant—the priests' cobras are consumed, the water and frogs defile the land, the gnats did their biting, and the boils were painful and disfiguring. But none of the effects were fatal. In all of the P accounts, Aaron is mentioned and the Egyptian priests compete, until they fail to make gnats and are blemished by the boils. At that point, the Egyptian priests can no longer perform their public duties.

The P plague stories end simply with references to the Pharaoh *strengthening* his own heart (except in 9:12 where God *strengthens* Pharaoh's heart). The same vocabulary and style can be found in the P redactorial verses in 8:15b; 9:35; 10:20; 10:27; and 11:9–10. (Only in 11:10 does God *strengthen* Pharaoh's heart.) Moses does not preside over the final details in these P texts.

The P accounts and P redactorial inserts show God controlling the Pharaoh in the period leading to the final climax at the Passover meal.

The stories from the Elohist (larger segments of the bloodred Nile water and frog plagues, and the accounts involving the flies, pestilence on cattle, hail, locusts, and the deep darkness) are longer, and the plagues are more burdensome or deadly. Moses is more prominent in bringing some of these to a conclusion. In general, the E stories seem to portray God's immense power over natural forces as though each specific plague would smash Pharaoh and all of Egypt right away (even though Pharaoh somehow staggers on toward the next episode).

Section Eight: Exodus 12:1—13:16

53. It is not difficult to imagine this as an annual sacrifice for some common purpose, such as celebrating their role as shepherds, or seeking protection for their flocks, which bear their new lambs just weeks before the challenging move to summer grazing grounds. It could have originated in nomadic or seminomadic (farming and shepherding) societies, perhaps from a time before Moses. In 12:2, the time of Passover in March or April is now elevated to the first month of the year (*month* can also be translated *new moon*). Propp describes at length the various calendar systems in the ancient Near East. Some were based on agricultural practices and often started the new year in the fall, within the lunar month nearest to the autumnal equinox. Rosh Hoshanah, although mainly a postbiblical holy day,

developed from this system. The great Day of Atonement, Yom Kippur, occurs ten days later.

Other systems set the new year in the month nearest to the spring equinox. Passover takes place at the time of this full moon, on the fifteenth of this first month, but the animals are selected and sequestered on the tenth. The first ten days of this month came to be used for intercalation (to realign lunar and solar calendars, in somewhat the same way that we add February twenty-ninth every four years to our solar calendar). In most ancient Near Eastern cultures, the time of the new year (spring or fall) did not have significant secular celebrations comparable to our own; there were too many varying local customs to allow focus on an abstract, geophysical point of time.

Male animals were not required in all animal sacrifices, but may have been preferred at times by priests designing ceremonies. Year-old males were expendable since herd management always involves selective breeding. Younger males would perhaps not be thought tarnished by work or breeding of their own. They most likely were held for the four days to determine their health and wholeness.

The blood was sprinkled on the dwelling doorways before nightfall, the time of greatest physical and spiritual danger. A doorway is the boundary point, the point of risk of invasion by evil spirits against the family within. In some cultures, leaven was considered to be an impure substance. Unleavened bread was required at all Jewish sacrifices, and is often baked for convenience and time saving even now. Many local herbs or greens had a tangy or bitter flavor, and eating them at this time may easily have been associated with their bitter slavery in Egypt (Exod 1:14). The prescription to roast the animal in whole form may stem from several notions. Raw meat usually contains blood and fat, both of which were burnt at sacrifices rather than consumed. The blood was avoided because of the life forces within. Roasting would sear away these elements, and in a way parallels whole burnt sacrifices. Roasting the whole animal on a spit or wrapped in leaves kept its shape intact, perhaps representing their flocks in some way, or recalling the simpler style of meals of true nomads. Some of the parts, such as the head and certain inner organs, were to be roasted but the text does not command that they be consumed.

Eating the meal the same night, and burning all leftovers, makes the meal and the time more special; the sacred character of all of it is enhanced. Leftovers eaten later could detract from the unity and the sharing in worship. Eating the meal in haste may be a logical imitation of the first Passover, and not a gross violation of etiquette, but it is not a realistic expectation for future centuries. Later Jewish commentary encouraged eating the meal at leisure. Current Passover meals have many specially prepared touches; if one family member rushes to finish, he or she can count on disapproving stares (or worse) from the cooks.

The two rules in 12:1–11 that did not endure were this matter of eating in haste, and the sprinkling of blood on the doorways. By the first century of our era, a major change had occurred; all the Passover lambs were sacrificed at the Temple in Jerusalem rather than in the villages and towns, and then eaten by the families in Jerusalem or immediately nearby.

54. The *judgments* of 12:12 were hinted at in 6:6. Now the LORD will humiliate the divine powers of Egypt by breaking that nation's grip on his people. The sprinkling of the blood on the houses is a way for the Israelites to participate in their own rescue. We could consider it a command to test their obedience, and an opportunity for them to be rewarded for their faithfulness. The Priestly traditions tend to use abstract nouns like *destruction* (*mashit*) in 12:13. The exact same form of the verb *shht* can be translated *destroyer*, as it is used by the Elohist in 12:23.

In the present context, these two verses, 12–13, are the reason for the instructions in 12:1–11. Since the feast is called *Passover*, and the verb *pass over* is used in 12:13, most readers would assume that all this is about to happen for the first time. They would not question the inner logic or possible antiquity of any of the ceremonial details at the beginning of the chapter; the details seem to be God's direct revelation in conjunction with his intention to slay the firstborn of Egypt.

55. This paragraph is presented as the direct, revealed wish of God. The observances involving leaven constitute a *festival* (*hag*), an event that almost always involves pilgrimage. (The word survives in Arabic and is used for the annual Moslem *haj* to Mecca.) The first and seventh days are special days of rest, except for the normal preparation of meals. We could say that the Israelites are starting a great pilgrimage from Egypt to their Promised Land, but in context, they are not able to observe actually all the rules for seven days at this point; future generations will follow the directives in full. The wilderness generation will rely on manna; Deuteronomy 29:6 notes that they did not eat bread all their years in the desert.

There is considerable emphasis on removing *all* supplies of old leaven, as well as having all believers eat only flat breads for the seven days before using new or starter leaven for the coming year. Leaven was considered dangerous, or at least bordering on the unnatural. A resident alien might be eligible to share voluntarily in the Passover meal, but he is fully obligated to follow the rules about removing leaven. Severe prohibitions about keeping old leaven speak of violators being *cut off*. This punishment might mean disgrace or banishment or at least some sort of priestly disapproval. Propp suggests that the phrase indicates an expectation that God will diminish the life span of the violator, or deny him descendants, land, and remembrance by posterity. Similar images come to mind when reading Leviticus 20.

It appears that the festival and the prohibitions against leaven are of major importance, at least as important as the Passover meal that got them started. The Unleavened Bread festival might have had ancient roots, even though now it is joined to the story of the death of the firstborn and the escape from Egypt. The narrative connection, the bread dough disturbed at the time of departure (12:34), is seen by many as an improbable folkloric device to tie the Unleavened Bread festival to the Passover story. Eventually the observance of this seven-day ban on old leaven no longer involved pilgrimages but was restricted to the home, while the opposite happened to the Passover meal, as was just mentioned in Answer 53.

56. In this passage from E, Moses himself is the lawgiver. We might guess that the *elders* led larger groups (rather than single families) in this ceremony, but this is only a possibility. Each family is to stay indoors all night; Propp notes that this makes the home a temporary sanctuary, a holy and safe place. Brushlike bunches of *marjoram* (less accurately, *hyssop*) are to be used to *touch* or *apply* the smears of blood to the houses. This verb is used in Exodus 4:25 and Isaiah 6:7 to refer to very specific acts of purification, and is not one of the usual words used for sprinkling blood. Propp notes that using the branches prevents the elders or heads of the families from actually being in contact with the blood itself (taking that as a priestly privilege). He notes that basins (verse 22) are often used during sacrifices to catch the blood, and that there are historical testimonies to sacrifices being done right in doorways so that the blood does not have to be moved at all. There is some alliteration in verse 23 with the LORD *passing over* (*pasah*) the *door* (*petah*). In the same verse, the *destroyer* is an angelic or personified agent of God himself. E notes the importance of explaining all these observances to the children in each generation, and in replying to the children E refers to the *Pesach* as a *sacrifice* (*zebah*), even though the slaying was not performed by priests (verse 27).

The E account in this section is more matter-of-fact, and much less solemn than the divinely revealed laws of 12:1–13. The E passage does not limit itself to Priestly concerns.

57. The prisoner and the slave woman each represent the lowest classes, who suffer losses of firstborn just as does

Pharaoh himself. Stylistic variations of this sort usually point to oral traditions. In this passage, we assume that the Pharaoh is now broken in spirit, but he will come looking for more trouble in chapter 14. His permission in 12:31–32 to go and worship (with all the people and flocks) may not be the same as a permission to emigrate. When he spoke to Moses and Aaron that night, it may be that he went to their camp, and called to them from outside their tent or dwelling. His request for a blessing does not reveal much of his inner thinking to readers; it may simply be a plea for an end to the plagues. In verse 33, (all) the other Egyptians do want the Israelites to emigrate, and the sooner the better. They seem to have more backbone here than they did in 10:7, where they briefly argued with Pharaoh but then went silent, or in 11:3, where we were told that the people held Moses and the Hebrews in favor. Now they are *stronger* in their desire to have the Israelites leave, just as the Pharaoh had *become stronger* in opposition earlier, either by himself or by God's design.

58. We cannot say when the Hebrews actually took possession of the jewelry and robes, but the verb forms indicate that it had already happened. The editors have seen fit to mention it now, during this night of nights, this chaos of death, devotion, and departure. The image adds to the excitement of the Exodus. The Yahwist tradition is firm in speaking of *taking plunder, booty,* or *prizes of war* (*nzl*).

   Propp suggests that elements of the story of the plagues could have been commemorated by later generations using humorous settings, even children's games. He ties this conjecture to the reference in 3:22 to adorning sons and daughters with the Egyptian jewelry and clothes. This may seem odd, but there is a parallel in festive synagogue celebrations of the feast of Purim, the story of Esther and Haman.

   Childs reviews classic explanations that the acquired jewelry and robes should be seen as back wages or a start-up bonus for newly freed slaves. Others have tried to explain in what way the favor of the Egyptians could have been

251

completely free and sincere. Childs points out that the verb for *asking* (*sh'l*) in this chain of references (3:21–22; 11:2–3; 12:35–36) is also the only Hebrew word for *borrowing*. Hence the problem that the Hebrews have been seen as borrowing under false pretenses, with no intention of returning the valuables. Childs finds all the mitigating explanations unprovable, and says that we should just live with the notion of plunder.

Exodus 12:33–39 depicts the disorganization of the departure, understandable on many levels—the panic of the Egyptians, the massive numbers of Hebrews (impossibly high numbers according to historians), the Passover ritual the same evening, and the camp followers and herds. The *mixed crowd* must have included Gentiles (other peasants or slaves, Egyptian or foreign). No reason is given for their joining in this mass migration, but it is easy enough to imagine them being of like mind, and wanting their own freedom or chance to escape poverty and oppression. Propp theorizes that no one had prepared provisions because they had never really trusted Moses and the LORD to come out on top!

59. Exodus 12:40–41 gives us exact dates, and confidently speaks of Israel's *armies* or *brigades* (*sabaoth*, commonly *hosts* in English). The second passage, verses 43–51, gets into technicalities of who will be eligible to share in Passover meals, and who will not. Circumcision is necessary in all these cases. The ideal of having one law for all, and there being complete obedience to that law, is put forward in a confident manner. The second mention of the *armies* of Israel ends the chapter.

Unity of purpose is the main theme in all this. Eating the meal with the family is important, and the rule of not breaking any bones of the lamb is restated. Propp suggests that keeping the roasted lamb intact might signify the identity or unity and safety of family, flocks, or nation.

These verses supplement the ones in 12:1–13, since both passages are in the Priestly tradition. The clarifications in 12:43–49 concern life in Israel centuries after the time of Moses.

60. Exodus 13:1–2 is a brief, undetailed law given directly to Moses by God; it is obviously from the P traditions. Little information is given about the firstborn in question, nor is their consecration explained to the reader. Propp points out that many ancient peoples offered firstfruits or firstling animals in worship, and that in nomadic cultures the oldest male child inherited leadership and priestly roles. So the honor given to firstborn males in the Old Testament may stem from pre-Israelite antiquity.

Exodus 13:11–16 contains further regulations by Moses. This Elohist strand identifies the firstborn in question as males. This leaves out any newborn boy with an older sister by the same mother. A man who has more than one wife might have more than one firstborn son.

Firstborn male animals are to be *set apart to the* LORD (verse 12). The Hebrew verb means to "pass something along" or to "transfer something." The mention of donkeys in verse 13 brings up the subject of unclean animals, which are not allowed to be offered in sacrifice for any reason. Donkeys may be a special case here, or perhaps they represent all unclean animals. Apparently, one may redeem a donkey by substituting one sheep in sacrifice, and firstborn boys should be redeemed the same way. Verse 13 speaks of killing a donkey if one does not redeem it, but donkeys were worth many times their number in sheep. As the reason for the custom is explained in verse 15, a parent is to reaffirm that consecration means that these firstborn male animals are to be sacrificed, and firstborn sons are to be redeemed.

Scholars dispute the actual practice of these regulations. They note Leviticus 27:27; Numbers 3:47–51; 18:15–16. In these passages, a small monetary donation may be made for the redemption, and Numbers 18:15 does not seem to envision the option of killing an unclean animal. Consecrating firstborn males often involved blessings, prayers, and small donations rather than sacrifices.

61. The first passage, from the P traditions, was told to Moses. The Elohist contributed the idea (12:34) that everyone's unleavened dough had to be hurriedly carried along with everything else in the great departure, and that simple unleavened flatbreads (*mazzot*) were made as best as could be (12:39). The E traditions continue in 13:3–10, now telling of Moses' instructions for the seven-day festival. The redactors were not concerned to avoid all repetitions in religious rules or regulations, nor even to eliminate serious discrepancies that developed over time. Their concern was to save in writing as many of their holy traditions as they could.

    If putting a sign on hand and forehead in 13:9 is to be taken literally, Propp notes the suggestion of some that perhaps smears of dried blood from the Passover lambs were applied. Propp offers another suggestion, translating somewhat differently—that in 12:34 the (leavened) dough *had not yet risen*, and, having been manhandled in the turmoil of departure, the dough fell, and so in 12:39 the people baked the dough *as mazzot, because it had not risen*. These are no more than conjectures, but the E passages about the festival of Unleavened Bread are closely tied into the narrative of the Exodus, whereas the Priestly laws in chapter 12 are cast more as divine revelation.

62. When one reads sixty-three verses that wrap around a paragraph only four verses long, the larger set of verses should have the greater impact. That is certainly the case here. The opening cascade of divine regulations about preparing the lambs and baking unleavened bread is a complete, almost disorienting change of topic, pace, and scope from what had taken place up to that point. Some of these rules have to do with the land of Israel centuries later. The brief allusions to the tenth plague in 12:12—13:27, and the event itself in 12:29–32, hardly revive emotions we had experienced when reading chapters 7—11.

    The hodgepodge of events and topics that follow—the bowls of dough, the acquisition of jewelry and robes, the vast procession, the count of 430 years, Passover eligibility rules involving circumcision, and further remarks about firstborn males—is somewhat overwhelming, but is much like the first part (12:1–28) in that the view is from later centuries.

Clearly the focus on the Passover meal is foundational, and speaks to Jewish people of every age. Christians must also think of Jesus sharing in this faith, and of the complexities and contradictions in their four gospels regarding his final days. As I look at these sixty-three verses now, I am struck by the experience the Hebrews in the story must have had—how they must have felt utterly dependent on God at this time. Reading the entire passage at one sitting (12:1—13:16) should strike any reader the same way; as the Pharaoh rages and Moses relays regulations centuries ahead of time, these Hebrew slaves or peasants were not masters of their own fate. Exodus 12:39 catches it perfectly, "They baked unleavened cakes of the dough they had brought out of Egypt; it was not leavened, because they were driven out of Egypt and could not wait, nor had they prepared any provisions for themselves."

Section Nine: Exodus 13:17—14:31

63. The waters forced to the east would have to skirt around the Israelites somehow to come back to harm the Egyptians (verses 21, 26–27). In addition, verse 27 mentions the Egyptians rushing *toward* the eastern waters, rather than rushing *away* from them (*back toward* the shore from which they entered the sea). These problems are not impossible to solve; however, they do help us to see the likelihood that the two walls of water and the waters pushed by the strong east wind represent two different versions of the same story, now merged into one more complex, dramatic account.

64. In 13:18–22, things mostly *happen to* the Israelites. God made them turn toward the wilderness leading to the sea.

Moses was given special credit for remembering to bring the remains of Joseph, who had made his people promise to bury him in the Promised Land. God led (*nhm*) them by the pillar both day and night; the pillar stayed with them.

The people also seem active; in fact they are described as being *prepared for battle* (13:18). The term, *hamushim*, might mean that they were organized by teams of fifty. Perhaps the image of eating the Pesach meal with loins girded (12:11) was a hint not only of their pending travel, but also of their readiness to defend themselves. Propp conjectures that the word *hamushim* in 13:18 could be an adjective meaning that they were *resolute*, even if not battle-ready.

Exodus 12:37–39 depicted a much more loosely knit throng, rushed and beset with their flocks and families. Exodus 13:17 strikes notes more in line with 12:37–39. In 13:17, Pharaoh is mentioned as the one who let them go; his role in the larger story is not yet over. God decides to send them on a southerly route, for "if the people face war, they may *change their minds* and return to Egypt." It is hard to combine the image of 600,000 men (12:37) with that of a group fearing local Philistines or Egyptian border patrols (13:17). We will touch on potential Israelite wavering again in Question 66.

65. All the dark interplay of wills and hard hearts between God and Pharaoh during the plagues comes back suddenly in this passage. The LORD tells Moses to have the people *turn back* and camp at a certain place. If this move reversed their direction, that could be taken as a clue by the Pharaoh that they were *wandering aimlessly* (*bwk*). Pharaoh then would be sure that the wilderness had *entrapped* them (or the Hebrew can mean that it is now a *barrier* to their progress). Going beyond the text, early Jewish commentators assumed that God gave these instructions as to where to camp in order to deceive the Pharaoh!

In verse 4, the LORD explains that he will *strengthen* (*hzq*) Pharaoh's heart, and he does so in verse 8. This verb came up frequently in the plague accounts. Further, in verse 4 God speaks of *gaining glory* or *being honored* (*kbd*) in this coming conflict. The root meaning of the verb is "to be heavy." This is the same verb that was used to describe the Pharaoh's heart becoming *heavy* or *dull* earlier. Now it is used in a passive form meaning "heavy with honor," as we might describe someone whose opinions or ideas *carry weight*. God ends with the claim in verse 4 that the Egyptians shall learn that "I am the LORD." This saying was used in 7:5 and 7:17, and has been an underlying theme all along.

Even with all this divine initiative, it is still surprising to read in 14:5 that the minds of Pharaoh and his officials *were changed* (passive form of *hpk*, a verb new to the story) when they heard that the people had fled. Apparently, we are to understand that Pharaoh still expected Moses and the people to come back after the three-day pilgrimage. Their exclamation, "What have we done, letting Israel leave our service?" seems to ignore all the devastation of the plagues and deaths. One irony is that this is the first time the Egyptians have used the proper name Israel since Exodus 5:2. The storyteller goes right on to mention at length the horses, chariots, soldiers, and officers who will pursue the slow-moving peasants with their flocks. Verse 8 mentions again that this is happening because the LORD *strengthened* Pharaoh's heart. It also states that the Israelites were *leaving boldly* (the Hebrew says their *hands* were *high*). This indicates their self-confidence or sense of power (perhaps an echo of the fighting image in 13:18). We know this boldness is not deep-seated, since they will panic as soon as they hear the approaching soldiers. Was their boldness based on thinking no one was coming after them? Had Moses relayed to them God's confident assurances of 14:3–4?

When we read 14:1–9 as a unit, the contrast of the Priestly reliance on God's total control in verses 1–4 and 8–9 clashes with the Elohist's depiction of the Pharaoh and his officials and soldiers, who seem hell-bent on recapturing their slaves (or avenging their own losses). The great battle at the sea is about to begin; the story will not wait for us to figure out who gets glory and who gets justice and who gets to understand what the LORD wants for all the people of the earth. The hardening of the heart problem has not gone away.

66. The whining self-pity of 14:11–12 may strike the average reader as exaggerated (or perhaps refreshing), but the mindset of the followers of Moses is very important. In verse 10, the text says "the sons of Israel lifted their eyes, and behold…"; this seems to indicate their surprise, despite what God had said in 14:3–4. Their *great fear* is mentioned, most likely stemming from their servility, despite the unity hinted at in 13:18 and 14:8. Their *crying out* to God could indicate prayer rather than panic; it seems they still have some confidence in God but not in Moses.

For the ancients, the ideal death involved burial on native soil; the classic nightmare was to be unburied in the wilderness. Their jibe at Moses in verse 11, "What have you done to us…?" parallels the Egyptian thinking in 14:5, "What have we done?" Both remarks are equally unusual in their contexts, and equally self-centered. We cannot tell if the Israelites are simply exercising hindsight about the risk of coming out of Egypt, or if they had had consistent doubts up to that point. Scholars note the cases in Exodus 21:5–6 and Deuteronomy 15:16–17 wherein a slave who is to be freed may elect to waive that freedom. How deep-seated is the fear of the future for these people in near panic before Moses?

This arguing against Moses will be repeated in Exodus (15:24–25; 16:2–8) and many times in Numbers. The series is called the "murmuring" tradition, and will deserve more examination as we proceed. At this point, we can say this brief protest by the people gives us a rare glimpse into their fears.

Moses' confident reply is striking. As a leader, he must say, "Do not be afraid, stand firm." *Stand firm* (*izb*) means "hold firm" or "watch carefully," rather than simply "stand still." The same verb is used of Moses' sister in Exodus 2:4. His assertion in 14:13, that God will do everything and that they will not see these Egyptians again, reminds us of the fireworks between Moses and Pharaoh in 10:28–29. The fact of God's intervention and the sight of the Egyptian casualties will form the concluding image in 14:30–31. Moses encourages them with the ringing motto that "the LORD will fight for you…"; even the Egyptian soldiers will say this in verse 25. Moses' final plea, "you should *be still* (*hrsh*)," seems to mean "be calm" or "watch silently." Propp suggests that it is possible to imagine Moses saying, "Shut up and watch."

It is difficult to explain the fact that now Moses is confident while the people are not. If Moses alone was the recipient of the revelation in 14:1–4, then perhaps his confidence stems directly from God's message in 14:4.

67. The opening remark by God, "Why do you cry out to me?" is spoken directly to Moses himself. If the import of the question is defensive or argumentative, we might speculate that Moses is here considered the representative of the people who have just cried out in fear, or we could guess at failures in Moses' own resolve. Perhaps he is discouraged by the murmuring against his leadership. The sense of the entire verse seems to be "Be a leader; get them moving."

The main picture in these verses (all from the Priestly traditions) is that of a hallway or ravinelike passage right through the entire sea, down to the dry seabed itself. Each side of the hallway or ravine is a miraculous vertical wall of water. God does all of this—*strengthening the hearts* (verse 17) of all the Egyptians, opening the hallway, and watching the Egyptians pursue, for his own glory and renown as well as to save his people.

This is the most well-known snapshot or iconographic image of the sea story, but it does presume that the Egyptian soldiers were willing to pursue the Israelites down this hallway. The fact that the LORD strengthened their hearts may be enough to explain their headlong rush, but we should also note verse 20, which speaks of cloud and darkness. Perhaps the soldiers were not fully aware of the nearby walls of water.

In later Jewish commentary, this miracle was told in even grander terms—rabbis imagined twelve parallel hallways in the sea opened at the same time, one for each tribe!

68. These E and J verses differ significantly from the previous P account. The angel and the pillar of cloud moved to form a barrier between both camps, perhaps hiding events at seaside from the Egyptians. At some point, the Israelites moved to or into the sea. In the middle part of verse 21, the east wind gathered up or pressed back one part of the water (or perhaps held back the upstream part of a river?); somehow God made the seabed dry. In verse 24 God *caused a panic* (*hmm*) among the Egyptian soldiers in camp (or in their moving ranks). It is not clear where the soldiers were positioned at this point. The next verse (25) says that God in some way hampered their chariot wheels, and he made them drive *with difficulty*.

The verb referring to the wheels seems to be *swr*, meaning "remove," but scholars have several other suggestions for translation. The description of wheels *clogging* in mud or wet sand is from ancient translations. There is also a word play between *swr* and the verb *'sr*, which is used in 14:6 to describe Pharaoh *preparing* or *harnessing* his horses and chariot. The pun could mean that Pharaoh *hitched up* the chariot and God later *hitched up* all the wheels. The phrase in verse 25, that the wheels turned *with difficulty*, is based on *kbd*, meaning "heaviness." This is the same root we have seen before for making hearts *heavy* or *dull*, and for God being *honored*.

The soldiers now use the proper terms *Israelites* and LORD, as they realize that the LORD is fighting for his people, as Moses had boasted that he would, in verse 14.

In these E and J verses, God's intervention involves the pillar of fire, an east wind blowing for many hours, a miraculous spirit of panic among the troops, and a disabling of the chariots. Somehow, part of the water was pushed back by the wind in some way. It is not as simple a snapshot as the P traditions, described in the previous answer.

69. In verses 26–29, the manner in which the waters return is not specified, but given the story so far, most readers would visualize a simple slamming shut of the two vertical walls of water forming the hallway or ravine. The Egyptians could have been drowned in seconds.

The briefer E and J sections of verses 27–28 are quite different. There may have been a cessation or change of wind that allowed the water under pressure to return at the same time as the Egyptians were advancing toward it. The vague description of God *tossing them into the sea* uses the Hebrew verb *n'r*, and can mean "tossing" or "shaking" them into the sea *from the outside*, or, following Propp's suggestion, *tumbling* them *within* the sea. In any case, this account also notes that all the soldiers died. There is no way to reconstruct clearly the events of 14:21–29; the conflicting statements all have a legitimate artistic impact.

The two passages both give God all the credit for leading the Egyptian forces to their utter doom, and for directing and dragging the Israelites to a complete escape.

70. Exodus 14:30 speaks of the LORD saving Israel *from the hand* of the Egyptians, and verse 31 notes that Israel saw *the great hand* with which the LORD worked against the Egyptians. Many translations do not retain this double image, but it does help to explain the joy of the Hebrew people.

The only other clear references in the earlier chapters of Exodus to such unity of faith are in 12:27, just before the death of the firstborn of Egypt, and in 4:31, at the end of Moses' initial meetings with the people and before they had to make bricks with their own straw.

Given these fourteen chapters, three references to firm belief and unity of purpose form a very small boast. Most of the story so far shows that the people protected by God and led by Moses were often timid, fearful, or passive. We should not mock them for this, but rather look in the mirror. How often have we thought about staying in Egypt rather than relying on God in the wilderness? The testimony in the Book of Exodus points to the initiative of God alone to change their lives of slavery; belief in God's initiative is one of the hallmarks of Jewish faith.

71. The editors may have wished to tell the sea story just one time, rather than twice. The same intention to combine sources is found in Genesis 6—9, the story of Noah and the Flood. Combining the hallway of water and dry seabed tradition with that of an east wind, miraculous panic, and damaged chariots make for a very complex story—one that is easy to listen to, but hard to diagram on a piece of paper. The editors were confident that complexity and repetition would not harm anyone's faith; they will present a third poetic version in chapter 15 that is again quite different. From a purely artistic point of view, the ambiguities (of where all the water was or how dark it was or where the Egyptian soldiers were at any one point) are positive elements contributing to a legitimate surrealism.

    When there were two or more traditions about the same event, Jewish priests, teachers, and scribes of later generations assumed that all the details should be saved. They were very familiar with great numbers of conflicting details, images, and nuances, and they enjoyed assembling larger and larger blocks of religious stories as a legacy for coming generations. Out of respect for all oral traditions, they were not interested in eliminating discrepancies, which were well known. After all, debating about small details is a way for everyone to deepen their faith and to learn more about how near God is to our lives.

Section Ten: Exodus 15:1–21

72. The hymn is really *about* the LORD and his victory. Some verses include praises spoken directly to God (especially

verses 6–7, 10–13, 17), but, as a victory hymn, the whole passage functions partially as a creed, and is meant to confirm the mutual bonds of faith of those saved by God. The "I" in verses 1–2 represents anyone singing or sharing in this hymn, not just the original composer or the original survivors at the shore of the sea.

73. The thanks for God's protection, and for intimacy with him, should be the constant disposition of all generations of believers down to the time of the one speaking this verse. The LORD is your *father's* God, and your *grandfather's* and your *great-grandfather's*. The last word in the opening phrase, "The LORD is my strength and my *might*," used to be interpreted to mean "song" or "music." (More recently, linguists have postulated new derivations more closely connected with the word *might* or *power*.) The older theory about the word *song* or *music* made some sense in that God can reach our hearts deeply, the way music can. Another rationale was that such reaching of hearts through *song* can effectively give one more motivation, and hence more power.

74. This brief acclamation sums up the basic note of holy war: God is the warrior; believers need only to watch him fight the battle. *The LORD (Yahweh)* is the one being praised in verses 1–4. In Hebrew thought, this name, like all proper names, has power in itself, and explains something of who God is. He is the one who cast the chariots and the riders into the sea. The second half of verse 4 makes the first half more specific, identifying the elite chariot squadron leaders and the Sea of Reeds wherein they drowned. Exodus 15:5 also adds to the drama.

Saying the name and singing the hymn can be used to spread God's fame throughout the world. Isaiah 42:8 expresses the same idea, "I am the LORD, that is my name; my glory I will give to no other, nor my praise to idols."

75. These verses indicate the heart and mindset of God, who continually tries to conquer sin, pride, and injustice. The

reference to God's *majesty* (*ga'on*) in verse 7 means the absolute self-esteem appropriate to a god, a legitimate loftiness or justifiable and holy pride. The adversaries whom he overcomes are those who stand up or rise up in defiance of this majesty. They misuse their free will to commit injustice and wrongly think of themselves as masters of their own destinies.

God's *fury* or *anger* (*haron*) will consume them as fire consumes *stubble* or *straw*. *Haron* means something that is *hot*, and is always used to identify Yahweh's anger. The point of the two verses is that God's legitimate self-esteem and radical disapproval of sin finally erupted into action against the Egyptian soldiers, and he (figuratively) burnt them like stubble. This is a mixed metaphor, within the context of chapter 15 and its imagery of flooding.

76. These seven verses joyfully praise God as the warrior and victor over Egypt. This stanza does not depict all the complex details of chapter 14; some of the verses refer to the struggle and victory but do not mention the winds and walls of water, nor the path taken by the Hebrews during the event. One main focus is on the deaths of the soldiers.

77. The contest described in 15:8–12 (or at least verses 9–12) is out of chronological sequence with the previous verses (15:4–7), since they have already mentioned the final victory. It does not take much for the reader to make the logical switch and to relive the battle.

The opening part of 15:8 refers to waters *piling up* as a result of a wind or breath sent by God. Related Semitic verb roots can mean "dammed up." This might allude to the strong east wind of 14:21.

The next section of 15:8 speaks of the *waters* (*nozelim*) *standing up in a heap*. The Hebrew verb is used at times of waters *flowing down* (Propp suggests the breaking tops of waves). In the Hebrew these waters then *became stationary* (*nzb*) *like a dam* (*ned*). This may well allude to the *walls* of water in 14:22, although there the noun is *homah* (wall), not *ned*.

Finally, the deep waters also *congealed* (*qp'*). This rare verb describes solids forming within liquids, but the final mixture need not be completely rigid. This might refer in some way to the dry seabed exposed by the moved waters. Propp and Cassuto suggest a miraculous instance of ice forming within the water, but not rising to the surface. In any case, the congealed waters seem to support the image of the water becoming stationary, like a wall.

78. The first three sayings clearly indicate a premature gloating —a mounting lust for engagement and victory. The entire set of sayings ("I will pursue, I will overtake, I will divide the spoil") takes only four compact words in the Hebrew.

 The next three sayings focus on the violence and death to come; the soldiers are not thinking of simply recapturing everyone. The phrase, "my desire shall have its fill," can have a more physical sense, "my *throat* shall be filled." Propp favors this physical sense, noting a rhyming effect between the Hebrew forms for *filled* and "the earth *swallowed* them" in 15:12.

 The last boast, that the Egyptians shall *destroy* them, means to "dispossess." The Egyptians want to impoverish them, and cut them off from any possible freedom to settle in another land. In a way, this phrase is parallel to the earlier "I will divide the spoil."

79. No. Exodus 15:10 describes a second stage, a second blowing of divine breath or wind. This might be related to 14:26, where the waters *returned upon* the Egyptians. In the song, the sea *covers* (*csh*) the enemy. The mention of the enemies sinking like *lead* intensifies their going down like a *stone*, used in 15:5.

80. This is basically an ecstatic interjection within the context of 15:8–12. The reference to other gods could mean the gods of Egypt or other nations, or perhaps subordinate angels in

the LORD's court. Noting the LORD's superiority over them supports the faith of the Hebrews of later generations.

The word *majestic* (*'dr*) in holiness can be translated *strong* or *splendid*. The same root is found in verse 6, *glorious* in power, and in verse 10, *mighty* waters. The word *holiness* in verse 11 can be taken on a less abstract level to refer to *holy places* or *holy beings* such as Mount Horeb (Sinai), the Temple, heaven, or even minor gods. This is one example of the way many words in this poem can have multiple senses, although one sense should predominate in each array.

81. In 15:12, God stretches out his hand, whereas Moses did that in 14:26. This image of the earth swallowing the soldiers concludes the second section of the poem, and also introduces the last part. The parallel with the consuming in 15:7 is clear, although different vocabulary is used in each place. Another twist mentioned by Propp is that we could understand the earth to be swallowing the minor gods, instead of the soldiers.

    Being swallowed up by the earth (or drowning) is the equivalent of entering Sheol. Propp suggests that in this poem the sea and Sheol are roughly equivalent. In Job 26:5–6 and 38:16–17, the underworld may be described as somehow being right below the bed of the sea.

82. The events in 15:13–18 have yet to come for Moses and his people standing on the shore, even though readers of later times know how everything turned out. So some of these verb forms might logically be best translated as futures. In 15:13, the verbs for *leading* and *guiding* can also refer to the tasks of shepherds. God's *holy abode* can mean *pasture, place of rest, camp*, and so on, and may hint at Horeb (Sinai), Kadesh, Jerusalem, or the Promised Land.

83. The surrounding nations stopped in their tracks in awe; they let Israel move past or through on their way to the Holy Land. This period of immobility or neutrality brings about worldwide publicity for the followers of the LORD.

In verse 15, the leaders *melt* (*mwg*); in verse 16, they stand by like *stones.* Both terms echo the images of water and stone elsewhere in chapter 15. All opponents of the LORD will be overpowered; they will stand aside, like the waters of the sea, and let the Israelites proceed on their journey.

At the end of verse 16, the LORD's people are the ones he *acquired* (*qnh*); the word can also mean "redeem" or "repossess," both of which make sense here. An identical verb root can mean "engender" or "create." With this many possibilities, English translations of the passage vary considerably.

84. Propp suggests that we should translate *may you bring them and plant them,* or *you will bring and will plant,* or we could use the command forms *bring* and *plant.* He argues that the context makes the past tense forms *you brought* and *you planted* the least likely.

   The vocabulary of the rest of verse 17 is complex. The mountain is God's true *possession* or *inheritance.* The mountain is the *place,* or the *firm seat* (*makon*). There the LORD has *made* (or *designated*) (*p'l*) his *abode* or *dwelling.* This last infinitive form of *ishb,* serving as the noun *abode,* can also mean "place to sit," and hence, "throne." The LORD himself *established* his sanctuary at this mountain; this verb is from the same root *kwn* as is found in *makon,* the *place,* the *firm seat.* Therefore, these are allusions of royalty, which will lead naturally to verse 18, where we celebrate the LORD as king.

85. The intent of 15:18 and the entire hymn is to celebrate God's dominion over all creatures. Exodus 15:3, 11 indicate this universal scope more than other verses, to be sure. Exodus 15:19 functions as a prose summary of the entire hymn. It also helps listeners to connect verses 13–18 back with verse 12.

86. Although the women are mentioned only at the end of the poem, we can reasonably assume that the women's per-

formance went on simultaneously with the singing by the men. Miriam's words in 15:21, clearly adapted from 15:1, may have been utilized as a continuous background chant during the song or as a periodic responsorial antiphon by the women's chorus.

Section Eleven: Exodus 15:22–27

87. In 15:22–25a, we can sympathize with the people, as their supplies of water dwindle. The oasis they reached was not adequate for their needs. Their complaint, by itself, does not seem to be made in bad faith, although we know that this is the first of many such murmuring stories, which, taken together, will reveal much of their true feelings during the journey.

Exodus 15:25b–27 follows logically only if we see God testing, interacting, and sharing some of Moses' frustrations. The making of regulations, the testing, and the warnings to obey have to do with the ongoing mutual relationship of this people and their LORD. The sweetening of the bitter water may be an indicator that the people have "passed" their first test, but there is more to come.

Section Twelve: Exodus 16:1–36

88. The angry complaints in verses 2–3 could be accurate; they may have been nearly out of food. Still, their case is cast in very melodramatic terms, wishing for God to end it all or for Moses and Aaron to accept much of the blame. Propp points out that the people took care of their flocks for the entire wilderness period, and used animals and grain in certain sacrifices. Perhaps self-pity and panic were mixed in with their perceptions. Childs notes that meat would have been an occasional luxury in most ancient diets, and mentions the harsh judgment against this murmuring in

Numbers 11:4 and Psalm 78:17–25, especially verses 19, 22. Their complaint is one of unbelief, a direct attack on God's interest in them.

In 16:4, God intends to *rain down* (*mtr*) food from heaven. While quails might possibly be included in this image, it refers in the main to the falling of the dew, which contained the sweet manna within. In all of 16:4–13 we can see God taking the initiative, designing the system to supply as much manna as needed, apparently without getting angry at the original complaint. Childs calls God's focus on manna in 16:4–5 a "hearty unconcern" about the Israelites' complaint.

89. The testing certainly involves collecting and using the manna properly, not trying to hoard or save any of it. The schedule for collecting and cooking reestablishes the natural weekly Sabbath cycle, presumably long in disuse. Relying on manna year in and year out can become a problem in itself, providing another opportunity to trust in God's support. Such testing helps God to understand his people, and to deepen his relationship with them.

The instruction might refer to the coming laws at Sinai. Deuteronomy 8:1–16 contains a moving sermon from Moses that speaks fondly of the humility coming from hunger, and of the manna that makes everyone aware of the life-giving power of every word that comes from the mouth of God, all "to humble you and to test you, and in the end to do you good."

90. It is quite clear that Moses is doing more than promising that God will send them food. Moses is passing the blame to God for bringing them out to the wilderness. The LORD "has heard your complaining against the LORD"; …he "has heard the complaining that you utter against him"; …"your complaining is not against us, but against the LORD." Twice he asks, "What are we?" Propp remarks that the context shows Moses and Aaron asking this question to

claim to be innocent of deceit and powerless to influence God's plans.

91. The LORD came in the glory of a bright cloud in verse 10, as announced in verse 7. We could say that God's words in verses 11–12 are a summary or review of what had been said earlier in verses 6–7. Another explanation is that Moses and Aaron had foreknowledge in verses 6–8. Such repetition is frequent in P, where a declaration (such as the coming glory) is happily repeated when the event does occur. The effect of the entire passage with all its repetitions is one of mounting solemnity.

92. The manna is thought to come down within drops of dew, which then evaporate, leaving behind this fine, white powder. The doughy substance can be gathered and baked or boiled. It would perish completely on the second day (except for the portion used on the Sabbath itself). Somehow, the collecting of it always worked out so that no one had shortages or surpluses. Gatherers did not even have to measure carefully this steady supply. They did have to collect it early in the day, since it would melt in the high heat. Exodus 16:31 adds some details as to its texture and taste.

93. Exodus 16:32–34 indicates that some manna was to be kept as a sacred artifact, commemorating the divine assistance for those forty years. It is described as sweet tasting; but unlike honey-laced dough, it did not ferment or decay. Nor did it dry out within this one jar, kept in a sacred place. That sanctuary must have been thought to have special life forces within it to keep the manna a fresh and viable sign.

In 16:34, the word for *covenant* is *eduth* (*'dwt*), which can also mean "reminder" or "testimony." Propp says that it means "covenant" in related languages, and here could be an idiom for (the Ark of) the Covenant. Aaron's staff will also be kept next to the covenant (Num 17:10).

Keeping an encouraging artifact of the wilderness years could point to the blessings that will come when they reach the Promised Land, but it can also be thought of as a sign of the obedience needed to sustain this relationship with God. The manna represents a relationship of trust, purified by testing.

During the many years remaining in their wandering in the wilderness, we must remember their daily dependence on and use of manna. There will be many more instances of murmuring and anger by these people, even while their lives were sustained by this daily gift of food coming down with the dew.

Section Thirteen: Exodus 17:1–7

94. Fretheim notes that on a long, difficult journey through a wilderness, the wilderness experiences can become a state of mind influencing all other thoughts. Every difficulty can become a difficulty of faith.

These verses are loaded with indicators of the emotions of the people and of Moses. The people quarrel and complain; they command him to supply water. Instead of using more polite phrases, they accuse Moses of hostile, even murderous, intentions. If Moses is not exaggerating, they may have been ready to kill him. Propp imagines the scene in verse 5 as a very uneasy truce, during which the elders agree to be witnesses at the site of the promised spring.

Moses is shown arguing by asking blunt questions, and in verse 4 he seems to run to God for help. His remark that he fears they will stone him soon may come as a surprise to the average reader, and may indicate Moses' near panic.

95. In 17:2, Moses accuses them of testing the Lord, which is a rebellious stance; Moses is basically telling them to shut up. In 17:3, they accuse Moses alone of bringing them out of Egypt. Such an accusation also denies God a role in that rescue. In 17:4, Moses seems to lose his nerve, crying to God for assistance. If he cried out in the hearing of the

people, that could have been part of his way of trying to persuade them to calm down.

By the end of 17:5, the people are willing to allow their elders to accompany Moses, so he must have forced a standoff at least, if not able to regain their complete trust. Propp takes the phrase in verse 5, "*Go on ahead* of the people," to mean rather, "*Cross before* the people." Such a deliberate or brave movement facing the people as he went to select the elders could have contributed to the standoff. The NRSV translation, "*Go on ahead*," is equally valid, since the same Hebrew phrase is used in Genesis 32:17.

96. Having the elders witness the striking of the rock and the flow of the water will allow them to convince the people of God's role in all this. God not only provides the water, but also stands before Moses at the rock (perhaps somewhat higher up). This gesture not only drives home that God is summoning the waters, but it also shows divine deference to a human being. Here, and in other places in the Bible where God does the same, ancient versions often reworded the verse to tone down the deference. For example, in Genesis 18:22 the text actually says that "the LORD remained standing before Abraham."

Propp argues that the rock at Horeb must be an extended part of the mountain of Horeb, the very site where the covenant will be made in Exodus 19. It may be the same source of water that will be used by Moses in Exodus 32:20. (An allusion can be found in Deut 33:8–9.) At no point in 17:5–6 does God seem angry or impatient.

97. In many biblical stories the name of a person or place is "explained" in a folkloric manner, using rough parallels in vocabulary. Moses (Exod 2:22) named his first son *Gershom*, for "I have been an *alien* (*ger*) residing in a foreign land." He called his second son *Eliezer* (Exod 18:4) because "The God of my father *was my help* (*'zr*), and delivered me from the sword of Pharaoh." Joseph called his first son *Mannaseh* (Gen 41:51), because "God has *made me forget* (*nshh*) all my

hardship and all my father's house." His second son (Gen 41:52) was *Ephraim*, because "God has *made me fruitful* (*prh*) in the land of my misfortunes."

At *Massah/Meribah*, even though the people were given water by God, Moses was shaken by their anger and named the spring *Test* (*rib*)/*Quarrel* (*nsh*), highlighting the seriousness of their doubting.

98. In chapter 15, the people complain once, without quarreling, and do not accuse Moses of hostile intentions. Moses does not cry out to God claiming that he was in danger of death; the LORD is patient but does test them in some way and calls on them to obey his laws. In chapter 17, the quarreling is more intense; the accusations are stronger; Moses says more, even if on the defensive. Here, too, the Lord was patient, selecting the elders as the only witnesses. This move by God counters the anger of the people and their desire to see things for themselves, especially to see God respond to their demands.

Section Fourteen: Exodus 17:8–16

99. What is missing is any preparation or help for the reader! The Amalekites attack immediately, without so much as a word of identification. We do not know if Moses is acting on his own or if he had received assuring guidance from God. The raising and lowering of Moses' hands, and the influence of those gestures on the outcome of the battle, are not explained at all. The suddenness of the scene and selected details of the early part of the battle leave us about as confused as were the ordinary people following Moses. Propp remarks that as often as we reread the story we can move from one theory to another as to the gestures and intention of Moses. How odd to reflect that some Israelite soldiers were injured or died at those periods when Moses was too exhausted to hold up his arms. The powerful image of someone standing like a thunderbolt-wielding

storm god is forever skewed when he needs two assistants to hold him and a stone to sit on! Moses is not the only hero here; the LORD and the Israelites are all involved.

100. Exodus 17:15 is fairly clear. Moses dedicates a memorial altar in honor of the victory, giving all credit to the LORD, whose help was so much more than a banner and pole can signify. Exodus 17:16a is a hard text to translate, but it must be another phrase in honor of the same victory and the same divine help.

Exodus 17:14 contains God's only direct speech in this story, with its solemn flourishes about writing things down and reciting them for Joshua (and future generations). Here God declares the Amalekites perpetual outlaws, who one day will be obliterated from history. Yet the editor in 17:16b indicates that they endured for centuries, a constant thorn in Israel's side, at least by comparison with the Egyptians, who never invaded their land.

In my previous book in this series on Genesis, I commented on Genesis 19:37–38, the passage mocking the Moabites and Ammonites. In Answer 115 of that book, I noted that it would be difficult to sustain a mocking attitude or animosity toward a group for centuries unless there were new or ongoing injustices or incidents. That is clearly the case here; the Amalekites are depicted as enemies of the Israelites down to the time of Saul and David, and even further to Hezekiah (1 Chron 4:43).

Section Fifteen: Exodus 18:1–27

101. The storyteller gives us some information about what Jethro knows, and reminds us of Moses' wife and sons. We are left to imagine the feelings each member of the family had for the others.

We are not told how Jethro came to hear of the rescue of the Israelites by their God, nor of how he knew where Moses and the people were encamped. Perhaps their adventure was the talk of the region. While Jethro's name is mentioned several times within this account, he is quite often simply identified as Moses' father-in-law (thirteen times). The original meanings of the names of Moses' two sons had to do with the strife Moses endured when he had to flee from Egypt in the first place. As Childs notes, in another sense Moses himself has more recently been an alien in Egypt, and most recently has been delivered by God from the sword of Pharaoh.

Exodus 18:6 is rather formal in tone; "He *sent word* (*said*) to Moses, 'I, your father-in-law, Jethro, am coming to you....'" Some of the ancient versions even enhance this formal style, "*It was said* to Moses, '*Behold*, your father-in-law, Jethro, is coming to you....'" Perhaps, instead of formality, Jethro is thrilled at the success of his son-in-law.

One might wonder how the marital status of Zipporah could become so murky within the very book that tells of the marriage and the children. Propp points out that there is very little emphasis in Exodus on Moses' progeny; he is not a patriarch in the pattern of Abraham or Jacob. His sons did not become leaders themselves. His unique leadership responsibilities isolated him not only from his own followers but also from his own family. Even in chapter 18, the mention of Zipporah and the sons is confined to the first six verses. Whether they are being returned from a safe haven or are being brought back by a father-in-law trying to reunite the couple, the sole focus from verse 7 on is with Jethro and Moses. Even in 18:27, as Jethro departs for his own country, we are told nothing about Moses' wife and sons.

102. In verse 8, Moses recounts the plagues and the escape through the sea, and the more recent hardships of their wandering in the wilderness. Exodus 9:16 and 10:2 speak of making the LORD's name resound in all the earth, and of the Israelites telling all these things to their children and grandchildren. Moses is fulfilling these ideals as he joyfully goes over details with Jethro. Fretheim calls this recounting "the gospel of God's deliverance."

Jethro was deeply impressed, and declares the LORD to be greater than all other gods; Jethro shows himself open to the worldwide plans of Yahweh. The phrase, "Blessed be the LORD," in 18:10 is an exclamation of thanksgiving for what God has done. This is not the place to ask if Jethro had moved to a monotheistic faith, but he does sincerely give God credit for saving this people for a special purpose. Childs is firm in holding that there is no evidence that Jethro became a convert, but he fits the Jewish ideal of one who fears God, one who admires the moral code and the justice that God urges on us all. We see some of Moses' human qualities here, his enthusiasm for all that has happened and his respect for his father-in-law. Jethro picked up that enthusiasm and felt what they had gone through, likely without need to give up his own faith and culture. Childs notes that many later rabbinic and Christian patristic writers assumed Jethro had become a convert.

Still within the tent-sanctuary, Jethro led the sacrifices that followed, and Aaron and the elders joined him in the meal of thanksgiving to God. In a way, this worshipful sharing of prayers and a meal partially fulfills God's earlier command in Exodus 3:12. In that same revelation in chapter 3, God promised to bring them one day to their own land, a land flowing with milk and honey (Exod 3:17). Watching Jethro praise God with Moses and all the people, we are reminded that Horeb was not the final goal, but the place for new graces for the trip ahead.

103. In 18:13–14, Jethro is a neutral observer; he is not taken aback by the fact of Moses settling cases, and does not seem to quarrel with the content of their law code. He does have a problem with the logjam of cases, all waiting for the one judge on duty from morning until evening. His question in verse 14, "What is this that you are doing...?" could also be translated "What is *this thing* (*haddabar*) (or *this situation* or *this process*)...?"

In fact, Moses did not understand Jethro's concern for the logjam. He simply explained what he did in each case;

he felt he had to conduct a judicial process that involved prayer and teaching. Moses replies that people come to *inquire of* or to *seek* (*drsh*) God, and that Moses *makes known* (*causes them to learn*) the statutes and instructions (*torah*) of God. Moses felt that his decisions in day-to-day disputes had this religious dimension to them.

The language used by Moses reminds us of the solemn conferences he will have with God at the Tent of Meeting in Exodus 33:7–11; 34:34–35. (In Num 11:16–17, 24–30, we find the related tradition of seventy elders being brought to the tent so that God could give them some of Moses' spirit so that they could help him govern.) However, having God spiritually empower elders and having Moses *inquiring of God* and issuing *statutes* and *torah* are major acts of mediation for the nation. Such procedures may be too advanced for two neighbors disputing about a few goats or chickens. On the other hand, as Childs notes, Moses' conscientiousness and sense of duty provide the context for the important human insights Jethro wishes to share with him.

Jethro does not discuss theological ethics here; he simply points to the fact that there are only twenty-four hours in a day. His first remark in verse 18, that Moses *will wear himself out* (*nbl*), goes on to include "these people with you." The logjam harms everyone, and the harm is potentially serious. In 2 Samuel 22:46, David speaks of subject peoples *losing heart* (*nbl*) as they approached him in his power. Commentators note that related forms of this verb can indicate cynicism or moral ruin. This being worn out will not be remedied by the occasional long weekend of rest.

In Deuteronomy 1:9–18, Moses will remind the Israelites that at Horeb he had asked for helpers to be chosen from each tribe, and had installed them as judges for all but the *hardest cases* (*qshh*) (verse 17). Moses recalled in Deuteronomy that he could not do everything himself (1:9, 12), although in that account there is no mention of Jethro or his counsel. Deuteronomy 1:17 shows Moses' confidence that God will guide each worthy judge in some way. Moses says, "You must not be partial in judging: hear out the small and the great alike; you shall not be intimidated by anyone, for the judgment is God's."

104. Jethro combines religious sensitivity with his common-sense observations. In 18:19, he adds the phrase, "May God be with you," and speaks of Moses being "for the people *before* (or *in front of*) God," and of Moses bringing "the cases to God." In 18:20, he encourages Moses to continue *warning* (*zhr*) about statutes and laws (*torah*), and making known to them the way to go and the things to do. These paraphrases and repetitions of key words represent Jethro's understanding of Moses' explanations in 18:15–16. Jethro is not telling Moses how to mediate God's wishes.

But Jethro proposes the selection of qualified judges, honest and devout, who can hear the *minor* (*qtn*) cases (18:22, 26). The cases reserved for Moses are called *large* (*gdl*) or *important* in verse 22, and *hard* (*qshh*) in verse 26. The goal is stated in 18:23, "If you do this, *and God so commands you*, then you will be able to endure, and all these people will go to their home *in peace* (*shalom*)."

So what is Jethro saying in 18:19–23? Propp suggests that the opening, "May God be with you," could be a *blessing* or *confident prediction*, but it might in context rather be seen as a *warning* to make these changes only with God's agreement. Moses will remain the main mediator and teacher. As other judges take over the minor cases, Moses will maintain his stamina and the people will have their cases completed in a timely fashion (*go to their homes in peace*). Jethro adds *if you do this and God so commands you* (verse 23). The reference to God's command in verse 23 could be an echo of the warning of verse 19 (with the word *if* doing double duty), or it could be another blessing or confident prediction, as before.

In summary, as Fretheim notes, there is nothing wrong with a good idea, regardless of its source. Jethro is wiser than Moses; he realizes that a judicial system must be built on the principle of subsidiarity. Jethro seems confident that the LORD will agree with him, and will also guide Moses to be more realistic in delegating judicial hearings that do not require ever new and intense discernments of the will of God.

105. The style of Exodus 18 is very pleasant. We get to sit by the campfire and listen to two decent men, not only related as in-laws but also gladly sharing many beliefs and values. They participate in thankful worship of the God of Israel at a ceremony led by Jethro, who is not from one of their own tribes. As Jethro offers his advice on how they could develop a workable system of judges, he is courteous and respectful of Moses' religious responsibilities and wants what will be best for all the Israelites, not just for his son-in-law. Moses needs this help, even if he does not realize it, just as he needed Aaron and Hur to hold his arms during the battle.

Jethro's visit comes at a time for worship and for rest, a time to look back on how far they have come in a few months and to marshal their hopes for the future. Let us take one example of looking back. In Exodus 18:13–26, the verb *to judge* (*shpt*) and the related noun *shopet* are used several times, and the judges whom Moses *set* (*sim*) *over* the people are called *officers* (*sare*) over thousands, hundreds, and so on. In Exodus 2:14, the angry slave had challenged Moses, "Who made (*sim*) you a ruler (*sar*) and judge (*shopet*) over us?" Look how far Moses and the Israelites have come—from a bumbling do-gooder thanklessly defending one Hebrew slave from another one to the leader of a vast throng of free people on a quest for a homeland, now so numerous that Moses needs to develop an adequate and stable judicial system for them.

We are observing one day in the life of a people, one day for a people supported by their God, who asks them to rely on him for food and water, for protection from raids, and for leading them on a long journey one day at a time. On this day they tell Jethro what God has done for them, solve some problems with Jethro's help, wish him well as he departs for his own homeland, and wait for the next indication of God's will for them.

There is a Latin phrase for this way of taking life's challenges one day at a time. While it was not likely a religious saying to begin with, it is still appropriate. The saying is "*Solvitur ambulando*," which means something like "Things will get resolved as we walk along."

Section Sixteen: Exodus 19:1–25

106. There are several repetitions within the first two verses, but the focus on the date and itinerary indicate the Priestly editors at work. P usually calls the mountain *Sinai* rather than *Horeb*. Camping *in front of* the mountain (verse 3) may mean *around* the mountain (a somewhat similar Hebrew phrase can be found in Num 2:2). This could clear up possible confusion in 19:12, where the boundary markers were set around the mountain rather than around the people.

In 19:3, Moses' initial ascent may have been of his own initiative, although most readers assume that he went up the mountain because he was called by God. Commentators have long noted that the mention of the people *camping* is immediately followed by the mention of Moses *going up*, and his *going up* is mentioned just before the statement that *the LORD called to him*.

Overall, it is fair to say that the opening verses get off to a fast start and mark a clear break in style and subject matter from Exodus 15:22—18:27. The daily routines of the wandering Israelites will be changed forever by this new conversation between God and Moses.

107. It is difficult to explain what is new and what is not new in the Sinai accounts. Scholars have long been impressed by the Exodus parallels in style to ancient Near Eastern treaty formulas, and at times have considered the briefer covenants with Noah and Abraham to be derivative of these in Exodus.

On the other hand, covenant theology is so deeply rooted in Genesis and Exodus that we need to appreciate the continuity of the relationship started with Abraham.

The previous reference in Exodus to a covenant (*berith*) was in 6:2–5. There Moses was reminded of God's appearances to Abraham, Isaac, and Jacob, and of God's covenant promise to give their descendants the land of Canaan. God spoke of the sufferings of the slaves in Egypt, and of his intention to free them because "I have remembered my covenant."

Fretheim argues for the continuity of the already established relationships between God and his people. The Sinai covenant must fit within the Abrahamic one. The Israelites have been tested and challenged to obedience before; obedience was the topic at Marah (15:25–26), and also in 16:28, regarding the manna. Obedience is a concern that grows out of a relationship already established by God. Before agreeing to obey these new laws, what God has done in the past had filled their lives. This community is already elected, redeemed, believing, worshipping.

What is new must be related to the phrases in 19:5–6, about being a treasure, a priestly kingdom, and a holy nation. These possibilities are prefaced by the preposition *if* in 19:5. Propp argues that we could even translate the following, "*(then) you shall be my treasured possession*" as "*if you will be....*" In this alternate translation, one would render the start of the next verse "*then you shall be for me a priestly kingdom.*" Whether we go with one *if* or two *ifs* in verse 5, this covenant is still a proposal, a free offer.

108. The *priestly kingdom* (19:6) could be taken in a narrow sense to refer to a kingdom ruled by priests, but commentators are confident that the author intended a wider sense, *a kingdom where everyone is as holy as a priest, or does priestly work*. In this chapter, everyone undergoes the extraordinary priestly purifications in 19:10–15, and all are part of the *treasured possession* in 19:5. The same idea of having a special call permeates Deuteronomy 14:1–21, especially

verses 1–2, 21. We may say that the people are called to become a *holy nation*, but in another sense, God's proximity to them imposes holiness on them almost by definition.

This call to holiness is a privilege and a responsibility. But what purpose is there to this holiness? For that we need to return to Abraham. Abraham and his descendants were to be a source of blessing in some way for all the nations (see Gen 12:3; 18:18; 22:18; 26:4–5; 28:14). At Sinai God is asking his people to be priests to the whole world, mediators and exemplars of justice. God's additional remark in verse 5, "the whole earth is mine," could help us to understand the other phrases.

Fretheim notes that the *if* in verse 5 is an invitation, not a threat, to be God's redeemed people for the world. Or to put it another way, *if you will obey* means "when you will obey" or "when you accept this covenant"—at that point, you take on the worldwide role. Now Israel as a community can respond as Abraham had, and be chosen for the benefit of humanity and nature. The passage in Deuteronomy 4:5–8 captures this worldwide role nicely.

"See, just as the LORD my God has charged me, I now teach you statutes and ordinances for you to observe in the land you are about to enter and occupy. You must observe them diligently, for this will show your wisdom and discernment to the peoples, who, when they hear all these statutes, will say, 'Surely this great nation is a wise and discerning people!' For what other great nation has a god so near to it as the LORD our God is whenever we call to him? And what other great nation has statutes and ordinances as just as this entire law that I am setting before you today?"

109. Perhaps the story is going at top speed because it is a foundational bedrock of their theology, and so needs little explanation; or perhaps the authors want to show that the enthusiasm of the people matches the enthusiasm of God. Childs points out that the blind agreement in 19:8 logically allows for further input in the coming chapters; the response will be fleshed out by the context, culminating in

24:3, 7. Fretheim considers the response not so much blind as free and generous. It must be seen in its immediate context, which is 19:4–6, and it is an open-ended commitment, a vote of high confidence in God's future goodness. By this unanimous acclaim, the people enter into a loyal, exclusive personal relationship building on what they had when Jethro visited Moses.

110. In 19:9, God wishes to have the people witness some of his speaking to Moses, in order for them to *trust* (*'amn*) Moses forever after. This wish might be called an opening bracket to the Ten Commandments of chapter 20, and the further request of the people for Moses to be their main mediator in Exodus 20:18–21 functions as a closing bracket.

All the people will hear and understand the commandments; Moses will be the coordinator, but God will be the direct speaker of the words.

Fretheim points out that at many other places in the Old Testament Moses has easier access to God. Storms and lightning did not always attend their conversations. In 24:9–11, the elders will meet God in a serene encounter. The majestic effects in chapter 19 are meant to impress the people whom we might call the general public, and to elicit their trust in Moses. God is linking his work to the human work of Moses (and to others in the future).

111. There is nothing in Exodus 19:1–9 to prepare readers for the wild, overwhelming events in the rest of the chapter. By God's instructions, the people are to make themselves (and their clothing) more worthy of the coming revelations. There is great emphasis on staying behind the boundary markers (ropes, stones, furrows?) set around the mountain. Any overeager human or hapless animal that crosses the boundaries is to be stoned or shot by arrows, and then left untouched (perhaps covered with stones?). (Even assuming that no one actually disobeyed and died, the grim prohibitions are discomforting to most modern readers.) The community is now prepared, or consecrated, or made holy or

worthy. Whatever term we use amounts to describing a group that is focused or isolated for special purposes.

The actual arrival of God in verses 16–19 is as complex as anything in chapter 14. The trumpets mentioned in verse 13 were most likely to be sounded by people acting on Moses' instructions. However, the trumpeters in verses 16 and 19 are not identified. Cassuto suggests that the hornlike sounds could have been generated by strong winds blowing through narrow mountain gorges.

In verse 16, all the people *trembled* (*hrd*); in verse 18, the mountain did the same. (The NRSV describes the mountain as *shaking violently*, but it is the same verb in Hebrew.) Propp remarks that we do not need to assume that the authors knew much about volcanic activity. The references to fire, smoke, and furnace, as well as to the storm images, are standard devices to indicate God's presence. Still the effect here is quite dramatic, since so many forces are called upon.

Qol is the word used for *voice* in 19:5, and at the end of 19:6, God tells Moses to relay these *words* (*debarim*) to the people. The verb *dbr* is used in 19:9 to describe God's *speaking* to Moses. The word for *thunder* in verse 16 is *qolot* (again the basic word for *voices* or *sounds*); the same word *qol* is used for the *blast* of the trumpet. In verse 19, we again have the *blast* of the trumpet, and God replying *in thunder* (*qol*) to the words spoken by Moses. In this last case, some translations have God speaking *in a voice*.

Childs explains that *qol* usually does not mean *words* in Hebrew. He asks what it might mean in 19:19 that God replied in *thunder, sound,* or *voice*. Did God speak words that were audible and intelligible to all, or did his communication sound more like thunder to the people? Fretheim admits that God's voice might have been hard for the people to understand, given all the activity in 19:19. Propp, following Cassuto, suggests that God raised his voice over the din in order to reach Moses and the people down below. The oddity that a word for *voice* could mean *thunder* but not *the speaking of words* is one example of the rich ambiguities possible in Hebrew style.

Childs notes that in Deuteronomy 4:10–12; 5:4–5, 22–24 this imprecision is cleared up. In those Deuteronomic passages, God is described as using words that can be easily understood. Perhaps the Deuteronomic writers wanted to clarify some of the artful mystery in Exodus 19.

112. In the past, commentators have found the additional warnings in J (19:20–23) and E (19:24–25) to be somewhat anticlimactic or superfluous. Moses may have felt much the same, as can be seen in verse 23. However, there are potentially valid reasons for the passage.

God is very concerned to protect his people from the harm of coming too close to his overwhelming otherness. Moses had been cautious at the initial meeting at the burning bush (Exod 3:6). It may also be that God felt Moses himself needed more protection at this time.

Alternatively, these instructions might have been part of a testing process, for the people and for Moses. Fretheim notes that initial stages of any personal relationship involve testing; later on, trust becomes second nature and testing diminishes. There seems to have been no failing or disobedience during this event.

Childs raises the question of what prompted the warnings in 19:12–13, 21–24. He assumes that the people were quite impatient and inquisitive, thus needing all the warnings. So God would have been aware of how close the people and priests were to crossing the boundaries, even if Moses had confidence in their obedience. This trip down the mountain may also have been necessary in order for Moses to escort Aaron across the boundary. Childs concludes that 19:20–25 makes the most sense if we consider chapter 20 as inseparably linked to chapter 19. The revelations in 19:19 are only beginning; the great commands of 20:1–17 will continue this unique, life-threatening call for them to become a holy nation. The people need protection from their own religious metabolism during all these hours at the foot of the mountain.

Fretheim notes that all the protections for the people from the overwhelming divine presence in chapter 19 help the people hold on to their free will, the free will to disbelieve or disobey. Some special protections are extended to Moses, Aaron, Joshua, and other elders for the sake of their missions to the rest of the people.

As modern readers, we need to distinguish the positive intent of the "special effects" in chapter 19 from our first impression that the people may have been terrified. Terror would paralyze free will, and is completely counterproductive as a motive for entering a covenant. To use a relatively recent example, the special effects might be considered analogous to the peaceable blinking lights and musical tones of the giant spaceship in *Close Encounters of the Third Kind*. These visual effects are ways to help us vividly imagine otherworldly beings making contact with us.

Section Seventeen: Exodus 20:1–21

113. God personally desires or insists on an exclusive faith relationship, involving no physical images whatsoever of any divine being. This may be a way of explaining the theology of his essential nature. He wants a close relationship with all humans. He is the only God, despite the fact that the majority of decent humans at the time of Moses thought that there were many gods.

God has the right to make his will known because he has already rescued the Israelites and lived up to the promises he had made to Abraham and to Moses. By speaking these words, God is asking for further commitment from the Israelites, even though he had rescued them without any further obligation on their part. God is in the process of molding a people for himself. He uses his deeds in history and these laws as two ways to do this. Throughout Exodus 20, the second-person verb forms, pronouns, and adjectives are all in the singular. Each individual is being addressed (thus the older translations "Thou shall not...").

Fretheim concludes that the apodictic style (briefest possible direct commands) shows God's concern for the health and order of the entire community, and that obedience should be the main motivation for observing these revelations. The LORD is again promising to be their God, and to maintain this personal relationship. The reference to Egypt and slavery points to their particular history; the laws will not be another form of slavery but rather a gift from their redeemer. They were already God's people before this; the sayings will be instructions regarding the shape such a redeemed life is to take in everyday affairs.

The command in Hebrew in verse 3 is *There will not be for you other gods* (or *another god* or *any other god*) *to my face*. Childs notes that the phrase *to my face* (or *before me* or *besides me*) is not adequately translated by the English phrase *except me*. *Except me* may not be strong enough in English, sounding as though God acted from vanity. The NRSV has *before me*.

For Childs and Propp, the command in verse 3 is not a statement claiming or defining monotheism; it simply describes God's relation to Israel by prohibiting worship of any other divine power at any time for any reason. Scholars use the term *henotheism* to describe an interest in one god to the exclusion of all others. Given Hebrew traditions, this way of expressing the predominance of Yahweh seems to be consistent and ancient. In his commentary on the patriarchs in Genesis, Westermann outlines the practical elements of ancient nomadic religion, which was usually henotheistic and austere.

Some scholars argue that there might have been a specific crisis point closer to the writing of Exodus wherein idolatry by some Israelites occasioned the restrictions of verses 3–6, but that is speculative.

114. Perhaps physical images promote polytheism, or create some other danger for the Israelites that are best avoided by simply outlawing images altogether.

The demand that there be no other gods for Israel is expanded in verses 4–6. Any such *bowing before* or *worshipping* (*serving, offering sacrifices*) other gods or use of any carved *idol* (*pesel*) or *visible image* (*temunah*) is called *iniquity* (*'avon*); those who do these things *reject* (*sn'*, "hate") God, while those who worship him alone and keep his commandments *love* (*'hb*) him. Most commentators take *visible images* to include paintings, murals, or embroidered symbols, although Propp feels that the text does not make this clear. Mental or verbal images are not included in this prohibition; after all, we need some methods to represent God to ourselves.

The language and style are blunt; no explanations or fine points are offered. God describes himself as a *jealous God* (*El Qana'*), which may sound odd to modern readers. (See Josh 24:19: the high point of that entire chapter. In verse 19, Joshua calls Yahweh holy *and* jealous; to worship him is to reject other gods at the same time.) Propp suggests other ways to translate the word *jealous*, including *zealous*, impassioned, or perhaps even *punitive*, given the context. The correct note of emotion in the title might be the *jealous possessiveness* of a romantic relationship.

The prohibition of statues and visible images applies also to representations of Yahweh himself, again without any explanations. Childs refers to Deuteronomy 4:9–20, especially verses 12, 15, where Moses reminds the people that at Horeb they heard God's voice but did not see any *form* (*temunah*) of him. For this reason, they are not to make any representations of Yahweh.

Historians of ancient religions note that idols were not usually worshipped in themselves, but were respected as vehicles for divine presence. The idolaters mentioned often in the Old Testament were not as simplistic or naïve as they were made out to be. Childs doubts von Rad's suggestion that Yahweh is too active to be constrained by carvings and paintings. Instead, Childs holds that the focus on what God has already done for them, from Abraham to the escape from Egypt, controlled Jewish thinking; no other visible image provided a worthy alternative to their sacred history.

Fretheim reasons that the Jewish tradition of taking 20:4–6 as a separate commandment shows how serious the topic was for them. Even the worship of Yahweh could become contaminated by the use of images, as it was to be in Exodus 32. Yahweh is not a remote observer of our fates, or someone who must constantly be flattered; he is a redeemer who makes decisions every day. No physical image can capture this change and development, this detailed application of justice and mercy.

Fretheim also considers 20:5 to be toned down considerably in 34:6–7; the latter passage focuses more on forgiveness and patience. Propp notes that the punishing of a sinner's descendants was a given in clan and tribal cultures where corporate identity predominated. Within the Old Testament such punishments were curtailed as time went by (Deut 24:16; 2 Kgs 14:3–6), and was challenged by some of the prophets (Ezek 18; Jer 31:29–30).

Propp mentions that the phrase in 20:6 for *showing steadfast love* (*hesed*) can be more clearly translated as *faithfully requiting*.

In discussing the Jewish prohibition of idols and images, Propp seeks some of the logic that may lie behind the law. Propp considers the use of religious images to be a universal human impulse, and that Jewish thinkers must have had reasons to go against that. He asks why Jewish monotheists would not allow themselves the use of images of their own LORD, within clear bounds. Propp considers the common Old Testament charge that idols were actually worshipped in themselves to be an exaggeration, and asserts that there is much evidence that "idols were understood only as pictures of the gods and receptacles for their divine presence." However, perhaps the Israelites had a better sense of the average ancient Near Easterner's inclination to actually worship an idol. The Israelites may have had a sense that the use of icons would demean God's freedom in some way, his free and personal decision to be their God (and to punish when faced with great sin). Fretheim calls our attention to 2 Kings 17, which vividly describes the destruction of the northern kingdom for its intense commitment to polytheism.

The overuse of images could also contribute to pantheism, which constricts the divine to the natural elements. Another problem is the desecration of idols in times of conquest and war, or desecration by unworthy craftsmen even as they are being made. Propp notes that many of these theological concepts likely were also considered by polytheists. He mentions some other ancient Near Eastern cultures that avoided making images of their gods. He goes on to recall archaeological examples of ancient Jewish art and the few references to images in the Old Testament itself, such as the bronze serpent (Num 21:8–9), gold calves (1 Kgs 12:28; 14:9), the cherubim or griffins in the Tabernacle and Temple (1 Kgs 6:23–28; 8:6–9; 2 Kgs 19:14–15), the bulls beneath the great basin (1 Kgs 7:25), and other bulls and lions (1 Kgs 7:29; 10:19–20).

Instead of physical images, Israel developed many stories about Yahweh, mostly comparing him to a strong adult male, although there are other compassionate parental images used in addition.

115. Naturally one would like to know what this commandment prohibits. Some oaths would be legitimate religious proclamations. In Deuteronomy 6:13, the people are told to *swear* (*shbᶜ*) by the name of the LORD. But deceitful oaths in law cases are crimes of perjury as well as blasphemies or sacrileges. So too superstitious conjuring, or prayers for impossible requests, or idle, rude uses of the names of gods all amount to trivializing disrespect or sacrilege. All these misuses damage social bonds, especially in court cases, and dishonor God at the same time. Note the strong language in Leviticus 19:11–12. In the context of 20:3–6, we can see God being zealous to banish other gods, ban all

attempts to make religious images of himself, and protect the honor of his own name or reputation.

Fretheim looks at some broader implications of this commandment. As we have seen in many places in Exodus so far, God wants his name known by the whole world (for example, Exod 9:16). Thus, believers must uphold the honor of God's name in their own lives, so that this name will ring true for the rest of the world. The use of God's name is a matter of mission. We must use it in prayer, in praise, and in the holiness of our own lives, so that it will mean something to others when they come to hear of him.

Therefore, the wording of Exodus 20:7 is general and inclusive, covering any misuse of the divine name. In the ancient world, covenants and oaths were considered pledges taken on pain of life and death. In 20:7, we are told that the LORD will not *acquit* (*nqh*) anyone who does this. The phrase means more than that God will not *forgive*; it means that he will not *declare excused from punishment* anyone who misuses them. The punishment is in a sense automatic; God would have to go out of his way to prevent it from happening.

116. The more we understand the mystery of creation and God's pride and enjoyment of it, the more we can ask ourselves how best to spend that day each week.

For many Jews and Christians, resting and going to worship ceremonies remain simple, but limited, guidelines. More brainstorming about how to make the Sabbath holy could be done, especially at the communal level.

Exodus 20:10 speaks of the Sabbath *to* the LORD or *for* the LORD. One offers up the day to God and loses potential income (from the care of crops, herds, and so on) in the same way one would lose income in donating an animal, bird, grain, or oil for a burnt offering. Everyone offers up the day, even the draft animals; they get to rest like everyone else. By extension, we could even say that the fields get a day off; no one is plowing, harvesting, or excavating for walls or wells. Fretheim captures this treatment of animals and fields by noting, "One moment in creation is recaptured when the world's creatures were at peace with one another. And it calls for, indeed anticipates, a new world order when once again it will be so and everything will be very good." Fretheim calls the setting aside of each seventh day "a sanctuary in time."

Propp quotes Abraham Heschel, who described this keeping holy the Sabbath as one of learning "to understand that the world has already been created and will survive without the help of man." When we rest in union as a whole people, we imitate and join with God's resting on the seventh day of creation.

In Deuteronomy 5:15, the motivational clause does not concern God's resting on the seventh day, but on his rescuing them from slavery in Egypt. Perhaps the mention of their rescue from slavery in Deuteronomy 5:15 points to another kind of rest, the rest that free people can have the chance to be themselves with their God. In Exodus 16:22–30, the newly freed slaves needed extra instructions about collecting manna for the Sabbath; they seemed quite unsure of their own customs at that point, unsure as slaves who had not even had time off from work to maintain their own heritage.

In the past and today, many Jewish families gather for Sabbath dinners. I recall reading of one example of rabbinic support for such gatherings. In small villages where relatives live just a few doors away, it is allowed to join houses set close together by connecting both with a long branch or pole or even by tying a piece of string between them. This flimsy physical connection makes the two (or more) houses the rabbinic equivalent of apartments within a larger house. Then one could carry dinner kettles, casseroles, and the like to grandmother's house for dinner without breaking the ordinary rules about carrying things outdoors. I do not think I need to explain why having such a family meal is an example of Fretheim's reference "to be in tune with the created order of things."

117. The command to *honor* parents is broad, but it does not simply refer to *obeying* them in every family decision during the parents' lifetimes. At times, adult offspring have to firmly negotiate boundary issues with their own elderly parents, and even hold to a stalemate, or intervene if they are endangering themselves.

The second part of verse 12 promises or assumes that loving care of parents will result in long lives for the children. However, on one level these promises are stock phrases, found often in Deuteronomy and elsewhere. Propp cites Deuteronomy 22:6–7 for the same promise of a long life in relation to a custom involved in scavenging for bird eggs! In Ephesians 6:1–3, Paul calls this "the first commandment with a promise." Still, honoring parents was considered a sacred duty. In Leviticus 19:3 we are told to *revere* (*ir'*) them. This verb is mostly used in reference to *fearing* God or *being in awe of* God, as in Genesis 22:12.

Fretheim agrees that the mention of long life is neither strictly promise or warning. It follows the style of Deuteronomy, a matter-of-fact moralizing style that assumes that good deeds will always be rewarded. Fretheim describes this as a loose causal weave, assuming the effect of such conduct being intrinsic to the deed. So those who honor their parents will someday be honored by their own adult sons and daughters.

Propp suggests that this commandment is important not only for individual families, but also for the moral unity and stability of the entire people. He notes that the promise in Exodus 20:12 is not just of long life, but also of family stability.

118. The command not to *kill* was understood to point to a vast biblical array of legal and moral distinctions regarding violence. The fact that the Hebrew verb used here covers a range of meanings that require several different verbs in English is simply a matter of coincidence. Linguists call that a mechanical barrier that often occurs in translating from one language to another.

To look at one part of the biblical collection, the example of Numbers 35 is worth reviewing. Numbers 35:6–13 describes cities of refuge, to which one who has killed (*rzh*) another without intent can flee. In a city of refuge, that person is protected from the *avenger* (the male relative who has obligations to protect or avenge a person's wrongful death). The avenger's obligations are legal, and approved in individual cases by judges. The topic of killing without intent is continued in Numbers 35:22–28.

On the other hand, Numbers 35:16–21 concerns another group who cause death. They are called *murderers* (*rzh*), and avengers are legally appointed as their executioners. Childs is of the opinion that in Numbers 35:20 and at the very start of 35:21 we have a later refinement in meaning, in which *hatred* and *lying in wait* and *enmity* identify the killers' motives. Otherwise, in verses 16–19 and the rest of verse 21 (after the mention of *enmity*) there is no mention whatever of motive. (That is why I used the term "those who cause death.") One who kills with an iron or wooden bar, stone, or one's own hand is held responsible.

Finally, as the judges decide cases of unintentional manslaughter two different terms are used to describe the same person. In 35:25, the unintentional killer (*rzh*) is protected from the avenger. Here the older sense of the verb ignores motive. In verse 24, while the trial is under way, the one described in verses 22–23 is called the *striker* or *hitter* (*nch*). This is the refinement of meaning mentioned above; motives have not yet been judged, so the person should not yet be called a *murderer*. The NRSV tries to be helpful here by using the word *slayer* in both verses 24 and 25.

At this point, I would like to include a chart of all of the relevant Hebrew vocabulary forms in Numbers 35. The verb *nch*, to "hit" or "strike" or "beat," can also mean to "beat to death" or "strike dead" in context, just as the same English words can be used. The NRSV uses *kill* or *strike* in most of the instances of *nch*, with the exception of *slayer* in verse 24, as mentioned.

Chart of Hebrew verbs/nouns and
NRSV translations in Numbers 35

Verse	English NRSV	Hebrew verb
Cities of refuge		
6	slayer	*rzh*
11	(slayer who kills without intent)	*rzh/nch*
12	slayer	*rzh*
15	(who kills without intent)	*nch*
Murderous killings		
16, 17, 18	strikes	*nch*
	murderer	*rzh*
19	murderer	*rzh*
[20 mentions hatred, lying in wait]		
[21 mentions enmity]		
21	strikes/who struck	*nch*
	murderer	*rzh*
Unintentional killings		
[22 mentions without enmity, without lying in wait]		
[23 mentions unintentionally (without seeing), not enemies, no harm intended]		
24	slayer	*nch*
25, 26	slayer	*rzh*
27	(he) is killed	*rzh/rzh*
28	slayer	*rzh*
Consistent, severe punishments		
30	one kills	*nch*
	murderer	*zh*
	be put to death	*rzh*
31	murderer	*rzh*

Most of Numbers 35 uses the verb *rzh*, which the NRSV rightly translates as *murderer* in verses 16–21 and 30–31. However, the same word has to be translated as *slayer* in verses 6, 11, 12, 25, 26, 28, in order to make sense in English.

We have come a long way from the brief command of Exodus 20! In later passages in the Bible where *rzh* is used, evil intention is always present (see Isa: 1:21; Hos 4:2; 6:9; Job 24:14; Jer 7:9; Ps 94:9). In all these cases, the word *murder* is a good translation.

Childs concludes that the verb *rzh* originally meant any killing that called for an avenger to come forward. As cities of refuge were set up and motives were given more consideration, the same verb had to cover all cases. Later on, *rzh* came to mean acts of violence for unworthy motives. Taking Exodus 20:12 in its broadest sense, as we should, the commandment prohibits such violence and rejects the right of any person to take the law into his own hands out of a feeling of personal injury. We cannot become self-appointed avengers. There was an appropriate public role for deputized avengers in ancient tribal societies with no police or jails, but that era is long gone.

119. The focus on adultery may have been driven by concern for the stability of family, clan, and tribe. But it also points to the larger array of laws regarding marriage, inheritance customs, the rights of women, and so on. For example, if a man forced himself upon a virgin who was not engaged, he was obligated to pay a fine to the woman's family, and to marry her without the right to divorce her at any later time (Deut 22:28–29; related rules can be found in Exod 22:16–17). This custom is mentioned in Genesis 34, where the man, Shechem, desired marriage with Jacob's daughter Dinah. While that incident ended with war and Shechem's death, Jacob had been willing to allow the marriage (Gen 34:30). A similar case involved David's daughter Tamar, overpowered and raped by her half brother Amnon, another son of David. Tamar suggested marriage instead of undergoing this violence, but Amnon refused. Her remarks in 2 Samuel 13:12–13, 16 are heartbreaking; used and then spurned, she could never marry. Later Absalom dishonored some of

David's wives during his rebellion; they were doomed to never having relations with David again, even though their dishonoring most likely involved no physical contact with Absalom (2 Sam 16:20–22; 20:3).

In the next chapter, Exodus 21:7–11, there are humane rules regarding wives chosen from slavery, and there are similar considerations for wives chosen from among prisoners of war in Deuteronomy 21:10–14. Those studying all marriage regulations in the Old Testament sooner or later must come to Numbers 5:11–31, which describes a trial by ordeal. This ancient procedure, about as useless for us now as a rusted blunderbuss or a gruesome pile of damaged dinosaur bones, was long ago outlawed by rabbinic authorities. The purpose was admirable, as one way to protect the institution of marriage, but the complications and inequities are obvious.

Adultery figures in other well-known biblical stories. Abimelech properly blasts Abraham for lying about Sarah (Gen 20), as had the Pharaoh before him (Gen 12). Joseph bravely resisted the lures of the wife of Potiphar (Gen 39). David acted dishonorably in his desire for Bathsheba, and then abused his office to arrange the death of her husband (2 Sam 11). Severe punishments followed.

Elsewhere in the Bible, lust and fornication are warned against and condemned, and adultery is frequently used as an analogy for polytheism, the worship of any god other than the LORD.

Fretheim points out that, given ancient Near Eastern history, we have inherited more biblical sanctions against women who act inappropriately than against men. For example, men alone were allowed to initiate divorces. Of course, in our own time both Jewish and Christian communities should treat men and women equally. Fretheim notes (235) that "this commandment insists that *issues of sexuality are not a casual matter* for the good order of God's world. From a positive perspective, this means a lively concern for healthy male/female relationships in all aspects of daily life. Respect, honor, and integrity should inform both attitude and behavior toward members of the opposite sex."

120. As with murder, all societies prohibit stealing as a matter of common sense and justice. Everyone loses when something is stolen. Fretheim reminds us of the damage theft causes. It harms society and the inner peace of the victim, and demeans the victim's work and dignity. The thief himself is avoiding an authentic life of honest labor and social bonding, and is ruining his own relationship with God. In many places in the Old Testament, the prophets criticized the growing gap between the rich and the poor (see Isa 1:21–23; Amos 8:4–6, and so on). Thus, general questions of social justice could be seen to fall under this commandment.

121. Fretheim notes that we need to think of the damage false witnesses do not only to one unjustly accused, but to the entire judicial system. As trust in a legal system wanes, more injustices abound. This commandment calls for honesty in our dealings with each other, and constructive speech in daily life to enhance collective goodwill and the good order of God's creation.

122. In the past, scholars who sought a narrow focus about stealing in Exodus 20:15 considered 20:17 to cover all the other categories of stealing. They were also doubtful that the emotion of *coveting* or *desiring* could ever have been prosecutable in itself. So they looked at some uses of the verb *hmd*, such as Exodus 34:24 and Psalm 68:17, where in context *covet* could mean to *take possession*. So they took this verb to mean that *you shall not take action to possess your neighbor's estate, wife, slaves, and so on.*

Propp considers this interpretation about *taking action* to be overdone. He finds nothing wrong in having a command that addresses base human motives of envy and acquisitiveness. Covetous desires can be the root of many a crime, be it theft, murder, adultery, or giving false witness. See Joshua 7:21, where the foolish Achan admitted that he had *coveted* and taken valuable and beautiful (but forbidden) spoils of war.

This final commandment encourages the suppression of envy and covetous greed as much as possible for the good of society. Propp goes further to say, "The last of the Ten Words approaches the Buddha's insight that desire is the source of all unhappiness."

Childs agrees with Propp that the motives of envy and acquisitiveness are at the heart of 20:17. He argues that we cannot force *ḥmd* to mean primarily action to the exclusion of covetous desires, and also finds the verb (*'wh*) for *desire* in Deuteronomy 5:21b to be basically interchangeable with *ḥmd*.

Fretheim notes that perhaps thinking of Exodus 20:17 as *law* is not adequate. Coveting cannot be policed; often it cannot even be observed. Yet 20:17 is an attempt at instruction, the development of an attitude of the heart. Such instruction reminds us of the fundamentally Godward orientation of all ten sayings. Only God can look upon the heart and judge the human spirit.

123. Exodus 20:1–17 as a literary unit is really a creed, which wanders from glimpses of God's nature to a schematic outline of what a believing, just community must practice in order to be more godlike. Most modern readers, familiar with the Ten Commandments as part of our Western civilization, probably think of it as a basic moral code, but that can lead to underestimating its depth and value as a creed, a proclamation of faith.

124. I think the Decalogue in its context can teach modern readers of the Old Testament the importance of belonging to a larger community of faith. While there are many times in life when an individual must wrestle with his or her own demons and temptations (to steal, hate, lie, use drugs, and so on), the Ten Commandments were never meant to be simply a check list for individuals to make sure they were not committing major sins. It was always part of a great

treaty between an imperfect society (both Jewish and Christian) and a generous and loving king. This imperfect society (both Jewish and Christian) has endured for thousands of years, and when some members hate, give false testimony, or abandon their families, the whole society is less able to live up to this creed and to this treaty.

125. The Decalogue was meant to be evocative; it is too compact to explain all our religious beliefs and ethics. This creed evokes goals, but cannot possibly clarify how to accomplish those goals. A simple list of gaps (which anyone could expand) is given here.

   The Decalogue does not in itself explain the following:

   a. how to have faith and to explain our monotheism to others
   b. how to promote the right use of God's name and the Sabbath
   c. how to promote social identity and justice, and to protect ecological resources
   d. how to uphold family, especially when one has had disappointing or harsh familial experiences earlier in life
   e. how to have a sound sexual life that fosters true love, and promotes the sexual morality of the larger society
   f. how to honor all women and men equally.

126. Propp notes that this paragraph could function as a flashback or overview, a description of how the people have felt since the start of Exodus 19:3. The solemn formula in 19:4, "You have seen what I did to the Egyptians," is balanced by that in 20:22, "You have seen for yourselves that I spoke with you from heaven."

   In Deuteronomy 5:22–33, this short passage from Exodus has been expanded, with God approving the people's attitude and their designation of Moses to bring God's words to them. In Deuteronomy, God allows the people to return to their tents while Moses listens to the laws that follow. Perhaps the people had a cautious sense of being exhausted by the sensory overload accompanying the revelation, or they may have been very open to a much larger set of case laws to come. We can take verse 19 to indicate their confidence and trust in God and in Moses.

The more important element in 20:19 is the people's affirmation of Moses as their mediator. God chose a public way of speaking to Moses in 19:9, and carried that out in 19:19. In 19:9, God said to Moses, "I am going to come to you in a dense cloud *in order that* (*b'bwr*) the people may hear when I speak with you and so trust you ever after." This was to convince the people that Moses was God's spokesperson and not simply speaking on his own. Then Moses took the lead in 20:20 to reassure the people, saying that God has come *in order to* (*lb'bwr*) test you and *in order to* (*wb'bwr*) put the fear of him upon you.

In 20:20, Moses speaks of God's purposes. Childs thinks this verse provides the narrator's own key to his understanding of chapters 19—20. First, God has come to *test*. The context is both the theophany of chapter 19 and the Decalogue of chapter 20. The test must include grappling with the burden of the Decalogue. Second, the *fear of God* does not simply refer to emotions felt when in the divine presence. Fear of God is the positive function of the law, the call to obedience in action in daily life. God provides in his law the very motives for obeying God and keeping from sin. The holy nation of 19:6 will be holy insofar as they obey the commandments and render acceptable worship. Election by God brings no comfortable special status, but an invitation both to share the redemption of God to the world, and to bear witness to his final judgment of sin.

Childs recounts that later rabbinic commentary stressed that other nations had been offered covenants and refused them; then Israel was offered one and accepted it. This was a way of explaining why Israel became the chosen people. A different rabbinic view was to say that the Decalogue was commanded in the absolute sense for the good of the world, and thus the Israelites were chosen without choice.

Fretheim also focuses on the interaction of the people with Moses. He notes that the people asked Moses to mediate "on the basis of their experience of need," and that this request was not imposed on them. Moses' reply was to explain God's concern for their welfare, to call their attention to the God who gives the law. Fretheim claims that their request "may interrupt the divine speaking, but it is precisely the interruption God hoped for." The people act from freedom, not fright; experiencing God's purposes will keep them from sin. This positive fear or awe of God will keep "obedience personally oriented." This obedience will be not for the sake of the content of the law, but for the sake of the lawgiver. "God has appeared personally before them to speak these words in order that they might revere and hold fast to God (the giver of the law). If they so focus their eyes on God, it is that which will enable obedience more than attention to the details of the law."

Section Eighteen: Exodus 20:22—23:33

127. The first-person style of these regulations may have the unintended effect of sounding self-centered. However, we can also take the personal references (*alongside me, for me, my name, for me, my altar*) as emphatically monotheistic. Fretheim notes that God has tied these rules directly to himself, and obedience will be a personal, loyal response to his initiative. God promises to come to them and bless their sacrifices; thus he in turn promises to be loyal. God is both lawgiver and promise maker.

No reason is given for the need for plain altars. Perhaps the plainness of the altars harkens back to the simple style of nomadic worship, where an earthen or unworked stone mound would be used once or twice at a camp and then left behind. Another explanation may be simply that Israelites wanted to differentiate their altars from those of neighboring cultures, which were often highly carved.

128. The period of slavery was limited for Hebrew men, and women had some rights to marriage, protection, and fair support at the time of divorce. Perhaps all we can say here is that the laws could have been harsher—that "half a loaf was better than none." The authors believed that their laws were just, and were inspired by their just God.

129. Given the range of rights and duties that slaves had, these laws seem to uphold the status quo, the common good of that slave-owning society. Slaves could not be acquired by kidnapping, nor beaten to death, nor maimed; one was worth thirty shekels of silver when restitution had to be made to the owner. But it was apparently understood that, at times, an owner could inflict limited corporal punishment, and leeway was allowed. Perhaps more precise restrictions would not have been able to be enforced, or violations reported. In the ancient world, slavery was so commonplace that many important slaves had slaves of their own.

130. The cases in Exodus 22:1–17 mainly remind us of the history of jurisprudence within the ancient Near East long ago. It is easy to imagine village and clan elders developing norms such as these.

Verses 18-31 as sayings from God remind us much more forcefully of God's concern for justice, but the style is a bit heavy-handed. It can almost sound as if God is micromanaging, commanding worship, and running a very tight ship. The authors did not intend this impression, but their confidence in these divine death penalties and prohibitions may make us uneasy.

As both sections were fit together into the larger chapter and into the Covenant Code, we are reminded of the legitimate symbiosis of faith and justice. We do believe in a God who wants justice for all people, flocks, and fields.

131. In this passage, one can find firm promises in verses 20, 23, 25b–31; warnings in verses 21, 24–25a, 32; and conditional

promises in verses 22 and 33. These last two are signaled by the word *if* (*if* you listen, *if* you worship their gods).

In the epilogue, the stages of conquest are grim; with God's help, the Canaanites are to be conquered and their shrines are to be demolished. We know in fact that the conquest was quite slow, and that many Canaanites wound up serving their conquerors, intermarrying extensively with them, and leading them down the easy path to polytheism. The hints at rebellion (verse 21) and syncretism (verses 24, 32–33) are obviously projections back from a later time. The Israelites wound up struggling with the lure of polytheism for several centuries after taking over Canaan.

132. The mixture of firm promises, warnings, and conditions adds realism to this profile of the centuries covering the conquest of the land, the period of the monarchy and the Exile in Babylon. God led his people to a land and gave it to them, but their unfaithfulness eventually brought about their own destruction and Exile.

Childs notes that in 23:20–33 there is no mention of the Covenant Code itself, and that in the partially parallel sermon in Deuteronomy 7 there is no mention of an angel. He argues that the epilogue was not designed to wrap up all of the Covenant Code, but only to conclude the ideas found in 23:14–19 (which Childs calls *the law of the land*).

Following Childs's view, the harvest festivals exemplify the proper use of the Holy Land. One is to control the use of leaven, tend the animals, gather the grains, fruits, and olives, and keep in mind that such blessed living in the land is the gift of Yahweh. The pilgrimages to the shrines should enhance everyone's faith, and help them pay due worship to their one God.

The epilogue reminds everyone that life in the Holy Land will not be an eternal vacation. The addictive allure of Canaanite polytheism and superstition, their impressive shrines and idols, and their marriageable sons and daughters must be resisted.

133. Most Christians feel free to build their own ethics without getting lost in the fine underbrush of Old Testament case laws, food regulations, and the like, although they do consider the Decalogue binding.

Some Christians take these dozens of ancient laws as part of a developing code of ethics, one within which "progress" has been made over the centuries, especially with the addition of the higher ethical goals put forth by Jesus.

Childs lists the following four principles of modern exegesis that Christians should keep in mind as a precaution against this way of thinking:

1. All the Old Testament laws are historically conditioned.
2. There is no clear pattern of "ethical progress" in these laws, with their changes and additions. They are all examples of a rich, complex tradition.
3. Most scholars would question whether Jesus ever intended to present a "higher ethic." His interactions with Pharisees and other Jewish leaders were more complex than that.
4. Jewish interpretation of the Mosaic law cannot be dismissed by Christians as "rigid" or "legalistic." It must be understood, first of all, on its own terms before engaging in a debate with Christian theology.

Childs notes that in analyzing Old Testament laws we Christians cannot simply search for what is "eternally valid" or "perfect." We need to relate specifically to the "structuring of the concrete historical life of the people of God, who in ancient Israel, in the first-century church, and today continue to participate both in the kingdom of God and in the world. All forms of law, Old and New Testament alike, must be ultimately judged in the light of the living God himself who has revealed himself in Jesus Christ through a life of complete faithfulness under the law."

Our goal is to understand that the laws in Exodus are historically conditioned and need to be taken on their own terms. We should consider the rights of a slave woman purchased to be the wife of one's son (21:9), restitution for injuries inflicted in a quarrel (21:18–19), freeing a slave whose tooth has been knocked out (21:27), the arrest of a daytime thief rather than his execution (22:3), the protection of aliens, widows, and orphans (22:21–22), interest-free loans to the poor (22:25), the avoidance of bribes (23:8), and the bringing of the best firstfruits to use at sacrifices (23:19) as an admirable seedbed of case law and principles of national unity and charity. The Covenant Code was never meant to be a structured Western system of moral doctrines and definitions.

Section Nineteen: Exodus 24:1–18

134. While we see Moses and the people awestruck and worshipping, we need to be able to imagine the other side of the coin when discussing freedom. The people could have avoided these new responsibilities, taken their flocks, and gone on their way without committing a sin of disobedience. They were skilled shepherds, with nomadic roots. Every day outside of Egypt brought a new chance to do whatever they wanted.

135. Exodus 24:1–2, 9–11 describes God allowing Moses, Aaron, his sons, and the elders to experience a great vision and moment of intimacy with himself. One needs a larger context to realize God's purpose in allowing this vision to happen. If we assume that it is the ending or ratification of the covenant begun in chapter 19, that makes perfect sense, even if the account of their vision seems a bit austere (undetailed), or if the group of leaders seems somewhat passive, people to whom something happened.

Exodus 24:3–8, by contrast, is more vivid in its description of Moses speaking and writing, its account of altar and offerings, its quotations of what the people said and how they said it all together, and its images of blood upon the altar and upon the people. This ratification is more akin to 19:3–8 or 19:3–25 in detail and style.

136. Readers may not understand all the levels of ancient Jewish ceremonial symbolism, but blood spilled at ancient secular covenant ceremonies represents the life and death commitment of the two parties. The fact that some of the blood is first thrown against the altar may make the altar or the blood more holy, more worthy of being a sacramental sign. The fact that the altar and the people undergo the same application of blood is surely a sign of their unity with God in this new covenant. Christians who are used to sacramental rituals such as holy water or incense should find it easy to imagine the impact of these ceremonies at Sinai.

The use of the animal blood at the ceremonies in chapter 24 could have had many meanings. I will mention some of the possibilities cited by Propp, in what I think are an ascending order.

Propp notes that initiation rites often feature a real or symbolic wound representing death, leading to rebirth or new status. At Sinai, the people were sprinkled with blood, and so could be said to be symbolically wounded.

Further, Propp recalls the purifying and protective power attributed to the blood of circumcision rites in the ancient Near East. While we are not dealing with circumcision here, perhaps the blood was thought to have some sacramental, protective force.

On another level, the people may be represented by the sacrifice of the animals; the people were in a sense now offered up to God.

Thinking of the obligations of the covenant, Propp notes, "Exodus 24 may be read as the mirror image of the *Pesach*. The blood ritual in Exodus 12 initiates Israel's freedom; the blood ritual of Exodus 24 terminates it. Released from involuntary servitude to Pharaoh, Israel voluntarily enters Yahweh's servitude."

Most commentators take the sharing of blood between the altar and the people as a sign of their new unity with

Yahweh. In ancient treaty forms, slaughtered animals represented the punishments each party agrees to receive if that party breaks the agreement. So here the people make a commitment to uphold the covenant, and so does God, in that the altar is also sprinkled.

Another use of blood was in ordination rites, which prepared priests to be able to approach God without suffering harm. In Exodus 29:19–21, Propp (309) sees the blood placed on Aaron and his sons at their ordination as "a symbolic wound that confers protection from the divine presence. From Sinai onward, all Israel is Yahweh's priests' kingdom and holy nation. In confirmation that the rite of passage has been efficacious, Exodus 24 describes Israel's representative elders beholding God unscathed." Fretheim finds the ordination rite for Aaron and his sons to be the primary model for the sprinkling of the blood in Exodus 24. He notes that in Exodus 29 and Leviticus 8 blood is also dashed against the altar, and certain amounts of sacrificial meat are to be eaten by the newly ordained and no one else. So in a sense all the people are ordained now to be a priestly kingdom, an example to all the nations.

137. This should have been a "honeymoon period." It should have been a time for reflection on all God's blessings: their movement from slavery to Sinai in just a few months, their religious duties spelled out, the importance of justice in everyday life. Perhaps there was some understandable impatience or eagerness to continue the journey to the land of Canaan. The honeymoon may have waned a bit the longer Moses was absent, given that the people had depended so much on him as leader and spokesman for God. Even so, they should have felt safe, confident, and trustful of God.

Section Twenty: Exodus 25:1—31:18

138. God acts as fund-raiser (more precisely, collector of the necessary metals, fabrics, wood, oil, and so on) and designer of the Tabernacle. The word for *offering* is *terumah*, the same word used for *wave-offerings* of some of the meat of sacrificed animals.

    The appeal for freewill offerings of gold, silver, fine wool and linens, fine leather, spices, and precious gems may come as a surprise to the average reader who probably imagines these recently escaped peasants to have little more than their basic possessions and herds with them, and perhaps a small amount of gifts from their Egyptian neighbors. There is room for exaggeration in all these details about the materials.

139. We are familiar with the idea that inside the Ark would be kept the stone tablets or rolls of parchment containing the other laws given to Moses. Exodus 25:16, 21 speak of the *eduth*, the witnessing materials. Propp suggests that the artifacts kept in the Ark would be undisturbed, and not used as master documents for research or legislation.

    The *cover*, or *seat* (*kapporet*), seems to be the most holy place for God's presence and further communications. The Ark is not simply a throne with an enclosed chest beneath. The *cherubim*, facing each other, spread their wings over the cover in such a way that the ensemble does not look exactly like a chair or throne.

    Cherubim are not always winged angels with human forms and faces, as in most Christian artwork. They often were winged lions or bulls, representing minor gods or forces of nature. Most commonly, they seem to be associated with storm gods; in ancient pagan art they can be seen supporting the arms of thrones, facing forward. Propp calls them *griffins*, to allow for these ancient meanings. The Tabernacle curtains also had embroidered or woven representations of these griffins or cherubim. We would have expected neither the statues nor the designs in fabric, given the biblical prohibitions against images, but the Tabernacle may be the "exception that proves the rule." Some of the psalms have majestic phrases about Yahweh and storms. See Psalm 18, especially verses 9–10.

140. The twelve loaves of bread somehow represented the worship of the twelve tribes, or perhaps served as symbolic gifts of food. They were consumed by the priests and replaced each week. The lamp stand may have been a nested set of three U- or V-shaped arms on a central trunk. Propp suggests that the lamps may have represented the stars (in many ancient religions thought to be minor divinities). It may also have been fairly dark inside the Tabernacle, even during the day, depending on how much light entered through the doorway or around the bottom hem of the tent materials.

141. The Tabernacle is a rectangular tent with a nearly flat roof, divided by an inner fine curtain into two rooms (one at the doorway, and the other farther inside). It measured eighteen by forty-five feet, and was fifteen feet in height. It was made of four different layers of material placed upon wooden, vertical, ladder-shaped supports resting in heavy metal bases. The fine inner fabric was linen and wool, covered by the ordinary goats' hair tent material, and with additional roofing of tanned (reddened) ram leather and, finally, special leather with a beaded surface.

The Ark was kept in the inmost (smaller) room (perhaps a third of the whole floor area), and the outer room (sometimes called the *Tent of Meeting*) held the table, lamp stand, and a small incense altar. There was a vertical freestanding fabric screen a few feet outside the entrance to the tent. Priests performed certain ceremonies in the outer room, and the high priest alone could enter the inmost room on the annual Day of Atonement (Yom Kippur), but at no other time.

142. The Genesis altars were very temporary ones. This one is meant to be noble, even though it had to be portable. It

seems to have been a square metal bin with partially scalloped sides that swept back to the original height at the four corners (called the four *horns* of the altar). The scalloped areas and latticework lower on the sides, or horizontal grates within, provided for the needed drafts of air for effective burning. The horns may have helped hold the wood and the sacrificed animals steady during the burning. Propp suggests that the bin may have been partially filled with sand or stones at each encampment to provide stability, but this ballast would have been discarded when the journey was resumed.

The assembled courtyard curtains measured 150 by 75 feet, with a height of a bit over 7 feet. The high walled courtyard protects the sacred space for the altar and the Tabernacle, requiring those who are to witness ceremonies to enter the courtyard rather than simply gawk across a low fence. The later Temples of Solomon and Herod the Great had massive courtyards and high outer walls, for the same purpose.

143. In 28:3, Aaron's vestments are said to *consecrate him for priesthood*. This is an overstatement, but he does need the vestments, since the mingled blood and oil in 29:21, 29 touch both Aaron and the vestments.

The *ephod* was apparently a vestlike garment that had in the past been used to decorate idols; in various places in the Old Testament, its use was prohibited. Propp suggests that P deliberately uses it in the legitimate cult, rather than avoid mentioning the existence of the garment altogether.

The two stones in the pouch (verse 30), the Urim and the Thummim, were apparently used as lots, to search for yes and no answers, as implied in a few cases in Judges and Samuel. There are other theories about how they were used. Eventually, the custom was discontinued. This may have been another example of P legitimizing an old custom rather than ignoring it.

The ephod is made of a mixture of wool and linen. Such mixtures are forbidden in Leviticus 19:19 and Deuteronomy

22:11. The prohibition may have been to limit such mixtures to vestments, or this may be another "exception that proves the rule."

Aaron's vestments are as complex as other fabrics used in the Tabernacle. Vested, he can be seen as the legitimate caretaker of the whole shrine. The inscribed onyx stones and twelve stones on the breastplate show that he represents all the people as he enters the holy places.

Note the solemn phrases in 28:30, 35–38, 43. Aaron *bears the judgment of the Israelites* and *takes on himself any guilt* in their offerings. His robe has bells at the hem, *lest he die.* He and the other priests must wear full linen undergarments, *or they will bring guilt on themselves and die.* Priests eat of the sin offerings, and risk contamination from blood sacrifices. On Yom Kippur, the whole Tabernacle and the priests must be purified. Propp notes that "the Tabernacle and its personnel function for the land like an antacid, absorbing the people's unsettling transgressions." This might also explain amnesty from cities of refuge when a high priest dies; his death may act as a sin offering for others. Therefore, the vestments may be a form of protection from dangerous contact with divine holiness, in addition to other traditional understandings of the logic of liturgical vestments.

144. Moses coordinates the consecration of the altar and the ordination of the first priests, even though he is never described as a high priest himself. He never wears priestly vestments. This was a unique situation; once a ritual system is under way, an altar or priests could be used in consecrating more priests or more altars. Here the seven days are needed to sanctify the altar and the priests a bit more each day, as the time comes nearer for God to become specially associated with the Ark and the Tabernacle.

In 29:10, 15, 19, Aaron and his sons lay hands on the animal. This may be a sign of the transfer of sin and impurity to the animal, as it now represents sinful humanity. Most of the sacrificed ox (verse 14) is to be destroyed outside the camp, as it represents the sins of the ordinands or of the entire nation. At various points blood is placed on the ordinands; this may represent God giving them back their lives since the animals represented them. Blood placed on their ears, thumbs, and toes purifies them and marks them for service. (A similar rite is used in Leviticus 14:14–20 for the cleansing of those who have had leprosy-like blemishes.) After this purification, the oils are used to consecrate them. Aaron and his sons eat of the ram of ordination each day as the donors of the animals, not as priests. Verse 33 speaks of *atonement.* The basic verb, *kpr,* can mean "purge, cover over, smear, appease, ransom, or annul." It forms the noun *kapporet,* the *cover* or *seat* of the Ark. Propp notes that many of this range of meanings can be used here. "With the Sin-offering and its blood rite, the offerant *ransoms* his life from Yahweh: *smearing* the Altar *cleanses* him and effects *reconciliation* with Yahweh, who *covers over* and *annuls* his sin/impurity."

145. Paying the flat tax was a way of promoting equal responsibility and participation in the faith. The custom lasted even into Roman times, with Roman soldiers accompanying the large overseas shipments of money to Jerusalem. Having only one sanctuary for the whole nation was actually economical, and maintaining the Temple never became an oppressive burden.

    Some of the original census-tax silver will be used in 38:25–28 for metal bases for the ladder-shaped supports in the Tabernacle. Reference to *ransom for their lives* in 30:12, 16 may have to do with another biblical tradition that taking a census can be sinful or dangerous under certain circumstances. At times census taking was considered inimical to tribal life and customs. Here the weight of all the silver coins will be an indirect way of estimating the total population of adult males within the nation. The word for *ransom* and the references to *atonement* in 30:15, 16 are all forms of the same word *kpr.*

The restricted formulae for the oil and incense made them special markers for these ceremonies. Such markers can enhance inner feelings all the more when they are not used in daily life outside the Tabernacle.

146. God has bestowed special skills on these two artisans, who will be able to design and monitor all the metallurgy, carpentry, weaving, and so on. Everything will be first class, done by local talent. God is proud of all the art and workmanship called for in his directives to Moses. The name Bezalel may mean *in God's shelter*; he was from the southernmost tribe of Judah. The name Oholiab may mean *the Father is my tent*; he was from the northernmost tribe of Dan.

Within a religious system, liturgy is its own justification. It is not the main instrument of evangelization, but rather the main instrument of communal worship and an incentive to communal and individual prayer. The statement in 31:3, *I have filled him with divine spirit* (or *with the spirit of God*), is quite striking. The only other use of the phrase by P is found in Genesis 1:2, *the spirit of God swept over the face of the waters.* Propp speaks of Bezalel the artist as a "theologian, exampling divine activity and rendering it active and comprehensible." The Sabbath is an invisible sign, built into time itself.

Section Twenty-one: Exodus 32:1–35

147. The people violate the first commandment by serving other gods, or at least serving an image representing Yahweh or some of his spiritual forces. They also reject Moses without proof that he cannot or will not return. They then draft or force Aaron to take on forbidden roles, and they engage in a prohibited festival, even if it was exclusively in honor of Yahweh.

Aaron sins by agreeing to cooperate, asking for the gold, casting the idol, building an altar, and proclaiming and supervising the prohibited festival.

The statement in 32:1 that the people *gathered* (*qhl*) *around* Aaron could also be translated *gathered against*, in a threatening sense (see Num 16:3; 17:7; 20:2). The people have already made up their minds that Moses has abandoned them or is not coming back for some other reason, and they want their plans put into effect by Aaron. They do not ask him for advice, but instruct him to make them images of *gods*. The reference to *this Moses* may be sarcastic, and to say that he was *the man who brought us up out of the land of Egypt* certainly ignores the fact that God, not Moses, brought them out (Exod 20:2).

Aaron presses for their gold to make the statue, whereas in 25:1–7 God had planned for Moses to ask for voluntary contributions for all the materials needed for the Tabernacle. There have been rabbinic attempts over the centuries to show Aaron as an unwilling participant who tried to delay events, but the story is moving so quickly that Aaron and the people seem to be on the same page.

Cassuto is very defensive of Aaron, saying that he made the calf as a vacant throne, not thinking of the slippery slope the people might follow to idolatry. Aaron only wanted to take the place of Moses in some way, not of God. Aaron's action was partly passive, and even in its active aspect lacked any evil intent. He collected the gold to delay the whole project. Cassuto paraphrases Aaron's remark in 32:24 by saying, "I did not specifically intend to fashion this calf, but it emerged from my hands fortuitously, just as anything else might have resulted." Moses understood the position, and realized Aaron's limited responsibility and the greater culpability of the people. Christians may be less uncomfortable than Cassuto with the idea of Aaron's great sin, given that they have the tradition of Peter denying knowing Jesus, and the other apostles fleeing the night Jesus was arrested.

In 32:4, Aaron may have done detail work with a chisel-like tool, or used that chisel to make a mold for casting. Propp argues that the calf (young adult bull) may well have been a wooden carving, overlaid with gold leaf or gold veneers. The people immediately use the statue as they would an idol, and speak of *gods* bringing them up from Egypt.

Fretheim suggests that the calf in Exodus 32 was an attempt to represent the angel of Exodus 23:20–33, but now this figure is more separable from Yahweh himself than was intended in chapter 23. The term *go before* is used of the pillar in 14:19 and of the angel in 14:19; 23:20, 23; 32:34; 33:2. The problem is that any focus on an angel means there will be less focus on Yahweh.

Aaron built an altar before the calf and declared that the next day would be a festival to the LORD. However Aaron may imagine the purpose of the calf, calling an unscheduled festival was not within his authority as the high priest. Jeroboam did the same, in 1 Kings 12:32–33, with no more authority or divine approval.

Exodus 32:6 mentions *burnt offerings* and *sacrifices of well-being*, the same types of sacrifices arranged by Moses in 24:5. There they were appropriate; here they are sacrilegious acts.

At the festival, the people began to *revel* (*zhq*). This Hebrew word normally means to "laugh" and "play"; in a few instances, it may have sexual meanings. Childs and Fretheim agree that there may be sexual overtones here, but Propp is doubtful that the authors are describing general sexual license. He thinks it might be a reference instead to certain married couples who chose not to follow the custom of abstinence immediately prior to religious ceremonies (see Exod 19:15).

148. Moses rightly puts greater blame on Aaron, since he was second in command and in God's favor all along. Aaron should not have *caused* the great sin, but should have opposed it even at the cost of his life. He is not only as responsible for the frenzy as all the people, but even more responsible because of his priestly rank. The remarks of Aaron in 32:22–24 are so self-serving that they do not deserve a response. Before an angry Moses, Aaron puts all

the blame on *the people, that they are bent on evil;* but when they first came to Aaron (32:1), he caught the prevailing winds instantly and did not challenge them at all.

In 32:22, Aaron is evasive, trying to shift the blame back to the people and to minimize his role in making the idol. He claims that the people freely gave him the gold. Aaron's remark that the people are *bent on evil* echoes 32:12, where God was cautioned not to have the Egyptians say the same about him ("It was *with evil intent* that he brought them out..."). Aaron does not attempt to negotiate for the people here; he is too concerned to get himself out from under Moses' anger. His last remark, that *out came this calf,* highlights his passive stance.

Moses interceded for his people with God and made some headway; Aaron had not even tried to temper the religious anxieties of the people. Moses terminated the conversation with Aaron, obviously frustrated and disappointed in him.

149. God tells Moses to go down at once (verse 7), but God wants to destroy the people (verse 10). He is clearly upset and angry that they have acted *perversely* and *quickly* and are *stiff-necked.* He is shocked and feels betrayed.

In this paragraph, God is presented as one searching for a strategy, always in consultation with Moses. Moses has the right to speak up. In 32:7, the LORD is furious, angrily telling Moses that they are *your* people whom *you* brought up. (We are reminded of the way one parent blames the other, saying that *your* son or *your* daughter has done something wrong.)

In 32:10, God also offers to have Moses become a second Abraham, so to speak. He would be willing to have Moses become a new ancestor whose descendants could avoid idolatry in the future. Then God snaps at Moses, "Now let me alone, so that my wrath may burn hot against them and I may consume them." To be *left alone* is what one desires when grieving.

Fretheim notes that *let me alone* could mean that the decision and will of God is not yet set. This may be an indirect invitation for Moses to say something, to not leave his LORD alone. As we will see in 32:11–13, Moses did contribute something to the divine deliberation. God allowed his relationship with Moses to limit his own free decisions. Childs agrees that God left the door open for intercession; he allowed himself to be persuaded to calm down.

Fretheim suggests that *consuming* the people does not need to mean genocide. Removing them from God's special care and concern would let them fend for themselves and likely lose their religious identity; this would be worse for Israel than their bondage in Egypt.

150. In verse 11, after God says that he wanted to be alone, Moses immediately takes the defense. Without seeing anything firsthand, he reminds God that they are "*your* people, whom *you* brought out of the land of Egypt...." Fretheim calls this an appeal to reason, but it may still be the weakest argument. Reminding God of all the work he had just done to bring the people out of Egypt might not move him to chance "throwing more good work after bad."

Next Moses portrays the satisfaction Egyptians would find in learning that their recent nightmare had come to this ironic end, in which the Israelites wound up being punished by their own God. This is not as odd an argument as it might first appear; there was a public, international religious dimension to the escape from Egypt, and there could be puzzlement or bad example if the Israelites never reached their new land. This is an appeal to God's reputation. (Propp speaks of the way kings have always been competitive with their fellow kings.) The plagues had made sense as public displays of God's desire for justice on a worldwide scale. Cutting off Israel now could raise questions for other nations. See the parallels in Numbers 14:13–16 and Deuteronomy 32:26–27. Deuteronomy 9:28 puts Moses' words more strongly—that the Egyptians would say God hated his people.

Yet unfavorable Egyptian public opinion cannot serve as the absolute loophole for getting out of this betrayal. However, Moses plays this card anyway, perhaps out of desperation.

The final argument, in verse 13, recalling the promises made to Abraham, Isaac, and Jacob, may contain the strongest argument, an appeal to God's promises in the past. They were "*your* servants…*you* swore to them by *your* own self…." The promises in Genesis were unconditional. Still, the recent covenant promise to use no images and to follow no other gods is in effect, and the offer to Moses to become the second Abraham can be a way God could "keep his promises" from long ago.

As far as the story line goes, all the reasons combined are inadequate. The betrayal was too extensive for Moses to counter in one brief plea. Propp admires Moses for trying to negotiate. He notes (554) that "[Moses] prudently declines what God offers [to become a new Abraham] in a fit of pique, knowing that Yahweh must of his nature be true to his promises. In many ways, Moses is the quintessential loyal counselor, bravely facing down his liege when the latter is bent upon foolishness. Moses' selfless dealings with God set into harsh relief Israel's recurrent ingratitude."

I would suggest that God may not be in a fit or on a foolish tangent; he has a right to be offended or frustrated with the people to whom he had given so much and who had freely sworn their obedience unto death just weeks before. Anybody would feel the same at flagrant violations of a contract or treaty entered with good will. Fretheim compares this to a divorce, which is worse than simply breaking up with a casual mate. Those who make the choice for Yahweh and then depart from it have done worse than those who do not choose him.

In verse 12, Moses had asked God to *change your mind about the evil* intended (NRSV paraphrases this as *change your mind and do not bring disaster*). In verse 14, the same phrase is used, *the LORD changed his mind about the evil* (*disaster*). The verb can mean "to allow oneself a change of heart." In context, this change of mind may well be limited. God does not speak again until verses 33–34, where he speaks of individual sinners and the day of punishment. In verse 35, death by disease came to more Israelites because of the making of the calf. Complete forgiveness does not appear until 34:10.

The process of reconciliation has just begun. Fretheim remarks that Moses brings decisive thinking, energy, and insights to the table. What Moses says and does takes on significance because of the relationship he already has with God. God changes his mind, not about the disloyalty, but about the amount of punishment he wishes to deliver. Therefore, God is open to change. He is open to the future so that his salvific will for all might be realized as fully as possible. Fretheim (287) concludes, "God's steadfastness has to do with God's love; God's faithfulness has to do with God's promises; God's will is for the salvation of all. God will always act, even make changes, in order to be true to these unchangeable ways and to accomplish these unchangeable goals."

151. The next paragraph describes Moses' descent from the summit, carrying the two tablets. These verses cover a few hours of time, and add suspense and irony. The narrator even takes time to describe the tablets in detail. The unbroken tablets may imply that the covenant has been kept on God's side. We do not know at this point how Moses will confront his fellow Israelites when he arrives at the camp.

Moses meets Joshua at his station; Joshua is not yet aware of the incident, nor of what Moses has been able to do so far. The festival can be heard before it comes into view. The saying about the noises of war might remind readers of Joshua's leadership in the battle with the Amalekites (Exod 17:8–15), during which Aaron and Hur held up the arms of Moses for victory. Childs finds the reference to Joshua simply a device to include the ancient poetic line of 32:18, after which Joshua has no further role in this chapter. Moses' poetic reply to Joshua contrasts the

ʿanot (noise) of winners and the *ʿanot* (noise) of losers to the actual *ʿannot* (singing). The three Hebrew words are all from the same verb, but the differences are hard to catch in English. For *ʿannot* the NRSV has *the sound of revelers*, thus uniting the verse to 32:7, where a different verb (*zhq*) was used. The sounds Joshua and Moses heard could have been of victors who had driven off bandits, or of people celebrating life, but they were in fact the sound of sinners, sinners committing idolatry and disobeying a life-and-death covenant.

152. In these seven verses, Moses the negotiator becomes the enraged leader, judge, and jury. He is very shocked at the calf and the dancing (even though he knew about these things before he arrived). He smashes the tablets, most likely dramatizing his own conviction that the covenant has been completely violated by the people. He pulverizes the calf and renders its debris forever impure by having the people drink that mixed with water. Cassuto takes this as an application of the trial by ordeal in Numbers 5, and argues that the three thousand men who were executed had been either the leading revelers or men who were visibly ill, having failed the ordeal. As he came to the calf to destroy it, Moses consulted no one and gave no explanations. See 2 Kings 23 for the extensive reforms of Josiah, which involved the destruction and desecration of many shrines and idols.

Moses grills Aaron briefly, and then discontinues that pointless interview, and observes that the people are still *running wild*, despite what he had done to the calf. We can imagine Moses being angry, frustrated, sympathetic with God's grief, and feeling betrayed by the very people he has worked with so long. We do not know if Moses had any further instructions from God prior to 32:33.

Fretheim is struck by the intensity of Moses in 32:17–27. He remarks,

> One wonders why there was none of this anger when he was informed by God of these events. He equivocates with Joshua, not telling him what he already

knows. Nor does he tell the people about his intercession with God and its effect; in fact, in verse 27 he
speaks a word for God that has no basis in the previous conversation. This suggests that the narrator
indends to overdraw Moses' reaction as somewhat
too zealous on behalf of Yahweh. (287)

153. In this passage Moses becomes judge, jury, and executioner. God may have changed his mind in verse 14, but
Moses himself uses stern measures at this point.

The evil momentum of this unofficial festival persisted.
The people *ran wild* (*prᶜ*) the Hebrew means to be
"untied" or "loose." The same word was used in Exodus
5:4, "why are you *taking* the people *away* from their
work?" The text reminds us that their running wild was
Aaron's fault, a sin of omission on his part at the least.

At this point Moses calls for each person to decide for or
against the LORD. This is an authentic invitation to cease
sinning and get back on track immediately. The majority
kept on celebrating, prolonging their apostasy and disloyalty. The men of the tribe of Levi, Moses' own tribe, come
forward, but no one else. If everyone had come forward,
perhaps there would have been no need for the severe punishments beginning in 32:28.

When Moses announces the use of deadly force to end
the misguided ceremonies, he uses the prophetic style,
"Thus says the Lord." For those coming upon this story
for the first time, this command to attack might be
astounding. The repenting of the Levites does not prepare
us for their execution of three thousand heads of families.
Nothing could prepare us for that image of execution,
since we rarely think in such corporate or communal terms
(see Deut 13; 1 Kgs 18:40; 2 Kgs 10:17). Fretheim notes
that the dramatic death sentence should "occasion critical
reflection by those of us who live in an age where virtually
anything that goes by the name of religion is tolerated."

The Levites carried out their orders and three thousand
people were slain, presumably from among the six hundred

thousand men mentioned in Exodus 12:37. The three thousand represent the rest. (A variant figure of *twenty-three* thousand is found in the LXX, and from there came into the New Testament in 1 Cor 10:8. Propp thinks a simple copying error in Greek led to this variant.)

The story does not explain when (or if) God had given such a stern command to Moses, nor if just one pass through the camp was the plan. It is possible to imagine Moses both initiating the executions and then calling a halt to them on his own.

One biblical tradition about the Levites (32:29) is that by carrying out Moses' orders and stopping these unholy rites, the Levites set themselves apart for the LORD's service. This was their ordination ceremony. Ordination should be for service and leadership as well as for conducting liturgical ceremonies. In fulfilling the duty laid upon them by Moses, the Levites showed more leadership than Aaron. Aaron was not defrocked, but the Levites were raised up to priestly rank and leadership. Childs notes that, in the light of Aaron's later prestige, it is all the more remarkable that this story was retained in the tradition.

154. Moses returns to his role as a negotiator; he seems compassionate, but he may be less sure of how things will turn out. The *perhaps* in verse 30 and the *if* and *if not* in verse 32 indicate more caution than anything he had said in verses 11–13. His request to offer his life in atonement for the life of his people is generous, but receives no reply. Apparently, God does not want such a trade. He refuses to accept Moses' offer, without commenting on the merit of the principle of one atoning for the many.

Some commentators take Moses' proposal to be blotted out of the LORD's book to be little more than a bluff, or perhaps hyperbole or emotional overstatement. Some wonder if Moses was simply indicating that he did not wish to be the sole survivor or the leader of just the surviving Levite families. These possibilities do not lessen his generosity or his identification with all the Israelites. I would side with Fretheim and take his offer of his own life as Moses' serious attempt to redeem his people.

Childs notes Moses' statement to the people in 32:30 that *perhaps* he can make atonement. By offering his life Moses bravely attempts to negotiate and fully atone, but this time it does not work. On the other hand, God's reply in 32:34 cannot simply be taken as the voice of eternal doom. In the larger context, Moses will pursue negotiations in chapters 33—34 and good will come of his work in the long run.

God listens to Moses, but leaves things unexplained and undecided. He speaks of the lives of those *who have sinned against me*, and of a coming *day of punishment*. The *plague* (epidemic) which follows took more lives, but we have no idea how many. He tells Moses to continue leading *the* people (not *my* people or *your* people), and promises that his messenger/angel will continue to assist. He does not describe how near or far from them he himself will be. In a way, God, like Moses, does not seem to be sure how things will turn out.

The last part of verse 34 is ominous. There will still be punishments to come. The Hebrew speaks of *visiting* or *settling accounts* (*pqd*), but the context is clear. There will be more atonement or expiation demanded for this disloyalty. The command for Moses to continue the journey, and the promise of the angel to guide, still seem to be demoting them in some way. Fretheim suggests again, as he had regarding 32:10, that God contemplates letting them fend for themselves and likely losing their identity. They would in the future suffer for their sins according to the normal moral order of things.

Exodus 32:35 ends the story with one more stern detail. A plague came upon them for the calf that they and Aaron had made. This verse illustrates the decision God had just made and the failure of the intercession. Childs takes this verse as a minor addition to the story; I think he fails to see that it adds emphasis to the preceding two verses and to the serious subject matter of the entire chapter.

The people must be in some phase of repentance. The executions by the Levites and the plague may have brought them to their senses. So Moses attempts to atone, and God permits the journey to resume, but the absence of any words or actions from the people in this passage hampers any further analysis on our part. Most likely the people have no idea how things will turn out. We readers are in the same boat. That is what the storytellers have done to us deliberately.

Section Twenty-two: Exodus 33:1–23

155. God seems crabby, perhaps trying to calm down. Once again God refers to the people whom *you* have brought up, but in the same verse he also recalls his promises to the Patriarchs. He then speaks of sending an angel to guide them, but in verse 3 he declines to accompany them himself. While the angel represents some assistance from God, the point is that God is still close to ending his special relationship with them. God seems to be uncertain, caught between disappointment and fidelity to his word.

God's remark, that he would consume them if he went along, is forceful. Propp calls God "dangerously irascible" here, which is putting it harshly, in my opinion. Childs says that God fears that his presence would be a threat to their existence because of their inclination to sin. Fretheim agrees, and calls this a marvelous picture of divine reluctance. It is best for both God and Israel for God to keep away. Fretheim also sees this as God's reluctance to be present at the Tabernacle within the sanctuary, as described in chapters 25—31. His solemn promises in 29:43–46 to dwell there are now on hold.

156. Verses 4–6 describe the reactions and gestures of the people. They dressed simply, as was the style for mourning or repentance, having heard God's *harsh words*. (The Hebrew has *bad word*.) Moses repeated the saying about God consuming them, adding the dramatic *if for a single*

moment. The several references to taking off their jewelry may be somewhat repetitious or confusing, but as Propp remarks, the people have to help Moses. Moses cannot seek reconciliation without their active repentance.

In 33:4, it seems the people took the initiative in not wearing jewelry under the circumstances. In 33:5–6, God asks for this sign from them; so then not wearing the jewelry might possibly be more a matter of obedience or fear. By including both traditions the editors leave things a bit more up in the air, which adds to the impression that God himself is up in the air about what to do next.

Thus 33:5 shows God aware of his own potential to consume them, his wish for their not using jewelry, and his plan to decide what to do next. Fretheim talks of God trying to find some new way into the future. Propp (598) puts it more amusingly with his statement, "Like an exasperated parent, Yahweh has exhausted his patience. He needs a vacation from his chosen people."

157. In 33:7, we are told that any individual Israelite could pray at the tent outside the camp. The people would all respectfully stand when Moses went to the tent, and when the pillar of cloud appeared, all would bow down in reverence. The people seem to be united and repentant, and again reliant on Moses as their leader and mediator with God.

This paragraph describes the *Tent (ohel) of Meeting (mo'ed)*, which is new to the story. Some argue that this was Moses' own residence, but others take it as a separate structure. Fretheim remarks that this passage slows down the main story.

This was an ordinary tent outside the camp, and not like the elaborate sanctuary Tabernacle planned in chapters 25—31, but not yet built. We could assume that God allowed this Tent of Meeting as a limited substitute for the Tabernacle, or we could imagine that Moses came up with the idea as a way to keep in contact with God, even if God did not wish to be in the midst of their camp. In 2 Samuel 7:6, God speaks of moving about *in a tent and a tabernacle.*

Childs notes that the passage unites God, the people, and Moses in one activity, and serves as a bridge to what follows. The sincere repentance of the people provides Moses with a warrant to intercede.

158. In this key conversation, Moses takes the initiative, speaking four of the six verses. He relies on the favor he already enjoys, being known by name, and asks not so much for a clarification of whom the LORD will send, but for a commitment that the LORD will, so to speak, send himself with them. Asking to see God's ways (verse 13) so that he may know him is another way of angling for this same commitment. When God agrees, Moses does not move to statements of praise and gratitude, but continues to make statements of negotiation, such as *do not carry us up from here*, and *how shall it be known* and *in this way we shall be distinct*. Therefore, the LORD ends in verse 17 by reconfirming what he had just said in verse 14. Moses has brought God around to agree to be present within the Tabernacle when it is constructed.

Propp points to a chiasmic structure in these six verses, a triple sandwich of matching pairs of verses. Chiasms are a common pattern in oral traditions, always emphasizing the central portion of the passage. Let us look at the three layers in turn, bearing with some repetition from the preceding paragraph.

1. The outer layer starts with verse 12, where Moses complains to God that God has not let him know who will go with them, even though God works closely with Moses (knows his name and extends favor to him). In the concluding verse 17, God agrees to do the very thing Moses had asked, and reconfirms that he does know Moses by name and favors him.
2. The second, inner layer starts with verse 13, in which Moses says, "[S]how me your ways, so that I may know you." Moses also speaks for the people: "Consider too that this nation is your people." Fretheim notes that this

is a strategic move; if God understands the importance of his relationship with Moses, what Moses thinks about the people is also important. Moses thinks that Israel should continue to be God's special people in spite of what they have done. In verse 16, Moses points four times to the people united with him (*"I and your people...*unless you go with *us...we* shall be distinct, *I and your people...."*).

3. At the inmost core, in 33:14, God agrees that "my *presence (face)* will go (*with you* is not in the Hebrew), and I will *give you* (singular) *rest."* Moses replies in verse 15 that God's *presence (face)* is everything; otherwise, moving on toward Canaan is pointless. The Promised Land will not be significant if they lose their special place in God's design for the entire world. Childs notes that Moses shakes off the offer of personal comfort or rest for himself, and demands that the response include the people. In all this Moses is putting his cards on the table.

159. The offer to send an angel (33:2; 32:34) was intended as a compromise from the beginning. Moses is not satisfied with any such reluctant compromise. He is determined to continue to seek full reconciliation between God and Israel.

160. This *favor (hen)* or *approval* is not to be confused with earned friendship or compatibility. However, it does have to do with hard work and reliability. Moses was drafted at the burning bush, put out in front of the Pharaoh and his own terrified and unpredictable fellow Hebrews, made spokesman for the covenant and messenger for hundreds of laws, trained in all the details regarding the planned Tabernacle, and left to clean up this disaster of the golden calf. Since he had never been fired, or given the chance to quit, he has some sense of God's approval and willingness to continue working with him. Moses is invoking this favor now as a way of influencing God's thinking. It is a legitimate strategy on his part, even though God does not "owe" him anything more.

161. When Moses says *show me your ways*, he could be asking for several different things. Propp mentions four of them: the *ways* (routes) to go safely through the wilderness to Canaan, the *intention* of God to go with them or not, the *ways* (behaviors) God expects of his people, and God's own *ways* (elements of his character). Most readers would concentrate on the second choice, the intention of God to go with them or not, given the immediate context.

162. While commentators differ on fine points in these two verses, the main point is that Moses is talking about the identity of the Israelites. They are not just another nation, culture, or language group. Their relationship with their God is the foundation for their being, going all the way back to Abraham. Moses is pleading for (not demanding) mercy so that this relationship can be fully repaired and renewed. The two verses show Moses at his boldest.

163. In 33:18, we might expect Moses to be grateful for God's agreements in these negotiations. Asking that he himself see God's glory seems to be a new topic, unless we consider it to be what Moses meant by *show me your ways* in 33:13. On balance, most commentators see the request as something extra.

    Even after this success in verse 17, Moses goes further. He asks to see God's glory. Fretheim notes that God is not bothered by Moses' request. That he allows Moses a vision at all is a demonstration of God's mercy and graciousness. God's freedom is thus a freedom *for* Moses. From Exodus 3 on, Moses has had several special moments with God, and has struggled with the Egyptians and with his own people to relay God's messages to them. Propp speaks of Moses' request here as emblematic of a "common human sense of alienation from the divine." We can never get enough of divine presence and reassurance.

    This may be so, but we should be alert to the context, and not just think of common human fascinations with divine forces. In our passage, perhaps this vision of glory could show Moses God's power to lead Israel, or it could help Moses to understand that forgiveness can lead to a second covenant (as will happen in chapter 34).

Propp refers to older rabbinic commentary that compared Abraham's question in Genesis 15:8, "O Lord God, how am I to know..." and Moses' question in 33:16, "How shall it be known...." In Genesis 15:17, a flaming torch passed between the sacrificed animals, while here (33:19) God says that all his *goodness* (*twb*) will pass before Moses. Verbal forms of the same word appear in Genesis 32:10 and Joshua 24:20, speaking of God's *good plans* for Jacob and of the *good* God had done to Israel when he led them out of Egypt. The noun form is well known from Psalm 145:7, "they shall celebrate the fame of your abundant *goodness.*"

Fretheim speculates that Moses was trying to see how God could come to their Tabernacle without being a dangerous presence. He notes that God redirects the request to see the glory by saying that he will make his goodness pass before Moses and he will proclaim his name to Moses.

In 33:19, God speaks of allowing Moses to see his *goodness* and to hear a *proclamation* of more of the meaning of the name Yahweh. God goes on to describe protecting Moses from seeing his face—but catching a glimpse of his back—but that theme is not continued in chapter 34. In 33:20—34:8, we get to listen to the same proclamation Moses heard, but there is no description of Moses seeing an image of the *goodness* or the *glory*. God is willing to proclaim his name. Whatever else Moses may have wished at this point is sidestepped. Moses is not a co-steerer here, although he asked for the privilege of seeing God's glory. He just tags along with God's instructions.

164. As God indicates that he will show his goodness and proclaim his name, he says, *I will be gracious to whom I will be gracious, and will show mercy on whom I will show mercy.* This theme will be expanded in 34:6–7. The statements are tautologies (also called *idem per idem* statements, a Latin phrase meaning "the same by the same"); we still use such

intentionally mysterious statements today, for example in "We shall see what we shall see."

Propp finds these divine tautologies evasive and unhelpful, evidence of God at times giving warnings or being uncooperative for some other reason. Here Propp focuses on the thin ice—the inconstancy of the people. He notes that some ancient rabbis did the same, citing one named Rashi. Propp puts it very bluntly: "In the immediate context, Yahweh is reaffirming his loyalty to Moses. He is also implicitly threatening that he may or may not favor Israel when they pray (Rashi). That is, while allowing Moses to manipulate him, Yahweh saves his dignity by emphasizing his sovereign right to arbitrary judgment." Cassuto is of the same opinion.

Childs takes Exodus 33:17–23 as both a climax to Moses' intercession and a preparation for the covenant renewal in the next chapter. Moses has to deal with God, who is both the one who judges and the one who forgives. He notes, "The Old Testament rather runs the risk of humanizing God through its extreme anthropomorphism…than undercut the absolute seriousness with which God takes the intercession of his servant. Moses, on his part, refuses anything less than the full restoration of Israel as God's special people."

Section Twenty-three: Exodus 34:1–35

165. The first tablets were made by God. They were spoken of in 24:12, given to Moses in 31:18, and spoken of again in 32:15–16; Moses smashed them in 32:19.

On the other hand, in 34:1, 4 Moses prepares two blank tablets to take up the mountain, and does some of the inscribing in 34:28a. In 34:1, God does mention that Moses smashed the original tablets.

Another difference from the earlier Sinai covenant in Exodus 19—24 is that no one else is allowed to accompany

Moses this time. The people are first mentioned in 34:30, when Moses returns to the camp.

Propp notes that God takes the initiative when commanding Moses to prepare the tablets. In 34:1, the Hebrew has *cut for yourself two tablets of stone.* Many English translations omit *for yourself.* Propp wonders if the phrase hints that God is still miffed at Moses. Moses has to prepare two blank tablets this time, to replace, as God mentions, the former tablets, *which you broke.*

166. In the formula in chapter 34, there are more phrases referring to God's mercy, and they are mentioned first. In 20:5–6, punishment was mentioned first, and there were much briefer references to mercy. The several mentions of *steadfast love* (*hesed*) refer specifically to the absolute loyalty of each covenant partner.

Propp notes that in verses 6–7 we do not get any details of the vision, but instead we get a "verbal portrait of Yahweh's personality. He knows how to cherish a grudge, but is more inclined to reward than to punish.... Now, after the Gold Calf fiasco, Yahweh realizes that he must make it clear that he both rewards and punishes."

Fretheim admits that the proclamation has a certain abstract, even propositional character to it. He sees it as a statement of basic Israelite convictions regarding its God. It is a canon of the kind of God Israel's God is, in the light of which God's ongoing involvement in its history is to be interpreted.

Fretheim compares this proclamation with the statements in Exodus 20:5–6 (and the brief allusion in 23:21). By contrast, in 34:6–7 the topic of punishment is moved to the end. This change in the word order could well mean that wrath is not a continuing aspect of the nature of God, but a particular response to individual events. *Jealousy* is not mentioned here, as it was in 20:5, and when jealousy is mentioned in 34:14 it is not coupled to punishment as such. In addition, the phrase in 20:6 about those *who love me and keep my commands* is not used here; we can assume the omission is intentional, to broaden the scope of God's love and forgiveness. So 34:6–7 has a new emphasis on divine mercy, forgiveness, and patience. Using *steadfast love* twice and dropping conditional phrases highlight the unconditionality of the divine love to Israel.

Fretheim also reminds us that the proclamation of God in 34:6–7 describes his relationship to all peoples. In Genesis 8:21—9:17, God backed off from any further total destruction of life and extended promises of mercy to a sinful world. Now he does the same with his own chosen people who had sinned so extensively by means of the golden calf. In Genesis and in Exodus the forgiveness is undeserved, grounded in God's grace. He does these things as creator. The striking forgiveness in Exodus 34 may well serve as a good example and have a good effect on others. This may be hinted at in 34:10 where God says that "all the people among whom you live shall see the work of the LORD."

In 34:7, divine forgiveness is spoken of as a fundamental way of conquering sin (*forgiving iniquity and transgression and sin*). Fretheim notes that what had earlier in 23:21 been stated as an impossibility (the angel pardoning transgression) is now proclaimed as a new way of God's relating to sinful creatures. In a sense, Moses' pleas for forgiveness will now benefit the whole world.

Note God's earlier statement in 33:19, *I will be gracious to whom I will be gracious....* Fretheim remarks, "This verse indicates that this divine decision is freely chosen by God. God's concern is *not* to stake a claim for a divine freedom *from* Moses or Israel, a freedom to be gracious toward some but not others if God so wills. It is a declaration of God's freedom *to move beyond previously stated stipulations* and reach out in mercy." It is a statement of God's graciousness *for* Moses, God's freedom *for* others, not *from* others. In 34:6–7, God makes this gracious move toward Israel because it is the divine nature to do so.

Fretheim finds another relevant parallel in the Book of Jonah. If God desires to have mercy even on such a renegade people as the Ninevites, God is free to make that move without being subject to Jonah's charge of being merely indulgent or unfair. Jonah quotes Exodus 34:6–7 in Jonah 4:2; he protests mercy for the Ninevites, while he was quite willing to accept it for himself.

Fretheim concludes that after the golden calf incident the people can claim no partial goodness or faithfulness that could merit lenience. They deserve death, by their own free assent to the covenant. Only now can grace be seen for what it in fact is: an incredible gift, extended only at the divine initiative.

167. In Exodus 34:8–9, Moses falls in worship after this proclamation, but immediately asks again for the LORD's complete pardon, using some of the phrases of 33:13–16. Propp takes verse 9 as Moses' last attempt to manipulate and argue. Fretheim comments that in 34:9 Moses notices God's mercy, speaking of going with *us*, pardoning *our* iniquity and *our* sin, taking *us* for your inheritance. Moses' prayer explores even more deeply these adjustments in God's own self-proclamation. They have fundamentally to do with a change in the divine relation to Israel's sinfulness. Moses did not identify himself as a sinful fellow Israelite in 32:30–32. Here in chapter 34 he asks God to go with them on the way, all of them relying on God's forgiveness. The request is for the exact opposite of 33:3–5, where God wanted to stay away from them to avoid consuming them.

Fretheim draws out parallels to the Flood story. After the Flood God promised in Genesis 8:21 never again to destroy all life, *for the inclination of the human heart is evil from youth.* God knows humans will sin as much after the Flood as before. Fretheim concludes that "if human beings are to continue to live, they must be *undergirded* by the divine promise. And so it is *because* of human sinfulness that God promises to stay with the world."

In Exodus 34:9, Moses says, "[L]et the LORD go with us. *Although* this is a stiff-necked people...." The word *although* (*ki*) can often be translated *because*. The nearby references to Israel as a *stiff-necked people* seem to confirm this possible use of *because* in 34:9. In 32:9, God used the term *stiff-necked* to describe those who had just made the golden calf. In 33:3–5, God wanted to stay away from such stiff-necked people to avoid consuming them. The word *for* in the phrase in 33:3, "I would consume you on the way, *for* you are a stiff-necked people," could easily be replaced by *because*.

In 34:9, Moses seems to be describing both the past and the future. He implies that Israel will continue to be stubborn and sinful even if God goes with them. Moses is not asking for an immorality discount or forgiveness mileage points, but he is saying that only if God chooses to be with them and forgive them can they move into the future with their distinct role in salvation, spoken of in 33:16.

In 34:9, Moses does not point to examples of Israel's repentance, such as the removal of ornaments in 33:4–6 or their use of the Tent of Meeting in 33:7–11. Instead, he does mention his own favor with God. Perhaps we could say that Moses' abject plea in 32:31–32 is being accepted here, without any need for him to be blotted out. So Moses becomes a successful mediator, as did Noah in Genesis 8:20–21.

168. The renewal of full relations is found in the solemn affirmations of 34:10. God promises to do *marvels* and says that his guidance will be an *awesome thing*. The first word was used of God's planned *wonders* (*marvels*) in Exodus 3:20, and both words can be found in the hymn in 15:11, "Who is like you, O LORD, ...*awesome* in splendor, doing *wonders*?" God says in 34:10 that marvels such as these have not been *performed* before in all the earth. The word *perform* (*br'*) is actually the word for *create*, as in Genesis 1:1.

Commentators see the scope of 34:10 in different ways. Propp stays with the immediate context, and takes the final phrase to hint at the coming disfigurement of Moses' face. Cassuto looks to the rest of the Pentateuch, and says that God is promising the Israelites protection, food, and water during the wandering years, victory over foes, and eventual conquest of the entire Promised Land. Childs connects this verse to Exodus 33:16. The renewed covenant will emphasize the distinctness of this people, who have been forgiven such a great sin as the wrongful use of the golden calf.

169. The authors are obviously projecting the grim lessons of later centuries of living in Canaan—projecting them back as God's words to Moses. Exodus 34:17–26 focuses mainly on right worship as the sure safeguard for their monotheism. The problem was not that the Canaanites of later centuries were especially opposed to monotheism or Israelite faith. The problem was that the Israelites, as newcomers to the Holy Land, began a significant change of lifestyle, relying more on farming and less on shepherding. The new and fearful challenges of farming and village life brought anxieties, which in turn led them to some of the simple answers that polytheism seemed to provide.

The precautions mentioned in 34:11–17 are Deuteronomistic in style, and echo those in 23:20–33. Once in Canaan, the danger for the Israelites will be intermarriage and the lure of polytheism. If they get into this trap, they will lose their distinctiveness (33:16). For example, any carved altars or shrines found there cannot be simply confiscated and put back into use; that would confuse the faithful. For a second example, in the ancient Near East wooden poles and stone pillars were originally markers of lingering divine presence after theophanies, but stone pillars eventually became goddess totems. The Israelites had used some of these markers of divine presence early on (Gen 28:11–22; 49:24; Exod 24:4; Josh 24:26), but eventually they became more strict in outlawing any custom that could hint at goddesses.

The reference to the LORD as *jealous* in 34:14 is an attempt to express the incompatibility between belief in one God and many gods. Fretheim says that by calling himself jealous God admits that Israel's faithfulness is a matter close to his heart; it touches his emotional life. He cares about them and so cares about what they do right or wrong. If they fail in the future, God cannot remain unmoved; he will feel pain and anger.

170. Commentators have difficulty with this passage. They struggle to understand why Moses used the veil much of the time because of the condition of his face, no matter whether it was shining or damaged and hornlike. While the veil is not mentioned again, the tradition is that Moses used it for the rest of his life.

If *shining* is the correct translation, Propp suggests that Moses' face is like the Tabernacle, manifesting and yet concealing Yahweh's splendor. Or Moses could represent Israel, the glory on his face a pledge and a symbol of the abiding of the divine glory with the whole people. We could also think of the analogy of looking at sunlight as it reflects off the moon. In a sense, Moses' was the face that led the people (33:14). His face, transformed by Yahweh, became something like the face of God.

Childs notes that 34:29–33 tells of the first incident, while verses 34–35 speak of his subsequent habit of using the veil. The veil covers his face only during the period in which he is not performing his office of receiving or communicating God's word. For Childs this use of the veil does not make much sense. Perhaps it is a vestige of some primitive priest-mask custom, but *reversed* in Exodus 34 to show Moses wearing the veil as a mask when *not* talking to God or to the people.

The shining was in some way a reflection of God's glory; the whole Sinai story is in another sense a reflection of God's glory. Childs (619) states, "God and his revelation stand at the center. But Sinai is also the story of Moses, the mediator between God and Israel, who continued to function as a mortal man and yet who in his office bridged the enormous gap between the awesome, holy, and zealous God of Sinai and the fearful, sinful, and repentant people of the covenant."

Fretheim also notes that no reason is given for wearing the veil. Like other commentators, Fretheim offers several speculative guesses. Perhaps it meant that Moses was not always functioning as a messenger—no doubt to the relief of both Moses and the people. Mentioning the use of the veil for the rest of his life might be a theological symbol, but not a historical reality. The shining gives prominence to Moses as a reflector of God's glory, a sign of delegated authority or of his embodying the divine words somehow. Divine words are radiant, intense, vital, warm, and passionate; they are for the common good. So Moses is a divine messenger, the face of God insofar as it can be made available to ordinary people. Further, his shining face prefigures the filling of the Tabernacle with the cloud of God's glory in 40:34–38.

Fretheim goes so far as to suggest that we may have a play on the gold calf image. Here we have a living human representation of God's glory with horns of light; we do not need a golden statue of an animal.

Thomas Dozeman takes another approach to this story of Moses and the veil, one that I find helpful. He thinks we should consider the shining skin and the veil as two different masks. Each mask is a *secondary face* that always points to a *primary face*. There are two main types of masks, according to Dozeman. A *mask of concretion* is one by which the primary face (in our passage that is God) is external to the wearer and to the mask itself. God invades and the wearer (Moses) with the mask is idealized, transformed, or transfigured. The wearer of this kind of mask has a role of service. The shining face of Moses is such a mask. As another example, one could think of actor Jim Carrey in the film *The Mask*; he is overtaken by forces when he dons the green mask.

The second type of mask, called a *mask of concealment*, is used by someone who has power or authority within himself. That mask hides the wearer, separates him from everyday culture, and enhances his power. In Exodus 34, the veil is such a mask, concealing the shining face of Moses, the wearer.

Moses veiled is thus kept separated from ordinary culture, since he is the unique social authority and lawgiver for the people. As other examples of masks of concealment one can think of Batman's mask, or the white stylized wig of a British judge, or (negatively) the hood of a Klansman.

If this line of thinking is correct, then Moses wears one or two masks at all times. Thus he really loses his personal identity; he always speaks for God, not for himself. He is not a hero, like Samson or David; God is the hero. His shining face indicates that his authority is transcendent. The two masks together indicate that Moses himself is never the focus; he is never a private citizen representing only himself. He represents God in cultic matters, and his service role is to transmit divine laws.

Section Twenty-four: Exodus 35:1—40:38

171. The description of the cascade of donations is rousing. These ten verses (35:20–29) constantly refer to *all the people,* the *men,* the *women,* the *leaders.* They are called *stirred of heart* (35:21, 26; 36:2), *willing (generous) of spirit* (35:21), or *willing (generous) of heart* (35:22, 29). Some of them have artistic *skill* (35:25, 26, 35; 36:1, 2). The Hebrew phrases for this skill are *wisdom* or *wisdom of heart.*

Bezalel and Oholiab are described again as endowed with every facet of wisdom, artistry, and craftsmanship, and inspired to *teach* (35:34). The Hebrew is that God *put it in his (Bezalel's) heart to teach.* Exodus 36:1–2 goes overboard to remind us of the ranks of gifted artists who will do their newest and best work, using not only their own skills, but the guidance given to them by God through Bezalel and Oholiab.

The passage ends with a few verses describing the great surplus of supplies that poured in; Moses and the leaders had to make a concerted effort to stop the donations. The melodramatic verb in 36:6, that the people *were restrained* from bringing more things, has a root meaning of *imprisoning.*

172. There is some creation language in this grand assembly of all the components of the Tabernacle.

Exodus 39:32: all the *work* (*abodath*) was *finished* (*clh*)
Exodus 39:42: the Israelites had done all of the *work* (*abodath*)
Exodus 39:43: Moses saw the *work* (*melacah*), and *behold*, they had done it...and Moses *blessed* (*brk*) them
(Exodus 40:33: Moses *finished* (*clh*) the *work* (*melacah*))

Similar words appear at the end of the creation account in Genesis 1:31—2:3:

Genesis 2:1: the heavens and earth were *finished* (*clh*)
Genesis 1:31: God saw everything, and *behold*, it was very good
Genesis 2:2: God *finished* (*clh*) the work (*melacah*)...he rested from all his *work* (*melacah*)
Genesis 2:3: God *blessed* (*brk*) the seventh day

We have already seen

Exodus 35:30–31: The Lord *has called* (*qr'*) Bezalel and filled him with *the spirit of God*
Exodus 31:2–3: I *have called* Bezalel...I have filled him with *the spirit of God*

The same words appear in

Genesis 1:2: *the spirit of God* swept over the waters
Genesis 1:5, 8, 10: God *called*....

Further, in Numbers 7:1 Moses *consecrated* (*qds*) the objects; this is paralleled in Genesis 2:3, where God *sanctified* (*qds*) the *Sabbath*.

With the exception of the word *abodath* (*work*) in Exodus 39:32, 42, a synonym for *melacah*, the other verbs and nouns seem to be deliberately borrowed from Genesis. The intention was not to raise Moses to a quasi-divine level, but to remind everyone of the cosmic significance of this Tabernacle and its furnishings.

173. In 40:1–15, Moses is to have all the Tabernacle and court-yard functioning by the coming first day of the first month, including completing the ordination ceremonies for Aaron and his sons. In 40:16–33, Moses does as instructed, and the first regular offerings were made (40:29). With every-thing in place, the glory of the LORD came (40:34–38) in cloud and entered the Tabernacle. The moving of the cloud would be the sign for moving the camp.

In other biblical stories, Moses does come close to God's glory. See Exodus 25:22 (receiving commands at the mercy seat); Exodus 33:9 (the Tent of Meeting); Exodus 34:34–35 (Moses' shining face after receiving new laws from God); Leviticus 9:23 (Moses and Aaron enter the Tabernacle together the first day, and everyone saw the glory of the LORD); and Numbers 7:89 (Moses often heard God speak from the mercy seat).

The statement that Moses was not able to enter the tent (40:35) is taken by Propp as a way to explain the intensity of this first coming of God's glory to the Tabernacle. From this point on, Aaron or other priests must enter the outer room every day. Fretheim speaks of the emphasis in Exodus 40:35 on the divine initiative; there is no room for Moses in this newly filled sanctuary. "Moses' activity is not responsible in any way for God's dwelling. The tabernacle is for God for the sake of Israel, not for human beings, however important."

Bibliography

Blenkinsopp, Joseph. *The Pentateuch.* Anchor Bible Reference Library. New York: Doubleday, 1992.

Brueggemann, Walter. *Theology of the Old Testament.* Minneapolis: Fortress, 1997.

Childs, Brevard. *The Book of Exodus.* The Old Testament Library series. Louisville: Westminster Press, 1974.

Cassuto, Umberto. *A Commentary on the Book of Exodus.* Jerusalem: Magnes Press, Hebrew University, 1967.

Dozeman, Thomas. "Masking Moses and Mosaic Authority in Torah." *Journal of Biblical Literature*, vol. 119.1, Spring 2000, 21–45.

Fretheim, Terence. *Exodus.* Interpretation series. Louisville: John Knox Press, 1991.

Lambrecht, Ian. *Second Corinthians.* Sacra Pagina series. Collegeville, MN: Liturgical Press, 1999.

Propp, William H. C. *Exodus 1—18.* Anchor Bible series. New York: Doubleday, 1999.

———. *Exodus 19—40.* Anchor Bible series. New York: Doubleday, 2006.

Raphael, Chaim. *Festival Days: A History of Jewish Celebrations.* New York: Grove Weidenfield, 1991.

Sanders, E. P. *Judaism: Practice and Belief, 63 BCE–66 CE.* Philadelphia: Trinity, 1992.

Sarna, Nahum. *Understanding Genesis.* New York: Schocken Press, 1970.

Westermann, Claus. *Genesis.* Three volumes; translated by John Scullion. Minneapolis: Augsburg, 1984–86.

green press
INITIATIVE